Understanding Programming Languages

T0172160

Cliff B. Jones

Understanding Programming Languages

 Springer

Cliff B. Jones
School of Computing
Newcastle University
Newcastle upon Tyne, UK

ISBN 978-3-030-59259-2   ISBN 978-3-030-59257-8   (eBook)
https://doi.org/10.1007/978-3-030-59257-8

This Springer imprint is published by the registered company Springer Nature Switzerland AG
The registered company address is: Gewerbestrasse 11, 6330 Cham, Switzerland

Preface

The principal objective of this book is to teach a skill; to equip the reader with a way to understand programming languages at a deep level.

There exist far more programming languages than it makes sense even to attempt to enumerate. Very few of these languages can be considered to be free from issues that complicate –rather than ease– communication of ideas.

Designing a language is a non-trivial task and building tools to process the language requires a significant investment of time and resources. The formalism described in this book makes it possible to experiment with features of a programming language far more cheaply than by building a compiler. This makes it possible to think through combinations of language features and avoid unwanted interactions that can confuse users of the language. In general, engineers work long and hard on designs before they commit to create a physical artefact; software engineers need to embrace formal methods in order to avoid wasted effort.

The principal communication mode that humans use to make computers perform useful functions is to write programs — normally in "high-level" programming languages. The actual instruction sets of computers are low-level and constructing programs at that level is tedious and unintuitive (I say this from personal experience having even punched such instructions directly into binary cards). Furthermore these instruction sets vary widely so another bonus from programming in a language like Java is that the effort can migrate smoothly to computer architectures that did not even exist when the program was written.

General-purpose programming languages such as Java are referred to simply as "High-Level Languages" (HLLs). Languages for specific purposes are called "Domain Specific" (DSLs). HLLs facilitate expression of a programmer's intentions by abstracting away from details of particular machine architectures: iteration can be expressed in an HLL by an intuitive construct — entry and return from common code can be achieved by procedure calls or method invocation. Compilers for HLLs also free a programmer from worrying about when to use fast registers versus slower store accesses.

Designing an HLL is a challenging engineering task: the bigger the gap between its abstraction level and the target hardware architecture, the harder the task for the compiler designers. A large gap can also result in programmers complaining that they cannot get the same efficiency writing in the HLL as if they were to descend to the machine level.

An amazing number of HLLs have been devised. There are many concepts that recur in different languages but often deep similarities are disguised by arbitrary syntactic differences. Sadly, combinations of known concepts with novel ideas often interact badly and create hidden traps for users of the languages (both writers and readers).

Fortunately, there is a less expensive way of sorting out the meaning of a programming language than writing a compiler. This book is about describing the meaning (semantics) of programming languages. A major objective is to teach the skill of writing semantic descriptions because this provides a way to think out and make choices about the semantic features of a programming language in a cost-effective way. In one sense a compiler (or an interpreter) offers a complete formal description of the semantics of its source language. But it is not something that can be used as a basis for reasoning about the source language; nor can it serve as a definition of a programming language itself since this must allow a range of implementations. Writing a formal semantics of a language can yield a far shorter description and one about which it is possible to reason. To think that it is a sensible engineering process to go from a collection of sample programs directly to coding a compiler would be naive in the extreme. What a formal semantic description offers is a way to think out, record and analyse design choices in a language; such a description can also be the basis of a systematic development process for subsequent compilers. To record a description of the semantics of a language requires a notation — a "meta-language". The meta-language used in this book is simple and is covered in easy steps throughout the early chapters.

The practical approach adopted throughout this book is to consider a list of issues that arise in extant programming languages. Although there are over 60 such issues mentioned in this book, there is no claim that the list is exhaustive; the issues are chosen to throw up the challenges that their description represents. This identifies a far smaller list of techniques that must be mastered in order to write formal semantic descriptions. It is these techniques that are the main takeaway of the current book.

Largely in industry (mainly in IBM), I have worked on formal semantic descriptions since the 1960s[1] and have taught the subject in two UK universities. The payoff of being able to write formal abstract descriptions of programming languages is that this skill has a far longer half-life than programming languages that come and go: one can write a description of any language that one wants to understand; a language designer can experiment with combinations of ideas and eliminate "feature interactions" at far less cost and time than would be the case with writing a compiler.

The skill that this book aims to communicate will equip the reader with a way to understand programming languages at a deep level. If the reader then wants to

---

[1] This included working with the early operational semantic descriptions of PL/I and writing the later denotational description of that language. PL/I is a huge language and, not surprisingly, contains many examples of what might be regarded as poor design decisions. These are often taken as cautionary tales in the book but other languages such as Ada or CHILL are not significantly better.

design a programming language (DSL or HLL), the skill can be put to use in creating a language with little risk of having hidden feature interactions that will complicate writing a compiler and/or confuse subsequent users of the language.

In fact, having mastered the skill of writing a formal semantic description, the reader should be able to sketch the state and environment of a formal model for most languages in a few pages. Communicating this practical skill is the main aim of this book; it seeks neither to explore theoretical details nor to teach readers how to build compilers.

Using this book

The reader is assumed to know at least one (imperative) HLL and to be aware of discrete maths notations such as those for logic and set theory — [MS13], for example, covers significantly more than is expected of the reader. On the whole, the current book is intended to be self-contained with respect to notation.

The material in this book has been used in final-year undergraduate teaching for over a decade; it has evolved and the current text is an almost complete rewrite. Apart from a course environment, it is hoped that the book will influence designers of programming languages. As indicated in Chapter 1, current languages offer many unfortunate feature interactions which make their use in building major computer systems both troublesome and unreliable. Programming languages offer the essential means of expression for programmers — as such they should be as clean and free from hidden traps as possible. The repeated message throughout this book is that it is far cheaper and more efficient to think out issues of language design before beginning to construct compilers or interpreters that might lock in incompletely thought-out design ideas.

Most chapters in the book offer projects, which vary widely in their challenge. They are not to be thought of as offering simple finger exercises — some of them ask for complete descriptions of languages — the projects are there to suggest what a reader might want to think about at that stage of study.

Some sections are starred as not being essential to the main argument; most chapters include a section of "further material". Both can be omitted on first reading.

Writing style

"The current author" normally eschews the first person (singular or plural) in technical writing; clearly, I have not followed this constraint in this preface. Some of the sections that close each chapter and occasional footnotes also use the first person singular when a particular observation warrants such employment.

Acknowledgements

I have had the pleasure of working with many colleagues and friends on the subject of programming language semantics. Rather than list them here, their names will crop up throughout the book. I have gained inspiration from students who have followed my courses at both Newcastle University and the University of Manchester. I'm extremely grateful to Jamie Charsley for his insertion of indexing commands. I owe a debt to Troy Astarte, Andrzej Blikle, Tom Helyer, Adrian Johnson and Jim Woodcock, who kindly offered comments on various drafts of this book. (All remaining errors are of course my responsibility.) My collaboration with Springer –especially with Ronan Nugent– has been a pleasure. I have received many grants from EPSRC over the years — specifically, the "Strata" Platform Grant helped support recent work on this book.

Contents

Chapter 1
Programming languages and their description

This chapter sets the scene for the rest of the book. Sections 1.1–1.3 outline the problems presented by programming languages and their related tools; Section 1.4 points out that there is material from the study of natural languages that is relevant to the problems of describing artificial languages such as those used to program computers; an overview of a range of techniques for recording the meaning of programming languages is given in Section 1.5 and Section 1.6 introduces the specific notation used throughout this book. In common with most of the following chapters, this one closes with a section (1.7) that contains further material — in particular such sections point to related reading.

1.1 Digital computers and programming languages

Consider the phrase "high-level languages for programming general-purpose computers"; starting at the end:

- The focus in this book is on digital –rather than analogue– computers. The qualification of "general-purpose" indicates that the behaviour of the computer is controlled by a stored program. The crucial idea that machines can be devised that are in some sense universal is credited to Alan Turing's famous paper [Tur36] on a technical issue in logic but few people would choose to program a "Turing machine".
- An essential question underlying this book is what is meant by "programming". A position can be taken that a program for device x should extend what can be expressed in terms of the basic repertoire of x. Thus an early computer that had no support for, say, floating-point numbers had to be programmed to simulate such calculations; even modern computers[1] do not normally offer instructions

---

[1] Many modern machine architectures follow the idea of the "Reduced Instruction Set Computer" (RISC); design and programming at the RISC level often requires re-building concepts that were in the instruction sets of earlier machine architectures.

© Springer Nature Switzerland AG 2020
C. B. Jones, *Understanding Programming Languages*,
https://doi.org/10.1007/978-3-030-59257-8_1

that compute, say factorial, so this is programmed in terms of multiplication etc.; similarly many sorting algorithms can be realised as programs.

- Even leaving aside the arcane language of Turing machines, programming at the level of machine code is tedious and error-prone (see Section 1.2). The reason for designing "high-level" languages (HLLs) is to get above this finicky way of expressing programs and make it easier and more productive for programmers to express their ideas.

Thus high-level languages for programming general-purpose computers are a means of generating (via a compiler) a series of instructions that can be executed on a digital computer and that realise concepts that are not directly available as expressions of the language.

1.2 The importance of HLLs

Picking up the point about the productivity of programmers from the preceding section, there was a panel discussion[2] on *Programming Languages and their Semantics* at a conference in Pittsburgh in May 2004 to which Vaughan Pratt put the intriguing question of how much money the panelists thought that high-level programming languages had saved the world. Pratt was aware of the difficulty of the question because he added a subsidiary query as to whether an answer to the main question would qualify for a Nobel Prize in economics. Without hoping –even with time to reflect– to provide a number, considering Pratt's question is illuminating. There are almost certainly millions of people in the world for whom programming forms a significant part of their job. Programmers tend to be well paid. A good programmer today can create –using a high-level programming language such as Java– systems that were unthinkable when programs could only be communicated in machine code. A good programming language can, moreover, ensure that many mistakes made by even an average-level programmer are easily detected and corrected. To these powerful savings, ease of program migration can be added: avoiding the need to write versions of essentially the same program for different machine instruction sets must itself have saved huge wastage of time and money.

It is also important to appreciate the distribution of costs around programs: even back in the days of mainframes, the majority of programs cost more to develop than their lifetime machine usage costs. Since that period, decades of tracking Moore's Law [Moo65] have dramatically reduced the cost of executing programs. With modern interactive applications, and factoring in the human cost of user time, the actual machine time costs are close to irrelevant. The productivity of programmers and their ability to create systems that are useful to the end user are the paramount concerns.

---

[2] The panelists were John McCarthy, John Reynolds, Dana Scott and the current author.

The mere fact that there are thousands[3] of programming languages is an indication that their design is a subject of interest. The additional observation that there is no one clear "best buy" suggests that designing a high-level programming language is non-trivial. One tension in design is between offering access to the power of the underlying machine facilities so that programs can be made to be efficient versus providing abstractions that make it easier to create programs. The problems of writing programs are also likely to be exceeded by the costs of their maintenance, where the intentions of the original programmer must be understood if the person changing the program is to do so safely.

A good programming language offers several aids to the programmers who use it to express their ideas:

- data structuring
- common forms of control can be built into a language (with only the compiler having to fiddle with the specific machine-level instruction sequences that realise the higher-level expressions)
- protecting programmers from mistakes

It is worth expanding on the issue of how programming languages provide abstractions. Most computers have a small number of registers, in which all basic computations are performed and instructions can only access one additional storage cell. A calculation involving several values must –at the machine level– involve a series of instructions and might require the storage of intermediate results. A first level of abstraction allows programmers to write arbitrary expressions that have to be translated into strings of machine operations.

Clear layers of abstraction can be seen with regard to data representation. The storage of a computer can most easily be viewed as a sequence of small containers (bits, bytes or words).[4] From its inception, the FORTRAN language supported declaring *arrays* of multiple dimensions whose elements could be addressed in a style familiar to mathematicians (e.g. $A[I, J * 3]$). Such operands have to be translated into sequences of machine instructions that compute the machine address in the sequence of addressable storage cells of the machine. The APL language pushed arrays to extremes and even PL/I provides ways of manipulating slices of n-dimensional arrays — such sub-arrays can then be manipulated as if they had been declared to be arrays of lesser dimensions.

Array elements are all of one type. Both the COBOL and Pascal languages offer ways of defining inhomogeneous *records*[5] that facilitate grouping data elements whose types differ from each other. Furthermore the whole inhomogeneous object can be used (e.g. as parameters or in input/output) as a single data item or its components can be addressed separately.

---

[3] As early as 1969, Jean Sammet's book [Sam69] recognised 500 programming languages; a web site that claimed to be listing all known languages got to 8,512 in 2010 then gave up.

[4] Of course, computer architectures normally include registers and might themselves provide abstraction such as "virtual memory" (supported by "paging"). Some of these features are discussed when issues relating to code generation are considered in subsequent chapters.

[5] Some languages, including PL/I, use the term "structures" rather than records.

List processing facilitates the creation of arbitrary graphs of data by allowing the manipulation of something like machine addresses as data. Early languages such as IPL-V, Lisp and Scheme had to develop a lot of techniques for *garbage collection* before list processing could be adopted into more mainstream languages.

The concept of *objects* is a major contribution to the abstractions, as offered in *object-oriented* languages such as Simula, Smalltalk and Java. Object orientation is discussed in Section 6.2 and its role in taming concurrent computation is the main topic of Chapter 9.

A similar story of programming languages developing abstraction mechanisms above the raw conditional jumps of machine level programming could be developed: conditional if constructs, compound statement lists, for and while looping constructs and –above all– recursion make it possible to present complicated programs as a structured and readable text. Tony Hoare reported [Hoa81, p.76] that he could not express his innovative Quicksort [Hoa61] algorithm until he learned the ALGOL 60 programming language.[6] This almost certainly contributed to his judgement on AL-GOL 60 in [Hoa74b]:

> Here is a language so far ahead of its time, that it was not only an improvement on its predecessors, but also on nearly all its successors. Of particular interest are its introduction of all the main program structuring concepts, the simplicity and clarity of its description, rarely equalled and never surpassed.

A final, but crucial, area where programming language designers have sought to offer abstractions is that of *concurrency*.[7] Most computers offer rather low-level primitives such as a compare-and-swap instruction; programming even at the level of Dijkstra's semaphores [Dij62, Dij68a] is extremely error-prone. The whole subject of concurrency in programming languages is still in evolution and its modelling occupies several chapters later in this book. References to histories of the evolution of programming languages are given in Section 1.7.

Here, the concern is with the problem of knowing how to record the meaning –or *semantics*– of useful abstractions such as those sketched above. Semantic description is a non-trivial problem and occupies Chapters 3–10 of this book. The payoff for mastering these techniques is large and can have effects far beyond the language design team. It is just not realistic to expect anyone to be able to design a programming language that will overcome the challenges listed above by sketching sample programs and then proceeding to compiler writing. In fact, such a procedure is a denial of everything known about engineering. The ability to record the meaning of a language at an abstract level means that designers can think out, document and refine their ideas far less expensively than by coding processors. Furthermore, the

---

[6] Although initially designed as a publication language (and the vast majority of algorithms published in the Algorithms section of Communications of the ACM were written in ALGOL 60) the language contributed so many fundamental concepts to programming language design that it has had enormous influence (see [AJ18, §1.4]).

[7] In contrast, so-called "weak" (or "relaxed") memory is a hardware feature which might inflict considerable damage on software development because it is hard to find apposite abstractions [ŠVZN+13, LV16].

far bigger bonus is that users of better thought-through languages will become more productive and stumble into far fewer unexpected "feature interactions".

Before techniques for describing semantics and the case for formalism are discussed in Section 1.5, it is worth considering the software tools that process programming languages.

1.3 Translators, etc.

Given that a programmer elects to write a program in a high-level language –say $\mathscr{L}$ – and that the hardware on which the program is to run only obeys instructions in its particular machine language,[8] some tool is required to bridge the gap. Two key tools are translators and interpreters.

Perhaps the more obvious tool is to write an *interpreter* program in machine language. Such an interpreter would read in the program written in $\mathscr{L}$ and simulate its behaviour step by step. This can be done, but pure interpreters tend to run rather slowly. The alternative is to write a program (again in machine language) that can translate any program of $\mathscr{L}$ into a sequence of machine instructions that have the effect of the original program. The obvious name for such a program is a *translator* but the commonly used term is to refer to "compilers" for $\mathscr{L}$.[9]

In practice, the description above is a simplification to make the distinctions clear.[10] Rather than producing pure machine code, a compiler can translate to the language of a *virtual machine* which is in turn interpreted on actual hardware. This idea has significant advantages in reducing the task of supporting multiple languages. Furthermore, compilers or interpreters can at least partially be written in high-level programming languages; this process is referred to as "bootstrapping".

It is worth reinforcing the point about translation by considering just a few examples. The focus in this book is on *imperative* programming languages.[11] In general-purpose languages, the key imperative statement is the assignment. (Other

---

[8] Grace Hopper said [Hop81]:

> In the early years of programming languages, the most frequent phrase that we heard was that the only way to program a computer was in octal.

[9] The origin of this word is explained in [Bey09] as deriving from the first attempts to automate program construction by collecting (compiling) a group of subroutines. It is surprising that this is the term that continues to be more commonly used for what is clearly a process of translation.

[10] In a detailed study [vdH19] of the ALGOL 60 implementation by Dijkstra and his colleagues, Gauthier van den Hove makes clear that, even early in the history of language processing, the question of compiling and interpreting was seen less as a dichotomy and more as a spectrum.

[11] Functional languages such as Miranda [Tur85] and Haskell [Hut16] make it easier to reason about programs as though they were mathematical functions. Early implementations of functional languages tended to perform considerably more slowly than imperative languages but this gap has reduced and some serious applications are now written in functional languages. Logic languages such as Prolog [SS86] make a further step both in expressiveness and in their challenge to offer performance. (In fact, Prolog still has imperative features.) The techniques presented in this book

imperative languages might move the arm of a robot, project an image or update a database.) Most of the statement types actually only orchestrate the order in which updates to variables are made by assignments.

As outlined above, straightforward expression evaluation has to be implemented by loads, stores and single-address operations of the machine. But a compiler will often try to optimise expression evaluation. For example "common sub-expressions" might be evaluated only once. Even in early FORTRAN compilers, expressions that occurred inside *FOR* loops but did not depend on variables whose values were changed in the loop could be evaluated once before the loop. More subtly, expressions such as those which compute array indexes in the loop could be subject to *strength reduction* so that the effect of multiplication could be achieved by addition each time round a loop. Many of these optimisations are known as "source-to-source" in the sense that there is an equivalent source program that represents the optimised code. There are other optimisations such as those concerned with maximising efficiency by minimising the number of loads and saves for registers (especially index registers for address calculation) that cannot be expressed in the source language. In either case, it is clearly essential that the "optimisations" do not result in a program doing something different from the programmer's legitimate expectations. In other words, any optimisations must respect the semantics of the given high-level language.

Similar points could be made about compiling control constructs. Most machines provide a primitive (conditional) jump instruction. High-level languages offer far more structured control constructs. The task of a compiler is to translate the latter into the former in a way that results in efficient code. But, again, that low-level code must respect the semantics of the programming language.

Three final points can be made about tools for executing high-level languages:

- The cost of building a translator for a high-level programming language is normally significant.[12] Many arguments can be advanced against undertaking this step too early in the design process for a new programming language. Clearly, if some language deficiencies or irregularities can be resolved less expensively by writing a formal semantics, this is a wise move. More worryingly, once a mistaken design choice is cemented in the code of a translator, the designer might be far more reluctant to undertake the rework to correct the infelicity.
- The division of a compiler into lexical analysis, parsing, dictionary building, . . . , code generation provides useful analogies for the task of formal description of languages — these are used in later chapters.
- There are also other important tools such as those that assist a programmer in debugging programs written in some language $\mathscr{L}$.

for describing the semantics of imperative languages would apply to both functional and logic languages (see for example [AB87, And92]).

[12] This can be reduced if translation to the language of an existing virtual machine is possible.

1.4 Insights from natural languages

The languages that are spoken by human beings were not designed by committees[13] — they just evolved and they continue to change. The evolution process is all too obvious from the irregularities in most natural languages. The task of describing such *natural languages* is therefore very challenging but, because they have been around longer, it is precisely on natural languages that the first systematic studies were undertaken. Charles Sanders Peirce (1839-1914) used the term *Semiotics* for the study of languages. Peirce[14] divided the study of languages into:

- *syntax*: concerning the structure of utterances in a language
- *semantics*: about the meaning of the language
- *pragmatics*: covering the intention of using the language

Heinz Zemanek applied the terminology to programming languages in [Zem66] but work on formalising the syntax of programming languages goes back to the ALGOL effort in the late 1950s.

As shown in Chapter 2, it is not difficult to write syntax rules for parts of natural languages but, because of their irregularity, a complete syntax is probably not a realistic objective. It is far harder to give a semantics of a language (than to write syntactic rules) and Section 1.5 expands on this topic, which then occupies the majority of the following chapters.

One way of appreciating the distinction between syntax and semantics is to consider some questions that arise with programming languages:

- Ways to fix the nesting of expressions (e.g. $2 + 3 * 4$ vs. $(2 + 3) * 4$) is a syntactic question.
- Another syntactic question is how to fix to which test the else clause in
  if $a = b$ **then if** $c = d$ **then** $x := 1$ **else** $x := 2$
  applies.
- Choosing which of the many possibilities of parameter passing modes is to be included in a language is a semantic question.
- Deciding whether to under-determine the results expected by a program is certainly a semantic decision and the role of non-determinism in programming languages is particularly important in the context of concurrency (see Chapter 8).

1.5 Approaches to describing semantics

Some general points about semantics can be made concrete by looking at a few specific programs. The following program (in a syntax close to that of ALGOL 60):

---

[13] Of course, there are a small number of exceptions such as Volapük and Esperanto.

[14] Pronounced "Purse".

```
begin integer n, fn;
    ⋮
    begin integer t;
    t := 0;
    fn := 1;
    while t ≠ n do
        t := t + 1;
        fn := fn * t;
    od
    end
end
```

computes the factorial of the (integer) value of the variable n and places the result in variable fn. A formal justification of this fact is contained in Section 7.3 but it is apparent that such a claim can only be based on an understanding of the meaning of the statements of the language in which the program is written. Thus it is clear that one role for a semantic description of a language –say $\mathscr{L}$– is to be able to reason about the claim that a program written in language $\mathscr{L}$ meets its specification. (This notion is examined in detail in Chapter 7.)

But, if it were the case that a programmer presented an argument –possibly even a formal proof– that a program met its specification and then a purported compiler for $\mathscr{L}$ introduced errors in the sense that the machine code created by the compiler was not in accord with the semantics of $\mathscr{L}$, the programmer would have every right to be aggrieved. So it is clear that a key role for a semantic description of a language is to remove this risk: any compiler or interpreter for $\mathscr{L}$ must realise the semantics of $\mathscr{L}$. (A formal statement of this notion is given in Section 3.3.)

Thus the semantics should mediate the bridge between programmers using $\mathscr{L}$ and implementers of language $\mathscr{L}$ so that the former group expect and the latter group deliver the same meaning. Faced with the large challenge of getting a computer to behave in an intended way, the semantics provides a "division of concerns": programs should be written on the assumption of the recorded semantics and processors for the language should reflect that semantics.

There are also other interesting questions. Consider the following alternative program:

```
begin integer n, fn;
    ⋮
    fn := 1;
    while n ≠ 0 do
        fn := fn * n;
        n := n - 1;
    od
end
```

This also has the effect of placing in fn the factorial of the initial value of n. If the earlier program included $n := 0$ after the while loop, the two programs might be considered to be equivalent in some sense. Making such notions of equivalence precise is another semantic issue. (These issues of what it means for programs to be equivalent become clearer with larger programs such as those for sorting: many sorting algorithms have been devised (see [Knu73]) but two such programs can be unrecognisably different from each other.)

It is time to discuss different approaches to recording the semantics of programming languages. If one knows one natural language, another language might be explained by translating it into the known language (although nuances and beauty might be lost in translation). So an option for giving the semantics of language $\mathscr{L}$ is to record a translation into a known language. This is, of course, exactly what a compiler does but unfortunately machine code is not an attractive *lingua Franca* for recording semantics. The problem with machine code as a vehicle for explaining semantics to a human being is that its own semantics might be opaque. Of more concern –and a clearer criteria– is that machine code is not *tractable* in the sense that there is no natural way of reasoning about texts in machine language. An approach that was originally called *mathematical semantics*, but is now commonly referred to as *denotational semantics*, defines semantics by mapping into mathematically tractable objects. This approach is described in Section 7.1 and commonly uses mathematical functions from states to states as denotations.

Denotational semantics is mathematically elegant but requires some fairly sophisticated mathematical concepts in order to describe programming languages of the sort that are used to build real applications. Taking a cue from the class of language tools that are known as interpreters points to a more direct approach to providing the semantics of a programming language. A so-called *operational semantics* provides a way of taking a program and a starting state and computing its final state. Again, it could be said that this is exactly what an interpreter written in machine code does but the key to a clear operational semantics is to write an *abstract interpreter* in a limited *meta-language*. Such meta-languages should themselves be tractable so that it is straightforward to reason about the description. The majority of chapters in this book employ operational methods of semantic description and Section 1.6 describes the meta-language used throughout this book.

The notion of a state is central to both denotational and operational semantics. The two approaches share the need to choose states that are as abstract as possible; both can therefore be viewed as offering *model-oriented* language descriptions. In contrast, it is possible to consider *property-oriented* approaches to semantics. One obvious way to convey information about the meaning of complex features of a programming language is to describe their meaning by relating them to simpler constructs in the same language. Early attempts to use this idea formally include [Bek64] and it can be seen in less formal descriptions in, for example, the way that [BBG+63] describes the for statement of ALGOL 60. This approach can be compared to the way in which a mono-lingual dictionary defines the more arcane words in terms of a limited subset of the vocabulary of a natural language. There is of course an inherent circularity about this approach in that a reader must be able to understand some expressions in a language but it is certainly possible to explain less familiar features such as "call by name" in ALGOL 60 by their translation to simpler subsets of a language. Notice that equivalences provide semantic knowledge without any notion of the state of a computation having to be described

A more radical –and now more widely used– approach that can be viewed as giving a property-oriented semantics is to provide ways of of reasoning about programs in a language $\mathscr{L}$. The idea of adding *assertions* to programs has a surprisingly long history (see Section 7.3.1) but the really important step was made by Tony Hoare who introduced an approach known as *axiomatic semantics*. Essentially, this approach provides rules of inference that facilitate proofs about programs and their specifications. Section 7.3 goes into some detail on such axiomatic approaches.

The tasks of reasoning about programs in a language $\mathscr{L}$ and justifying the correctness of a translator for $\mathscr{L}$ are distinguished above. It can be argued that one or another approach to semantics is better suited to the different tasks (this topic is reviewed in Section 7.5). But it should be clear that, if more than one approach is used, they must be shown to be coherent in the sense that they fix the same semantics.

The bulk of this book uses operational semantic descriptions because the aim is to equip the reader with the ability to describe useful programming languages. (Chapter 7 reviews the other potential approaches.)

The above division of approaches to giving semantics can even be discerned when looking at informal descriptions of programming languages that are contained in most textbooks, although it is also true that most modern textbooks put heavy reliance on examples that the reader has to somehow "morph" to solve their actual problem.[15] What then is the case for promoting formality in descriptions of programming languages? Although main-line programming languages (and –today– their indispensable libraries) are orders of magnitude larger than the formal metalanguage described in Section 1.6, the desirability of them being as tractable as practical carries over to programming languages. For example, programmers are unlikely to use language constructs safely if a phrase in a language has unexpectedly different meanings depending on the context in which the phrase is embedded. A clear test of a language being tractable is the ease of writing out formal rules of inference for the language.

Furthermore, if users can be given a clear mental model of the state of a programming language, they can understand the meaning of each construct by seeing how it affects that state. With both considerations (properties and models of a language), one way of testing clarity is to be able to record the ideas formally. As with any piece of knowledge, such a record makes it available for review and subsequent study. A compiler or interpreter for language $\mathscr{L}$ is itself "formal" — but its construction costs far more than does a formal language description and a compiler is certainly not tractable in the sense that it would be convenient to reason from the compiler about programs in $\mathscr{L}$.[16]

---

[15] This "use case" approach applies to many physical objects and their manuals fail to give the user any picture of the internal state of the object with which they are trying to interact.

[16] A more subtle facet of the question of relying on a compiler comes from the thorny issue of non-determinism: most HLLs actually permit a range of results (e.g. because of concurrency or to leave implementors some flexibility): even if a user is interested in the result of a program on

As indicated in Section 1.2, a premature leap from example programs for a new language to beginning to write a compiler for the language does not constitute sound engineering. A process of experimenting with language choices within a formal model can iron out many potential consistencies more quickly and far less expensively. The formal model can also serve as the starting point for a systematic design process for compilers once the language has been thought out.

Chapter 11 lists a number of formal descriptions of extant programming languages. One possibility opened up by making these descriptions formal is to provide tools that use them. There is quite good support for reasoning about program correctness from various forms of property-oriented semantics, although this normally applies to restricted subsets of major languages such as SPARK-Ada. There are far more tools based on formal ideas that check specific properties of programs in languages (e.g. possible dereferencing of null pointers, deadlock detection).

Having listed the technical criteria of being able to reason about programs written in $\mathscr{L}$ and acting as a base for compilers for $\mathscr{L}$, there remains a bigger objective. The main aim of this book is to ensure that formal models are more widely used in the design of future programming languages. It is to be regretted that most of the current main-line programming languages have semantic traps that surprise programmers and/or complicate the task of providing compilers for the language. Such anomalies can be detected early by writing formal semantic descriptions before tackling the far more costly job of programming a compiler.

What then is the impediment to writing, for example, an operational semantics of a language? Section 1.6 introduces a meta-language that should not prove difficult for any programmer to understand. With that one meta-language, he or she can describe any (imperative) programming language. Chapter 3 covers the basic method of writing an operational semantics and subsequent chapters consider new challenges and eight known techniques for coping with them. Experience of teaching these methods over the years suggests that the real hurdle is learning to employ the right degree of *abstraction* in tackling language descriptions. That can probably only be learned by looking at examples, and Chapters 3–9 provide many such examples.

1.6 A meta-language

The term *object language* can be used to refer to the language whose syntactic and semantic description is to be undertaken[17] and the script letter $\mathscr{L}$ is used when making a general point rather than discussing a specific object language such as FORTRAN or Java. In contrast, languages that are used in the description of an object language are referred to as *meta-languages*.

---

a single input item, knowing that the result is as required in one implementation of $\mathscr{L}$ does not guarantee that the program will give the same result on a different correct implementation of $\mathscr{L}$.

[17] The qualification "object" indicates that it is the object of study; this is not to be confused with "object code", which is what a translator generates when it compiles a source program.

A meta-language is itself a formal language. To serve the purpose of describing a range of programming languages:

- A useful meta-language must be capable of describing a large class of object languages — it must be "rich enough" for its intended task.
- A meta-language should be far smaller than most programming languages.
- Crucially, any meta-language should be tractable in the sense that there are clear rules for reasoning about its expressions.

The meta-language used in this book is derived from (but is a subset of) the notation used in the *Vienna Development Method* (VDM). A brief outline of the origins of VDM is given in Section 3.3.

The reader is assumed to be familiar with set notation;[18] Figure 1.1 indicates the symbols used as logical operators in VDM. Fortunately, textbooks use fairly uniform set notation and the only points worth mentioning from Figure 1.1 are:

- rather than use a special symbol (ϕ), VDM uses $\{\}$ for the empty set because it is just a special case of an enumerated set with no elements;
- the type of all finite subsets of some type X is written X-set;
- the set of all (finite or infinite) subsets is written (conventionally) as $\mathscr{P}(X)$;
- the name of the set of natural numbers is $\mathbb{N} = \{0, 1, \cdots\}$, the set of all integers $\mathbb{Z} = \{\cdots, -1, 0, 1, \cdots\}$ and the set of Boolean values $\mathbb{B} = \{\text{true}, \text{false}\}$.

T-set	all finite subsets of T	
$\{t_1, t_2, \ldots, t_n\}$	set enumeration	
$\{\}$	empty set	
$\mathbb{B}$	$\{\text{true}, \text{false}\}$	
$\mathbb{N}$	$\{0, \cdots\}$	
$\mathbb{Z}$	$\{\cdots, -1, 0, \cdots\}$	
$\{x \in S \mid p(x)\}$	set comprehension	
$\{i, \cdots, j\}$	subset of integers (from i to j inclusive)	
$t \in S$	set membership	
$t \notin S$	$\neg (t \in S)$	
$S_1 \subseteq S_2$	set containment (subset of)	
$S_1 \subset S_2$	strict set containment	
$S_1 \cap S_2$	set intersection	
$S_1 \cup S_2$	set union	
$S_1 - S_2$	set difference	
$\text{card}\, S$	cardinality (size) of a set	
$\mathscr{P}(X)$	power set	

Fig. 1.1 Set notation

Notation for VDM sequences is introduced in Section 2.2 (see Figure 2.2) and maps in Section 3.1 (Figure 3.1) when they are needed.

---

[18] Many useful textbooks exist on the notations of discrete mathematics including [Gro09].

A call for abstraction pervades work on modelling computer systems in general and in giving the semantics to programming languages in particular: as such, "abstraction" is a *Leitmotiv* of this book. For example, if the order of a collection of objects has no influence on the semantics of a language, it is far better to employ a set than a sequence. It might be possible to express the semantics in terms of a sequence but the description will have to cope with messy details; far more tellingly, any reader of the formal description is left to determine whether the order does in fact influence the semantics by reading every line of the description. In contrast, as soon as a reader sees that something is modelled as a set, it is abundantly clear that the order of its elements can have no semantic effect.

$\mathbb{B}$	$\{\text{true}, \text{false}\}$
$\neg E$	negation (not)
$E_1 \wedge E_2$	conjunction (and)
	E_1, E_2 are conjuncts
$E_1 \vee E_2$	disjunction (or)
	E_1, E_2 are disjuncts
$E_1 \Rightarrow E_2$	implication
	E_1 antecedent, E_2 consequent
$E_1 \Leftrightarrow E_2$	equivalence
$\forall x \in S \cdot E$	universal quantification
$\exists x \in S \cdot E$	existential quantification

Fig. 1.2 Logic symbols

The symbols used for logic (technically, *first-order predicate calculus*) vary between textbooks and Figure 1.2 indicates the symbols used in this book.

It is common to set out proof rules that define valid deductions about the logical operators. Examples that are assumed below include a definition of implication:

$$\boxed{\Rightarrow \text{-}I} \; \frac{\neg E_1 \vee E_2}{E_1 \Rightarrow E_2}$$

equivalence as bi-implication:

$$\boxed{\Leftrightarrow} \; \frac{\begin{array}{c} E_1 \Rightarrow E_2 \\ E_2 \Rightarrow E_1 \end{array}}{E_1 \Leftrightarrow E_2}$$

What can be thought of as a definition of disjunction in terms of conjunction is characterised by the bi-directional rule:

$$\boxed{\textit{de-Morgan-1}} \; \frac{\neg(\neg E_1 \wedge \neg E_2)}{E_1 \vee E_2}$$

is one of de Morgan's laws; another is:

$$\boxed{\textit{de-Morgan-2}} \; \frac{\neg(E_1 \vee E_2)}{\neg E_1 \wedge \neg E_2}$$

There is, however, an interesting extension in VDM to conventional logic in that a *Logic of Partial Functions* (LPF) is used. The reader should have no difficulty with an innocent reading of the propositional connectives listed in Figure 1.2 but LPF offers a principled extension to cope with the situation where operands can be "undefined". An obvious example is the proposition $5/0 = 0$ which –since division by zero means that the arithmetic term $(5/0)$ fails to denote a number– is taken as "failing to denote a truth value". Far more useful examples of partial expressions arise in both specifications and reasoning about such documents and attention is drawn to examples in later chapters — but it is important that the obvious interpretation of such logical expressions works; more detail is given in Section 1.7.3.

1.7 Further material

1.7.1 Further reading

An excellent source of material on the history of programming languages themselves is the series of conferences on *History of Programming Languages* [Wex81, BG96, RH07] — the first of these is a real gem. The PL/I language is mentioned several times throughout the current book and some of these mentions indicate the ways in which the interactions between language design decisions can result in confusion. George Radin's [Rad81] account of the creation of PL/I throws some light on how committee compromises can complicate a language. However, the use of PL/I to illustrate excesses in language design comes more from the current author's familiarity with PL/I than as a claim that it is the language that suffers the worst interaction of language features.

Another way to read the words of the masters is to access the Turing Award talks — printed versions include [Knu74a, Hoa74b, Sco77, Bac78, Wir85, Mil93, Ive07]; further wise words are in [Hoa81, Wir67]; specific language discussions include: [Knu67], [PJ03] and [Hut16].

An extremely useful book on concepts in programming languages is [Sco00] and it could be useful to read Michael Scott's book alongside the current text. Another book that covers a range of languages and provides useful historical background is [Seb16]. References on approaches to the formal description of programming languages are given in the closing sections of later chapters of the current book.

There are actually two aspects of VDM itself: it offers a formal development approach for any form of program and it has specific support for the denotational description of programming language semantics. The current book uses only the simplest common features of these two aspects. A general book on VDM is [Jon90] and the ISO standard for VDM is described and referenced in [PL92]. The semantics of full VDM is complicated by the fact that it was designed to write denotational semantic descriptions (see Chapter 7); the subset used here for operational semantics should be clear.

1.7.2 Classes of languages

This book tackles the semantics of imperative languages such as ALGOL and Java. Descriptions of functional and logic programming languages (e.g. Scheme [ASS85], Prolog [SS86]) would use the same ideas but it is worth saying a few words about the differences. Rather than design algorithmic solutions to solve problems, it would be attractive to write logical assertions and have a program find solutions. Even in the restricted world of mathematics or logic[19] this is impossible in general, but Prolog-style logic programming moves in this direction. Unfortunately, in order to circumvent the problems of massive search spaces, imperative features have been included in Prolog itself [SS86].

An intermediate approach between fully imperative and logic languages is the class of functional programming languages. In the extreme, such languages avoid all imperative constructs such as assignment. This makes it possible to reason about functional programs as though they are mathematical functions. Among other things, this avoids the need for a Hoare-style logic. Most functional languages actually offer some limited ability to "change the world".

1.7.3 Logic of Partial Functions

As indicated above, the logic used in the VDM meta-language is an extension of standard first-order predicate calculus (see for example [MS13]). The need for a *Logic of Partial Functions* (LPF) comes from the frequency with which reasonable expressions in specifications involve terms that can fail to denote a value.

Writing the specific expression $5/0 = 0$ would be bizarre but the following is more reasonable:[20]

$$i > 0 \land j \neq 0 \;\Rightarrow\; i/j \leq j$$

where the troublesome $i/0$ is one instance of i/j.

Far more useful examples arise in both specifications and reasoning about such documents and attention is drawn to examples in later chapters, but it is important that the obvious interpretation of such logical expressions works — for example, while the antecedent of the preceding implication does not guard the consequent in classical logic, the implication in LPF has the desired effect.

For example, the head (first element) of an empty list is undefined and applying a mapping (finite function) to an element not in its domain fails to denote a value. LPF offers obvious extensions to the normal meanings of propositional operators as in Figure 1.3 where an operand that fails to denote a truth value is marked as an asterisk.

---

[19] It is by no means obvious how to develop or validate specifications of systems that interface to the physical world. Some work in this area is described in [JHJ07, JGK+15, BHJ20].

[20] Such an expression is better written with type constraints and these are used below but do not cover all cases.

The reason that the reader should have no difficulty with these extended meanings is that key properties such as the symmetry of conjunction and disjunction hold:

$$\vee\text{-}sym \, \frac{E_1 \vee E_2}{E_2 \vee E_1}$$

$$\wedge\text{-}sym \, \frac{E_1 \wedge E_2}{E_2 \wedge E_1}$$

In fact, the key difference with conventional propositional logic is that the so-called "law of the excluded middle" $(P \vee \neg P)$ only holds in LPF where it is established that P denotes a truth value.

a	b	$\neg a$	$a \wedge b$	$a \vee b$	$a \Rightarrow b$	$a \Leftrightarrow b$
true	true	false	true	true	true	true
*	true	*	*	true	true	*
false	true	true	false	true	true	false
true	*		*	true	*	*
*	*		*	*	*	*
false	*		false	*	true	*
true	false		false	true	false	false
*	false		false	*	*	*
false	false		false	false	true	true

Fig. 1.3 LPF extensions of propositional operators

Quantifiers are in no way mysterious. Over finite sets, they are just convenient abbreviations:

$$(\exists i \in \{1, \cdots, 3\} \cdot p(i)) \, \Leftrightarrow \, (p(1) \vee p(2) \vee p(3))$$
$$(\forall i \in \{1, \cdots, 3\} \cdot p(i)) \, \Leftrightarrow \, (p(1) \wedge p(2) \wedge p(3))$$

Even the infinite cases should present no difficulty:

$$\forall i \in \mathbb{N} \cdot \exists j \in \mathbb{N} \cdot i < j$$

With all of the quantifiers, the scope is assumed to extend as far as possible to the right; parentheses are not required for this case but they can be used to define different grouping.

This leaves only the end cases with the empty range for the bound variable to note:

$$\exists i \in \{\} \cdot p(i) \, \Leftrightarrow \, \text{false}$$
$$\forall i \in \{\} \cdot p(i) \, \Leftrightarrow \, \text{true}$$

which are obviously related from the quantifier versions of de Morgan's laws:

$$de\text{-}Morgan\text{-}3 \, \frac{\neg(\exists x \cdot p(x))}{\forall x \cdot \neg p(x)}$$

$$\boxed{de\text{-}Morgan\text{-}4}\ \frac{\neg\left(\forall x \cdot p(x)\right)}{\exists x \cdot \neg p(x)}$$

There are other logics that attempt to handle terms that fail to denote a value and a comparison is given in [CJ91]. Details of the specific LPF used in VDM are addressed in [BCJ84, JM94]. Kleene (in [Kle52]) attributes the propositional operator definitions in Figure 1.3 to [Łuk20]. Other papers that address the issue of undefinedness include [Kol76, Bla86, KTB88, Bli88].

Chapter 2
Delimiting a language

The body of this book addresses the task of describing –or designing– the semantics of programming languages. This chapter prepares the way for that task by introducing the division between *syntax* and *semantics*. A tiny language is introduced which, because it has few surprises, can be used to explain the description method. As more complicated language features are considered in later chapters of this book, they are treated independently as far as is possible (e.g. input/output is modelled in Section 4.3.1 and a similar extension could be made to the concurrent object-oriented language in Chapter 9).

For an extant language,[1] it is necessary to delimit the set of allowed programs before their meaning can be discussed: Section 2.1 outlines "concrete syntax" notations for fixing the textual strings of an object language (such strings include various marks that make it possible to parse the strings); Section 2.2 addresses a way of defining the "abstract syntax" of programs without the symbols needed to facilitate parsing. This chapter also covers most of the VDM notation used in the current book. The topic of semantics is first tackled in Chapter 3 and runs throughout the remainder of this book.

2.1 Concrete syntax

Any interesting language allows an unbounded number of different "utterances". It is therefore not possible to enumerate all of the allowable strings of characters in a language.

It is not difficult to devise meta-languages with which to define the set of plausible programs of a language. Many of the notations used are close relatives of *Backus*

---

[1] A *Leitmotiv* of the remaining chapters of this book is the value of using formal models in the design of languages but this topic is postponed until the basic description tools have been covered in the current chapter.

© Springer Nature Switzerland AG 2020
C. B. Jones, *Understanding Programming Languages*,
https://doi.org/10.1007/978-3-030-59257-8_2

Normal Form[2] (also known as *Backus-Naur Form*).[3] *BNF* was used in [BBG⁺60] to define the concrete syntax of ALGOL 60. A slight elaboration of BNF is Niklaus Wirth's *Extended BNF* — EBNF is described in [Wir77].

Despite claiming that devising syntactic meta-languages is relatively simple, the first "challenge" is:

Challenge I: Delimiting a language (concrete representation)
How can the set of valid strings of an object language be delimited?

Syntax is about content and "concrete syntax" concerns the linear sequence of characters that are allowed in the object language. A well-designed concrete syntax can also suggest a structure that points to the semantics of the object language. Crucially, a concrete syntax must be devised that makes it possible to "parse" strings[4] but it is easier to consider the generation of strings first.

Starting with a simple example from natural language, a grammar can be written as a set of BNF rules:

⟨*SimpleSentence*⟩ ::= ⟨*Pronoun*⟩ ⟨*Verb*⟩ ⟨*Spread*⟩.
⟨*Pronoun*⟩ ::= I | You
⟨*Verb*⟩ ::= like | hate
⟨*Spread*⟩ ::= Marmite | Peanut Butter

This defines a set of eight sentences:

$$\left\{ \begin{array}{l} \text{I like Marmite., I like Peanut Butter.,} \\ \text{I hate Marmite., I hate Peanut Butter.,} \\ \text{You like Marmite., You like Peanut Butter.,} \\ \text{You hate Marmite., You hate Peanut Butter.} \end{array} \right\}$$

Looking more carefully at the BNF rules, each rule starts with a "non-terminal", which is marked by enclosure in ⟨···⟩; the non-terminal that is being defined is separated from its definition by "::="; this is followed by the definition, which is intended to fix the set of possible strings; all but the first rule above list options separated by a vertical bar (|). Such a definition can be made of a sequence of items that can be either "terminal" strings or non-terminal symbols that should be defined in other rules. Terminal (in the sense that no further production is needed) symbols just stand for themselves; non-terminal symbols can be replaced by any string that is valid from their production rule.

The rules above are not unique in generating the strings — all of the above and more are generated by:

⟨*SimpleSent*⟩ ::= ⟨*Word*⟩ ⟨*Word*⟩ ⟨*Word*⟩.
⟨*Word*⟩ ::= I | You | like | hate | Marmite | Peanut Butter

---

[2] Marking the insight of John Warner Backus (1924–2007) who proposed the notation.

[3] Acknowledging Peter Naur's (1928–2016) contribution to the development and use of BNF.

[4] It is noted below that designing languages that are easy to parse is itself a technical challenge but is not within the scope of the current book — references to this material are given in Section 2.3.

One way to move from a finite language like ⟨*SimpleSent*⟩ to languages with an unbounded number of possible strings[5] is to use recursion — for example:

⟨*Paragraph*⟩ ::= ⟨*SimpleSent*⟩ | ⟨*Paragraph*⟩ ⟨*SimpleSent*⟩

A potential problem can be seen if a pronoun ("He") that requires a different form of the verb ("likes") is added to the language. Writing:

⟨*Pronoun*⟩ ::= I | You | He
⟨*Verb*⟩ ::= like | likes | ···

can generate the ungrammatical string "He like Marmite." This could be resolved by splitting ⟨*SimpleSentence*⟩ but the more general issue of "context dependancy" is addressed below in Section 4.2.

Moving to describing the concrete syntax of an example programming language, it has to be recognised that there is a huge variety of syntax styles across the many known programming languages and debates about such stylistic differences often generate more heat than light. Interestingly for the main purpose of this book, most such syntactic argument has no impact at all on semantics. It is for this reason that, from Section 2.2 onwards, semantic discussions are based on abstract syntaxes.

When however example programs are presented, concrete syntax is used. The stylistic choice here is that a vaguely ALGOL/Pascal flavour of concrete syntax is used for sequential programs and a move towards Java syntax is made for concurrent (object-oriented) languages.

For the initial simple language, a complete ⟨*Program*⟩ might be bracketed by keywords and contain (yet to be defined) lists of allowed variable names and statements:

⟨*Program*⟩ ::= **program vars** ⟨*Ids*⟩: ⟨*Stmts*⟩ **end**

The design choice recorded in this rule is that the names of variables used in ⟨*Stmts*⟩ of a ⟨*Program*⟩ must be declared in the list of identifiers given after the keyword **vars**. For now, variables can only contain natural numbers ($\mathbb{N}$) — multiple types are addressed in Chapter 4. Lists of identifiers are separated by commas:

⟨*Ids*⟩ ::= ⟨*Id*⟩ [, ⟨*Ids*⟩]

Here, the square brackets of EBNF are used to show that the bracketed portion can be omitted. This could equally be written as:

⟨*Ids*⟩ ::= ⟨*Id*⟩ | ⟨*Id*⟩, ⟨*Ids*⟩

No grammar is given here for ⟨*Id*⟩ — were this done, it would probably require that the first character was a letter followed by a string of digits or letters.[6]

---

[5] EBNF provides the alternative of showing that a group of things can be repeated:

⟨*Paragraph*⟩ ::= ⟨*SimpleSent*⟩*

But recursion is stronger than iteration because the former can describe arbitrary nesting such as bracketing in (()())

[6] Some languages limit the length of identifiers.

Statements are separated by semicolons — notice that this syntax eliminates writing a semicolon after the last statement in a list:[7]

$\langle Stmts \rangle ::= [\langle Stmt \rangle \, [; \, \langle Stmts \rangle]]$

Statements can be one of three types (for now):

$\langle Stmt \rangle ::= \langle Assign \rangle \mid \langle If \rangle \mid \langle While \rangle$

The idea that the left- and right-hand sides of $\langle Assign \rangle$ should be separated by an equality sign is anathema to mathematicians who point out that:

$x = x + 1$

is a nonsense. ALGOL 60 uses $:=$ between the left-hand side reference and the expression which is to be evaluated and assigned to that reference:[8]

$\langle Assign \rangle ::= \langle Id \rangle := \langle ArithExpr \rangle$

There is an interesting parsing issue associated with $\langle If \rangle$ — but this is discussed below — for now a closing bracket (**fi**) is given to complete the conditional statement:

$\langle If \rangle ::= $ **if** $\langle RelExpr \rangle$ **then** $\langle Stmts \rangle \, [$**else** $\langle Stmts \rangle] \,$ **fi**

This is far from the only way to make a grammar unambiguous but some such device is necessary to ensure that parsing is unique.[9] Similarly:

$\langle While \rangle ::= $ **while** $\langle RelExpr \rangle$ **do** $\langle Stmts \rangle$ **od**

Moving on to the definition of the two forms of expression:

$\langle ArithExpr \rangle ::= \langle BinArithExpr \rangle \mid \langle NaturalNumber \rangle \mid \langle Id \rangle \mid (\langle ArithExpr \rangle)$

notice that the fourth option for $\langle ArithExpr \rangle$ allows the insertion of parentheses to distinguish the priority of operators between $x * y + z$ and $x * (y + z)$.

$\langle BinArithExpr \rangle ::= \langle ArithExpr \rangle \langle BinArithOperator \rangle \langle ArithExpr \rangle$
$\langle BinArithOperator \rangle ::= + \mid *$
$\langle RelExpr \rangle ::= \langle ArithExpr \rangle \langle CompareOperator \rangle \langle ArithExpr \rangle$
$\langle CompareOperator \rangle ::= = \mid \leq$
$\langle NaturalNumber \rangle ::= \langle Digit \rangle \mid \langle Digit \rangle \langle NaturalNumber \rangle$
$\langle Digit \rangle ::= 0 \mid 1 \mid 2 \mid 3 \mid 4 \mid 5 \mid 6 \mid 7 \mid 8 \mid 9$

---

[7] Writing the semicolon between $\langle Stmt \rangle$ is in contrast to terminating every statement with the punctuation symbol (as is done in most (European) languages, where a full stop marks the end of a sentence). Many years ago, Jim Horning reported an experiment in which he compared the number of mistakes made by programmers under each rule: in his experiment, the terminating semicolon was actually the cause of fewer slips than its placing as a separator.

[8] Some languages use "$\leftarrow$" between the left- and right-hand sides of assignments.

[9] Appendix A.1.2 shows how Java disambiguates conditional (and looping) statements. Tony Hoare proposed the more radical idea of writing the test between the two statement sequences:

$\langle If \rangle ::= \langle Stmts \rangle \lhd \langle RelExpr \rangle \rhd \langle Stmts \rangle$

This proves convenient for showing algebraic properties of conditionals.

Notice that ⟨*RelExpr*⟩ offers only a restricted way of obtaining a Boolean value; it would be easy to add a more general form of logical expression to the syntax.

The intention is that any given ⟨*Program*⟩ is finite (i.e. instead of taking recursive options all of the time, the option to use terminal symbols is eventually chosen) but the set of possible programs is infinite.

As with the natural language example above, there are other ways of defining ⟨*ArithExpr*⟩. One option would be to have a single set of strings for ⟨*Expr*⟩ that allowed all four operators. This would define a larger class of strings.

Grammars like those above can be used to generate the strings of a language; in fact, a single generator program can easily be written that takes a grammar as input and can generate (random) strings of the given syntax. Christopher Strachey showed that a simple grammar could be used to generate English paragraphs that could pass as love letters and IBM had a project in the 1960s that created random PL/I test cases: "APEX" generated random strings from a grammar of PL/I.[10]

Using grammars as generators of languages finesses the issue of "ambiguity". Even writing the deliberately ambiguous grammar:

⟨*Ambiguous*⟩ ::= a | a⟨*Ambiguous*⟩ | ⟨*Ambiguous*⟩a

allows many different ways of generating strings of the letter "a" but their unique generation can be recorded. If however the task is to analyse a string to determine how the rules could be used to generate such a string, the ambiguity issue is serious. Such analysis programs are called *parsers* and writing general-purpose parsers is a significant challenge.[11]

Language issue 1: Avoiding syntactic ambiguity
The concrete syntax of a programming language should be unambiguous.

Consider a grammar for conditional statements as in ALGOL 60:

⟨*A-If*⟩ ::= **if** ⟨*RelExpr*⟩ **then** ⟨*Stmts*⟩ [**else** ⟨*Stmts*⟩]

This is intended to permit programs that omit **else** parts of conditional statements but it can generate the ambiguous string:

if $a = b$ **then if** $c = d$ **then** $x := 1$ **else** $x := 2$

in two distinct ways. Indentation can be used to suggest these options:

if $a = b$ **then**
    if $c = d$ **then** $x := 1$
    else $x := 2$

---

[10] In fact, the grammars for APEX used a "dynamic syntax" to cope with context dependancies — see Section 4.4 for references.

[11] This can be compared to the fact that determining the factors of a composite number is far harder than multiplying numbers together.

and:

> **if** $a = b$ **then**
>   **if** $c = d$ **then** $x{:} = 1$
> **else** $x{:} = 2$

and these have different meanings.[12]

This is why some form of bracketing is added to the syntax of conditionals — here it is the closing keyword **fi** but it can equally be (as in Java) some explicit bracketing around the two sequences of statements contained in each conditional statement — see Appendix A.1.2.

The front end of a compiler or interpreter for a language has to:

- decompose the sequence of characters into distinct "tokens" (keywords, identifiers and constants);
- create a parse tree that shows how the sequence of tokens can be generated from the grammar of the language (and produce, hopefully useful, diagnostics if the input string is not valid with respect to the grammar of the language).

The grammar of a language must not be ambiguous in such a way that different generating sequences have different meanings.

Language issue 2: Defining priority of operators
The concrete syntax given above for $\langle ArithExpr \rangle$ makes no attempt to show the priority of multiplication and addition; in for example [BBG$^+$63] the syntax makes clear that the potentially ambiguous $a + b * c$ should be parsed as though $a + (b * c)$ had been written; this is achieved by adding extra phrase classes for $\langle term \rangle / \langle factor \rangle$.

An alternative approach to disambiguate expressions is by adopting a canonical linearisation of a tree such as that known as "reverse Polish" notation (e.g. $+ a * b c$).

There is a further issue when considering the parsing problem for compilers and that is the efficiency of parsing. The PL/I language designers declined to reserve the keywords of the language (and there were rather a lot!) and had no way of distinguishing keywords from identifiers. This has the consequence that a sequence of characters that looks as though it might be a keyword might actually be the start of an assignment to a variable of that name. Such ambiguities in a grammar complicate the design of its processors and damage their performance (this is further complicated in PL/I because declarations are not required to be at the start of a block).

Language issue 3: Avoiding syntactic inefficiency
The concrete syntax of a programming language should be such that parsing can be efficient — this amounts to minimising backtracking.

---

[12] This is sometimes referred to as the "dangling else" problem. With his typical pragmatism, Niklaus Wirth simply ordained that, in Pascal, the else clause related to the closest if.

Section 2.2 shows how the use of an "abstract syntax" avoids these complications, so they are left aside here. There are however many concrete syntax issues for language designers to resolve.

> **Language issue 4: Style of syntax**
> Many issues have to be resolved in designing the style of the concrete syntax of a programming language — a few examples are:
>
> - are blanks significant?
> - are keywords to be reserved or distinguished by some special markers?
> - how are comments to be distinguished from the intended program in which they occur?
> - should two-dimensional layout have an effect on parsing?

The payoffs from studying grammars include:

- General-purpose parsing algorithms can be written that handle arbitrary grammars — as distinct from writing a hand-crafted parser for each language.
- Parser generators take as input a concrete syntax and produce a parser that yields efficient parsing speeds.
- Tools can be constructed that transform grammars into ones that are equivalent but admit more efficient parsing.
- The important topic of error recovery in parsing can be studied systematically.

Syntactic meta-languages used to define concrete syntax (such as BNF) are of course languages themselves and, as such, have their own syntax and semantics. Without going into a fully formal definition, the semantics in terms of the set of strings is outlined above. To make the point about the syntax of a syntactic meta-language, Niklaus Wirth's "railroad diagrams" can define exactly the same sets — an example is given in Figure 2.1 and they are employed in the description of the Modula-3 language.

One important issue is being postponed and that is that the BNF syntax notation cannot describe the requirement that the statements in a program can only use identifiers that have been declared; Section 4.2 describes ways to handle such "context dependancies".

2.2 Abstract syntax

The concrete syntax notations covered in Section 2.1 give both a way of producing the texts of programs and a way of parsing such texts. But, even for simple languages, such a concrete syntax can be "fussy" in that it is concerned with details which make it possible to parse strings (e.g. the commas, semicolons, keywords and those marks that serve to bracket strings that occur in recursive definitions). Peter Landin used the lovely term "syntactic sugar" (which can be sprinkled on the essential content).

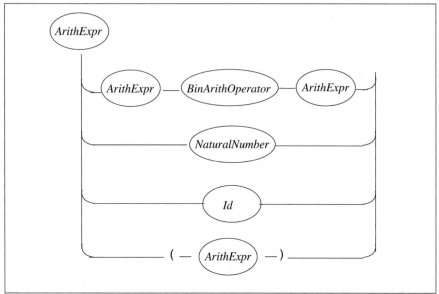

Fig. 2.1 Concrete syntax using "railroad diagrams"

For a programming language such as C or Java, there are many different ways of writing semantically indistinguishable programs. In PL/I, variable declarations can be placed anywhere in a block but their position has no meaning; most languages allow comments that have no influence on semantics. It should thus be clear that the concrete syntax is not a convenient basis for semantic descriptions. The concrete syntax does have to be defined but, since the syntactic variants have identical semantics, basing a semantic description on a concrete syntax clouds it in an unnecessary way. Here, the first big dose of abstraction is deployed and all of the subsequent work is based on an "abstract syntax".

Challenge II: Delimiting the abstract content of a language

Semantic descriptions mostly ignore textual details of programs. Furthermore, an abstract syntax can make it clear what can*not* happen (e.g. order of declaration of identifiers cannot have an influence because the abstract declaration contains a set). How can the abstract syntax of a language be defined?

It is again useful to relate what is done in a language description to the tools that process programs. The parsing phase of a compiler or interpreter generates (a representation of) a tree form of the program to be compiled. An *abstract syntax* defines a class of *objects* that retain as little superfluous information as possible. In most cases, such objects are tree-like in that they are (nested) VDM composite objects. To achieve abstraction, sets, sequences and maps are used whenever appropriate.

This section reviews more VDM notation. The concepts will almost certainly be familiar to any reader. The VDM notation for sets is listed in the previous chapter (Figure 1.1). Sequences (sometimes referred to as lists) provide another useful abstraction whose operators are listed in Figure 2.2.

T^*	type defining finite sequences (elements are of type T)
len s	length of a sequence
$[t_1, t_2, \ldots, t_n]$	sequence given by enumeration
$[\,]$	the empty sequence
$s_1 \frown s_2$	sequence concatenation
hd s	the element at the head of a sequence
tl s	the sequence comprising the tail of a sequence
inds s	the set of indexes to a sequence
elems s	the set of elements in a sequence

Fig. 2.2 Sequence notation

Just as with X-set, instances of X^* are always finite. Notice that the head of a sequence is the first element, thus hd $[a, b] = a$, whereas the tail of a sequence is a sequence without its first element: tl $[a, b] = [b]$. Either of these operators applied to the empty sequence is undefined and this serves as a reminder of VDM's use of a *Logic of Partial Functions* — see Section 1.6.

The indexes of a list are the set of natural numbers that can be used as indexes:

inds $s = \{1, \cdots, \text{len } s\}$

and that makes the elements of a list easy to define:

elems $s = \{s(i) \mid i \in \text{inds } s\}$

Selecting an indexed element of a sequence uses a notation identical to function application: $s(i)$. Notice that $s(\text{len } s + 1)$ or $s(0)$ again both fail to denote values.

Consider the task of checking that a list does not contain the same element more than once. In VDM, it is standard to be explicit about the type of a function which is recorded in its signature:

uniquel: $X^* \to \mathbb{B}$

A definition of *uniquel* that follows the verbal description above is:

$\textit{uniquel}(s) \quad \triangleq \quad \forall i, j \in \text{inds } s \cdot i \neq j \implies s(i) \neq s(j)$

The $\triangleq$ is an equality but is used for a definition rather than a simple assertion such as $1 + 1 = 2$. An equivalent definition of *uniquel* would be

uniquel : $X^* \to \mathbb{B}$

$\textit{uniquel}(s) \quad \triangleq \quad \text{len } s = \text{card elems } s$

The definition can even be written recursively to illustrate that VDM function notation allows both case constructs and conditionals:

$uniquel : X^* \to \mathbb{B}$

$uniquel(s)$ $\underline{\triangle}$ cases s of

$\qquad\qquad$ [] $\qquad\qquad\qquad\to$ true

$\qquad\qquad$ $[hd] \frown rest \to$ if $hd \in$ elems $rest$

$\qquad\qquad\qquad\qquad\qquad$ then false

$\qquad\qquad\qquad\qquad\qquad$ else $uniquel(rest)$

$\qquad\qquad\qquad\qquad\qquad$ fi

$\qquad$ end

Functions such as *uniquel* that yield Boolean results are referred to as *predicates*.

The concept of records is present in many programming languages (PL/I called them structures); its use in meta-languages dates back to John McCarthy's [McC66]. In VDM these sources are pulled together to make several facets automatic. An example record class is defined as follows:

$Example$ :: $field$-1 : X

$\qquad\qquad$ $field$-2 : Y

Such a record definition automatically defines a function *mk-R* for record type R — for building objects of *Example* from values of type X and Y:

$mk\text{-}Example : X \times Y \to Example$

The set of all *Example* objects is:

$Example = \{mk\text{-}Example(x,y) \mid x \in X \wedge y \in Y\}$

These implicit *mk-* functions can be thought of as labelling the values of the objects such that $mk\text{-}A(\cdots)$ can never yield the same values as $mk\text{-}B(\cdots)$ — thus the sets A and B are disjoint.

The record definition also automatically defines *selectors* (which are written as suffixes) so that:

$e = mk\text{-}Example(x,y)$

$e.field\text{-}1 = x$

$e.field\text{-}2 = y$

(Section 3.1 shows how the use of the *mk-* constructors in parameter lists can almost eliminate the need to use selectors explicitly.)

Record definitions often occur in places where recursion can lead back to the record type; here again, the intention is that only finite instances are considered.

The use of | to define unions of types is carried over from concrete syntax notation. In abstract syntax:

$[X] = X \mid \{$nil$\}$

where nil is a unique elementary object. Notice that, in contrast to record values where the constructor makes the set unique, equality rules are genuine set equalities. So with:

$$X = A \mid B$$
$$Y = B \mid C$$

it is not true that X and Y are disjoint.

SimpleProgram :: *vars* : *Id*-set
                          body : *Stmt**

Stmt = *Assign* | *If* | *While*

Assign :: *lhs* : *Id*
                  rhs : *ArithExpr*

If :: *test* : *RelExpr*
         then : *Stmt**
         else : *Stmt**

While :: *test* : *RelExpr*
                body : *Stmt**

ArithExpr = *BinArithExpr* | $\mathbb{N}$ | *Id*

BinArithExpr :: *operand1* : *ArithExpr*
                        operator : PLUS | TIMES
                        operand2 : *ArithExpr*

RelExpr :: *operand1* : *ArithExpr*
                  operator : EQUALS | LESSTHANEQ
                  operand2 : *ArithExpr*

Fig. 2.3 Abstract syntax of *SimpleProgram*

The abstract syntax of *SimpleProgram* is given in Figure 2.3. Remember that *Stmt** includes empty sequences — this obviates the need for a special skip statement in the language.

So, if $1 \in \mathbb{N}, i \in Id$ then:

$$mk\text{-}BinArithExpr(i, \text{PLUS}, 1) \in ArithExpr$$
$$mk\text{-}RelExpr(i, \text{LESSTHANEQ}, 1) \in RelExpr$$

and then with:

$$s_1 = mk\text{-}If(mk\text{-}RelExpr(i, \text{LESSTHANEQ}, 1),$$
$$[mk\text{-}Assign(i, mk\text{-}BinArithExpr(i, \text{TIMES}, 1))],$$
$$[mk\text{-}Assign(i, i)])$$
$$s_1 \in Stmt$$

And, finally

$$mk\text{-}SimpleProgram(\{i\}, [s_1]) \in Program$$

Writing out such objects is clearly longwinded for actual programs so example programs will normally be given in (some arbitrary) concrete syntax. The case for using abstract syntax as a basis for semantic descriptions becomes ever clearer as the languages covered in later chapters become more realistic.

Looking at Figure 2.3, notice that:

- the fact that the *vars* component of *SimpleProgram* is defined as a set (of *Id*) makes it immediately clear that their order has no semantic significance;[13]
- *Stmt* is defined recursively (via *If* and *While*);
- the concrete syntax markings in ⟨*If*⟩ statements are no longer required because the record nesting resolves ambiguity;
- *ArithExpr* is also defined recursively;
- the nesting of records fixes the tree structure of expressions, obviating the need for parentheses;
- the use of the mathematical set $\mathbb{N}$ as an option for *ArithExpr* is reasonable because there is a simple finite representation for any natural number (more care would be needed if an abstract syntax used real numbers ($\mathbb{R}$));
- PLUS etc. are constants that stand for unit sets containing a string.

Comparison of Figure 2.3 with the concrete syntax developed in Section 2.1 is useful but, on such a simple language, shows only limited progress; the difference between the abstract and concrete syntaxes of a language like Java or PL/I is much more marked because they offer many alternative ways of writing semantically identical programs. Another advantage of basing semantic descriptions on abstract syntaxes is that it is possible to envisage programs being printed in differing concrete forms (e.g. the original FORTRAN syntax for *DO* statements was built around coding pads and statement numbers but it could be generated from an abstract syntax that covers the for of ALGOL 60). The description is, in a sense, getting closer to the underlying "language concept". Christopher Strachey's observation was: "one should work out what one wants to say before fixing on how to say it".

Notice that the problem identified with concrete syntaxes that there is no constraint that the statements in a *SimpleProgram* should only use identifiers that are declared in its *vars* part also pertains to the abstract syntax. A reader who objects that the declaration of variable names in the *vars* part of *SimpleProgram* is not being used for checking is asked to remain patient until he or she reaches Section 4.2. There is however an important language issue:

---

[13] The ECMA/ANSI PL/I standard [ANS76] eschewed the use of sets — its authors arguing that sequences would be more familiar to programmers. Unfortunately this leaves the reader with no choice but to read hundreds of pages to determine whether the order of a sequence actually has any influence on the semantics. If not, this fact could have been made completely obvious by employing a set.

> **Language issue 5: Constructive redundancy**
> Mistyping an identifier in a language with no declarations can result in it being treated as the name of a distinct variable. Where possible, a simple typo should not make a program execute wrongly — simple mistakes should be detected by a compiler before execution is undertaken. One form of redundancy is that all variable names should be listed so that any undeclared names can be identified as errors.

Early versions of FORTRAN had no (redundant) variable declarations — the type (integer or real) of a variable was determined by the first letter of its identifier. Furthermore, blanks had no influence on strings punched as programs. A valid FORTRAN DO statement might be written:

DO 15 I = 1,100

where 15 is the statement number of the end of the loop, "I" is the intended control variable, 1 its initial value and 100 the intended final value of the iteration. Unfortunately, given the above decisions on FORTRAN, typing the comma as a full stop allowed the interpretation of an assignment of a floating point number to an (undeclared) variable (i.e. DO15I = 1.100). The claim that this resulted in the loss of a Mariner space probe has been discredited but the fact remains that lack of redundancy is extremely perilous.

2.3 Further material

Projects

Even at this stage where only syntax description is covered, there are many projects that the reader could pursue:

1. Many programming languages include some form of iterative for statement; an example in ALGOL 60 is:

   for $j := I + G, L, 1$ step 1 until $N, C + D$ do $A[k,j] := B[k,j]$

   A concrete syntax can be found in [BBG+60] or [BBG+63]; write an appropriate abstract syntax.
2. Add a class of Boolean expressions to *SimpleProgram*. The basic elements of Boolean expressions could be elements of *RelExpr*; a few simple propositional operators would be for (unary) negation and (binary) disjunction.
3. *SimpleProgram* has conditional statements; it is easy to envisage conditional expressions such as:

   $x := 5 +$ if $a = b$ then 2 else 3 fi

   It is even possible to have conditional references as in:

   if $a = b$ then x else y fi $:= 5$

Write appropriate abstract syntax definitions.

4. Languages such as C/C++/Java allow constructs of the form $x++$; as statements such increments might be viewed as useful clues to a compiler; written within expressions their semantics causes side effects. Discuss how this complicates even the abstract syntax of the language.[14]

More ambitiously, readers could find the concrete syntax of a favourite programming language and write out a complete abstract syntax for that language. A word of warning is in order: the reader might have to hunt beyond books bearing titles such as "Programming in $\mathscr{L}$". Unfortunately, it is now far less common to find BNF in language textbooks; they tend to limit themselves to covering "use cases" of programs that one has to perturb. The best source of a formal concrete syntax is likely to be the standard for $\mathscr{L}$.

Further reading

Although the next chapter turns to the main subject of this book (i.e. semantics), there are many interesting publications on syntax. A good starting point might be [MP99]; the subject of efficient general-purpose parsing is covered in [SJv19].

Historical notes

The argument that it is better to base a semantic description on an abstract –rather than a concrete– syntax is set out in [McC66]. McCarthy defined the constructors and selectors explicitly; the group in IBM Lab Vienna moved to these functions being implicit as soon as the record description is given.

Oxford researchers often based the semantic description of (small) languages on a concrete syntax. Where they moved closer to an abstract syntax, they used a disjoint union operator rather than records with constructor functions.

---

[14] More exotic forms might tax the understanding of someone who has to maintain a program containing statements such as $x := ++x * x++$.

Chapter 3
Operational semantics

Chapter 2 shows how to delimit texts in a language by using a syntax meta-language. This chapter moves on to the problem of fixing the meaning of texts in languages by using a semantic meta-language.

Three main object languages are described formally in subsequent chapters. In order to introduce the meta-language involved, a very simple language is described in this chapter. This initial language has only one type of variable and a limited repertoire of statements. An initial approach to describing the semantics of deterministic languages is contained in Section 3.1; this is enriched, in Section 3.2, to the style used to tackle the description of all of the remaining language concepts in the book. This enriched style copes with non-determinism in languages and the need is illustrated by the inclusion of a non-deterministic iterative statement.

3.1 Operational semantics

The presentation of a semantic description should be related closely to the abstract syntax of the language: in this case *SimpleProgram*, whose syntax is given in Figure 2.3. This leaves the question of the order in which it is easiest to read a semantic description.[1] Rather than start from the top of the grammar it is easier to see what needs doing in the semantic description by working first on the expression constructs and working up to the program level.

> **Challenge III: Recording semantics (deterministic languages)**
> How can the semantics of a deterministic language be recorded?

The abstract syntax of *ArithExpr* in Figure 2.3 is recursive because both operands of *BinArithExpr* are themselves elements of *ArithExpr*. Any instance of *ArithExpr*

---

[1] There is no single best solution to the question of order. The appendices of this book illustrate different orders of presentation of language descriptions. Clearly some interactive tool could escape the linear constraint of printed pages.

© Springer Nature Switzerland AG 2020
C. B. Jones, *Understanding Programming Languages*,
https://doi.org/10.1007/978-3-030-59257-8_3

is finite because its leaves are either natural numbers or members of *Id*. A recursive function that evaluated arithmetic expressions whose leaves were all constants ($\mathbb{N}$) would require only the expression as an argument. The fact that variable names occur in expressions (*Id* $\subseteq$ *ArithExpr*) indicates that the meaning of an expression depends on the current values of any such names: the fact that such values are changed by assignment statements is the essence of imperative programming languages.

Associations of values with some sort of key are a useful tool in most abstract models and their types are recorded in VDM as *Key* $\xrightarrow{m}$ *Value*. As with VDM's *X*-set, maps are always finite. The basic operators on maps are given in Figure 3.1. A map value is really just a finite set of pairs:[2] the domain of a map (dom *m*) is the set of values that are the first element of any pair in *m*; similarly, rng *m* is the set of values contained as the second element of any pair in *m*.

$D \xrightarrow{m} R$	finite maps from D to R
dom m	domain of a map
rng m	range of a map
$m(d)$	map application
$\{d_1 \mapsto r_1, d_2 \mapsto r_2, \ldots, d_n \mapsto r_n\}$	map enumeration
$\{\mapsto\}$	empty map
$\{d \mapsto f(d) \in D \times R \mid p(d)\}$	map defined by comprehension
$m_1 \dagger m_2$	map overwrite

Fig. 3.1 Map notation (basic operators)

Applying a map to a value ($m(d)$) yields the second element of a pair whose first element is equal to d. Because maps are like functions, there can be at most one such pair. Map application $m(d)$ is undefined if there is no pair in m whose first element is d.[3]

Further intuition about maps comes from noting that sequences are a special case of maps: T^* can be thought of as $\mathbb{N} \xrightarrow{m} T$. The sequence operator inds s gives the domain of the map m and elems s yields its range; selecting an element of a sequence ($s(i)$) is the same as applying the appropriate map to i.

It is somewhat of a tradition in semantic descriptions to use the Greek letter Sigma (Σ) for the set of all states and $\sigma \in \Sigma$ for specific values; this convention is followed here — thus the state required for *SimpleProgram* is:

$$\Sigma = Id \xrightarrow{m} \mathbb{N}$$

Maps are many:one associations in that different identifiers can map to the same value but any identifier can, in any particular $\sigma \in \Sigma$, only map to one value in $\mathbb{N}$.

Given this, the signature of the function to evaluate expressions is:

$$eval: ArithExpr \times \Sigma \to \mathbb{N}$$

---

[2] General functions (e.g. *square*) can be used where infinite associations are required; these can be understood to define infinite sets of pairs.

[3] Limiting the propagation of such undefined terms is one of the benefits of the "Logic of Partial Functions" (LPF) mentioned in Section 1.5 and described in more detail in Section 1.7.3.

In any large body of formulae, it is useful to record the types or *signatures* of functions along with their definition. It would be possible to write a definition of the *eval* function that evaluates arithmetic expressions with respect to a state as:

$$eval : ArithExpr \times \Sigma \to \mathbb{N}$$

$eval(e, \sigma) \quad \triangle$
    if $e \in BinArithExpr$
    then if $e.operator = \text{PLUS}$
        then $eval(e.operand1, \sigma) + eval(e.operand2, \sigma)$
        else $eval(e.operand1, \sigma) * eval(e.operand2, \sigma)$
        fi
    else if $e \in Id$
        then $\sigma(e)$
        else e
        fi
  fi

Map application is written in the same way as function application; thus the value of a given *Id* (say *a*) can be accessed in σ by writing $\sigma(a)$.

Thus:

$$eval(mk\text{-}BinArithExpr(1, \text{PLUS}, i), \{i \mapsto 2, j \mapsto 4\}) = 3$$

The meaning of VDM's conditional expressions should be clear but the next convention removes the need for them in this context.

Even for such a small language, the definition of *eval* above looks slightly heavy and this style becomes inconvenient for larger descriptions. A pattern matching style was used in early VDM language descriptions and it is much more convenient to split the definition of a function like *eval* by cases (and use the pattern to define local names for the values of fields) so that the definition of *eval* is given in cases such as:

$eval(mk\text{-}BinArithExpr(op1, \text{PLUS}, op2), \sigma) \quad \triangle$
    $eval(op1, \sigma) + eval(op2, \sigma)$

The six cases are given in full in Figure 3.2. This style becomes very natural for larger language description. Formally, the constructors (*mk-*) and any constants (e.g. PLUS) are defining when a match occurs and any other identifiers become bound to the values present in the specific argument passed. Thus:

$\exists op1, op2 \in ArithExpr \cdot$
    $e = mk\text{-}BinArithExpr(op1, \text{PLUS}, op2) \Rightarrow$
                            $eval(e, \sigma) = eval(op1, \sigma) + eval(op2, \sigma)$

Repeating the example above:

$eval(mk\text{-}BinArithExpr(1, \text{PLUS}, i), \{i \mapsto 2, j \mapsto 4\}) =$
                      $eval(1, \{i \mapsto 2, j \mapsto 4\}) + eval(i, \{i \mapsto 2, j \mapsto 4\})$

$$eval(mk\text{-}BinArithExpr(op1, \text{PLUS}, op2), \sigma) \quad \triangleq \quad eval(op1, \sigma) + eval(op2, \sigma)$$

$$eval(mk\text{-}BinArithExpr(op1, \text{TIMES}, op2), \sigma) \quad \triangleq \quad eval(op1, \sigma) * eval(op2, \sigma)$$

$$eval(mk\text{-}RelExpr(op1, \text{EQUALS}, op2), \sigma) \quad \triangleq \quad eval(op1, \sigma) = eval(op2, \sigma)$$

$$eval(mk\text{-}RelExpr(op1, \text{LESSTHANEQ}, op2), \sigma) \quad \triangleq \quad eval(op1, \sigma) \leq eval(op2, \sigma)$$

$$e \in \mathbb{N} \implies eval(e, \sigma) = e$$
$$e \in Id \implies eval(e, \sigma) = \sigma(e)$$

Fig. 3.2 The function *eval* given by cases

It is a useful by-product of employing the pattern-matching style that the names of the object fields are rarely needed as selectors.

So far, *eval* looks as though it is doing little more than identifying the syntactic mark PLUS with the mathematical notion of addition. This is partly the result of the object language in the current chapter having been kept deliberately simple in order to explain the meta-language. Notice however that the definition could be modified to take the modulus (with respect to the word length of a physical machine) of the mathematical result.[4]

There is a snag with the final case in Figure 3.2: applying a map to a value that is not in its domain does not denote a value (this is one of the common causes of non-denoting expressions, as mentioned in Section 1.5). The obvious purpose of the *vars* part of *SimpleProgram* in Figure 2.3 is that all variables should be declared. It would then be possible for the semantics to initialise all declared variables[5] (otherwise variables having values before they are accessed in expressions depends on the flow through assignment statements). The question of context dependancies such as requiring that all identifiers are declared is addressed in Section 4.2; handling issues such as run-time errors is discussed in Section 4.1.

Moving to the description of the semantics of statements (*Stmt* in Figure 2.3), the description can again be split into cases. As mentioned in the general discussion of what constitutes an imperative language, the key state transitions are brought about by assignments with conditional (*If*) and iterative (*While*) statements orchestrating

---

[4] Interestingly, few formal language descriptions do this. The issue of "computer arithmetic" is addressed in [vW66a] and then [Hoa69]; and [Sit74, CH79] tackle proofs about "clean termination" — see Section 7.4.

[5] An argument against initialisation is the cost (to a programmer who is careful).

the order in which the assignments are executed. Given that statements are to change the state, it is reasonable that a semantic function *exec* should have the signature:

$exec: Stmt \times \Sigma \rightarrow \Sigma$

The map operator that can be used to update a map is the overwrite (†) and it is used as follows:

$exec(mk\text{-}Assign(lhs, rhs), \sigma) \quad \triangleq \quad \sigma \dagger \{lhs \mapsto eval(rhs, \sigma)\}$

Thus:

$$exec(mk\text{-}Assign(j, mk\text{-}BinArithExpr(1, \text{PLUS}, i)), \{i \mapsto 2, j \mapsto 4\}) =$$
$$\{i \mapsto 2, j \mapsto 3\}$$

It is important to appreciate that where an identifier is placed affects how it is interpreted: on the right of an assignment, the identifier denotes its value in the current store; on the left, the identifier is the name of the variable to be updated. Christopher Strachey used the terms "right-hand value" and "left-hand value" to distinguish these uses. Having precise terms is useful because there are other places where the distinction is important (e.g. different parameter mechanisms use either the left- or right-hand value — see Section 5.4). This discussion is returned to in Section 5.2.

The abstract syntax of *Stmt* in Figure 2.3 is recursive (via *Stmt**) so –just as with *eval*– the *exec* semantic function is recursive: it is straightforward to define:

$exec(mk\text{-}If(b, th, el), \sigma) \quad \triangleq$
    if $eval(b, \sigma)$
    then $exec\text{-}list(th, \sigma)$
    else $exec\text{-}list(el, \sigma)$
    fi

$exec(mk\text{-}While(b, body), \sigma) \quad \triangleq$
    if $eval(b, \sigma)$
    then $exec(mk\text{-}While(b, body), exec\text{-}list(body, \sigma))$
    else σ
    fi

The topic of non-termination is discussed in Section 3.3.

Finally, an *exec-list* function can also be defined by cases:

$exec\text{-}list([], \sigma) \quad \triangleq \quad \sigma$

$exec\text{-}list([s] \frown rl, \sigma) \quad \triangleq \quad exec\text{-}list(rl, exec(s, \sigma))$

The function *exec-list* fixes the semantic order of execution of statements as left to right. The way this is done fits exactly the description that the semantics is given by an *abstract interpreter*. An operational description mimics the operation of an abstract machine. As the object languages being described acquire more features in later chapters, extra constraints on the preferred operational style come into play.

3.2 Structural Operational Semantics

The preceding section provides an intuition for operational semantics using functions. As pointed out in Section 3.3, this fits the historical development of ideas. The approach is also convenient with respect to providing tool support for a semantic description: such an operational semantic description could be implemented using a functional programming language such as Haskell [Hut16] or Scala [OS16] or supported by the VDM Toolset.[6] This section addresses the challenge of non-determinism where a language description has to define the range of acceptable answers for acceptable implementations of a language.

> **Challenge IV: Operational semantics (non-determinism)**
> How can an operational semantics describe a non-deterministic language in a way that clearly relates the structure of the semantics to its abstract syntax?

The most compelling case for non-determinism in programming languages comes from languages that support concurrent execution: such languages do not fix the relative progress of threads and this, in general, means that a program can legitimately deliver different results even from the same starting state. The task of a language description is to define all allowable outcomes. The way in which relations can cope with non-deterministic language features and notations to describe relations conveniently are introduced in this section and illustrated on the semantic description of a non-deterministic loop construct.

Functions have the crucial limitation that they define a unique result for their arguments — thus writing $f(x)$ denotes a unique value. Although uniqueness of result might be thought of as an appealing property for program semantics, there are a number of ways in which *non-determinism* arises in programming languages:

1. many languages leave the order of expression evaluation up to the implementation — where expression evaluation can give rise to side effects (e.g. because of function calls), a language description has to show the resulting non-determinism;
2. some (even sequential) languages include specific non-deterministic constructs (e.g. Edsger Dijkstra's so-called "guarded commands" — see Section 3.3);
3. most importantly, it is difficult to add meaningful concurrency to a language without introducing non-determinism.

---

[6] See http://overturetool.org/publications/books/vdmtools.html

The first category is messy and discussion of this language feature is postponed until Section 6.5. Category two can be introduced at will and an example different from "guarded commands" is given below. It is really the third of these categories that is both most interesting and is the strongest reason for switching to a way of presenting semantics that copes naturally with any form of non-determinism. The material on concurrency (including a concurrent object-based language) is addressed in Chapters 8 and 9; here an alternative way is chosen to introduce non-determinism into the simple language.

3.2.1 Relations

A mathematical function defines an infinite set of pairs. For example, the function:

$$square : \mathbb{Z} \to \mathbb{Z}$$
$$square(i) \quad \triangle \quad i * i$$

gives the set of pairs:

$$\{(i, i * i) \mid i \in \mathbb{Z}\}$$

Although the VDM type $\mathbb{Z}$-set only includes finite subsets, the mathematical notation for power sets can be used:

$$square \subseteq \mathscr{P}(\mathbb{Z} \times \mathbb{Z})$$

The function *exec* in the preceding section takes a pair of arguments but it is straightforward to extend the notion of a function to one whose domain is also a set of pairs:

$$exec \subseteq \mathscr{P}((Stmt \times \Sigma) \times \Sigma)$$

Although a function applied to different arguments can denote the same value:

$$square(2) = square(-2) = 4$$
$$\{(2,4), (-2,4)\} \subseteq square$$

the set of pairs has the many-to-one property that prohibits two possible results for the same argument value.

One part of the specification for sorting mentioned in Chapter 1 is the concept of a permutation. Here, a function cannot be defined that yields any permutation of its inputs because there are many such results. It is, of course, possible to define a function that yields all permutations:

$$permutations : X^* \to (X^*)\text{-set}$$

Alternatively this can be formalised by defining a predicate:

$$is\text{-}perm = X^* \times X^* \to \mathbb{B}$$

Similarly, it would be possible to define a non-deterministic statement using a function that yields a set of possible result states:

$execS: Stmt \times \Sigma \to \Sigma$-set

but composing such functions becomes notationally messy and relations offer a more natural mathematical extension.

Functions are a special case of *relations* and relations do allow many:many connections. To illustrate the idea, suppose that the top-level notion of a program in Figure 2.3 were changed to contain a set of statements that could be executed in arbitrary order:

$NonDeterministicProgram$ :: $vars$: Id-set
$\qquad\qquad\qquad\qquad\qquad\quad body$: $Stmt$-set

One program (in an unimportant concrete syntax) might be:

vars x:
$\{x:=1, x:=2\}$

The valid executions of the body of this program give rise to a many:many relationship between states:

$\{(\sigma, \sigma \dagger \{x \mapsto i\}) \mid i \in \{1, 2\}\}$

The semantics shifts from being given by a function: $SimpleProgram \times \Sigma \to \Sigma$ to a relation between pairs of $NonDeterministicProgram \times \Sigma$ and Σ. This relation will in general be an infinite set.

3.2.2 Inference rules

There are many ways in which such a relation could be defined — as with the permutation example (*is-perm*), it could be characterised by a predicate:

valid-transition: $Stmt$-set $\times \Sigma \times \Sigma \to \mathbb{B}$

and defined as follows:

$s \in stmts \land$
$exec(s, \sigma) = \sigma' \land$
$valid\text{-}transition((stmts - \{s\}, \sigma'), \sigma'') \Rightarrow$
$\qquad\qquad valid\text{-}transition((stmts, \sigma), \sigma'')$

A more readable notation (than writing the predicate *valid-transition* in functional style) is to define the relation as an infix operator marked by an arrow that indicates the type of the first argument — for statements:

$(stmts, \sigma) \xrightarrow{st} \sigma'$

this can be thought of as stating that configuration $(stmts, \sigma)$ "can transition to" state σ'. For:

$$\xrightarrow{st} : \mathscr{P}((Stmt \times \Sigma) \times \Sigma)$$

it is possible that both:

$$(\{x := 1, x := 2\}, \{x \mapsto 3, y \mapsto 4\}) \xrightarrow{st} \{x \mapsto 1, y \mapsto 4\}$$

and:

$$(\{x := 1, x := 2\}, \{x \mapsto 3, y \mapsto 4\}) \xrightarrow{st} \{x \mapsto 2, y \mapsto 4\}$$

hold.

"Natural Deduction" presentations of logic [Pra65] use inference rules such as:

$$\boxed{\wedge\text{-}E} \; \frac{E_1 \wedge E_2}{E_i}$$

$$\boxed{\vee\text{-}I} \; \frac{E}{E \vee E'}$$

Even in logic, some of the inference rules require multiple hypotheses ($E_i \vdash E$ means that E can be deduced from E_i):

$$\boxed{\vee\text{-}E} \; \frac{\begin{array}{c} E_1 \vee E_2 \\ E_1 \vdash E \\ E_2 \vdash E \end{array}}{E}$$

Similar rules can be used to define semantic relations conveniently — for example:

$$\frac{\begin{array}{c} s \in stmts \\ (s, \sigma) \xrightarrow{st} \sigma' \\ (stmts - \{s\}, \sigma') \xrightarrow{st} \sigma'' \end{array}}{(stmts, \sigma) \xrightarrow{st} \sigma''}$$

Just as with Natural Deduction, the rules are "schema" into which matching values can be substituted. Figure 3.3 shows two valid deductions from the rule above and establishes formally that the simple program $\{x := 1, x := 2\}$ can give rise to different final states.

The essence of the rule notation is that the relation under the line in a rule holds if all of the hypotheses above the line hold. More is said about this reading as inference rules below but for now the rule above can be read as:

Given that *stmts* is a set of *Assign* statements and an $s \in stmts$ can be found (thus *stmts* is a non-empty set), if (s, σ) can transition to σ' and *stmts* without s can transition from σ' to σ'', then it is valid to conclude that $(stmts, \sigma)$ can transition to σ''.

In fact, the rule style becomes so natural that most people use it even for simple sequential (deterministic) languages and it is first applied to the language as given in Figure 2.3. The same pattern-matching idea is used. With:

$$(x := 1) \in \{x := 1, x := 2\}$$
$$(x := 1, \{x \mapsto 3\}) \xrightarrow{st} \{x \mapsto 1\}$$
$$(\{x := 2\}, \{x \mapsto 1\}) \xrightarrow{st} \{x \mapsto 2\}$$
$$\overline{(\{x := 1, x := 2\}, \{x \mapsto 3\}) \xrightarrow{st} \{x \mapsto 2\}}$$

$$(x := 2) \in \{x := 1, x := 2\}$$
$$(x := 2, \{x \mapsto 3\}) \xrightarrow{st} \{x \mapsto 2\}$$
$$(\{x := 1\}, \{x \mapsto 2\}) \xrightarrow{st} \{x \mapsto 1\}$$
$$\overline{(\{x := 1, x := 2\}, \{x \mapsto 3\}) \xrightarrow{st} \{x \mapsto 1\}}$$

Fig. 3.3 Two deductions from a non-deterministic rule

$$\Sigma = Id \xrightarrow{m} \mathbb{N}$$

$$\xrightarrow{st} : \mathscr{P}((Stmt \times \Sigma) \times \Sigma)$$

$$\xrightarrow{stl} : \mathscr{P}((Stmt^* \times \Sigma) \times \Sigma)$$

$$(s, \sigma) \xrightarrow{st} \sigma'$$
$$(rl, \sigma') \xrightarrow{stl} \sigma''$$
$$\overline{([s] \frown rl, \sigma) \xrightarrow{stl} \sigma''}$$

Unlike the description with functions in Section 3.2.1, the description here is given top-down.

The style of semantic description used in Figure 3.4 was dubbed "Structural Operational Semantics" by its originator Gordon Plotkin.[7] (The figure only gives the description of the statements of the language; Appendix A includes the SOS rules for expressions.) The adjective "structural" indicates that the semantic rules should follow closely the structure of the (abstract) syntax of the language. This objective offers greater benefits when the semantic objects of the language need to be more complicated, such as with environments in Chapter 5.

The idea that SOS rules define inference relations ($\xrightarrow{st}$ / $\xrightarrow{stl}$ / $\xrightarrow{ex}$) is very important and Figure 3.5 illustrates two possible chains of inference for:

$$fn := 1;$$
$$\text{while } n \neq 0 \text{ do}$$
$$\quad fn := fn * n;$$
$$\quad n := n - 1$$
$$\text{od}$$

The SOS rules for expressions ($\xrightarrow{ex}$) are given in Appendix A. Apart from the argument that the use of inference rules offers uniformity of presentation, there is a technical reason for defining $\xrightarrow{ex}$ as a relation: the fact that it can be undefined (in the case where a reference is made to an undeclared identifier) means that it is

---

[7] See Section 3.3 for references and a sketch of the history.

$$\frac{}{([\,],\sigma) \xrightarrow{stl} \sigma}$$

$$\frac{(s,\sigma) \xrightarrow{st} \sigma'}{(rest,\sigma') \xrightarrow{stl} \sigma''}$$
$$\frac{}{([s]^\frown rest,\sigma) \xrightarrow{stl} \sigma''}$$

$$\frac{(test,\sigma) \xrightarrow{ex} \mathsf{true}}{(th,\sigma) \xrightarrow{stl} \sigma'}$$
$$\frac{}{(mk\text{-}If(test,th,el),\sigma) \xrightarrow{st} \sigma'}$$

$$\frac{(test,\sigma) \xrightarrow{ex} \mathsf{false}}{(el,\sigma) \xrightarrow{stl} \sigma'}$$
$$\frac{}{(mk\text{-}If(test,th,el),\sigma) \xrightarrow{st} \sigma'}$$

$$\frac{(test,\sigma) \xrightarrow{ex} \mathsf{false}}{(mk\text{-}While(test,body),\sigma) \xrightarrow{st} \sigma}$$

$$\frac{(test,\sigma) \xrightarrow{ex} \mathsf{true}}{(body,\sigma) \xrightarrow{stl} \sigma'}$$
$$\frac{(mk\text{-}While(test,body),\sigma') \xrightarrow{st} \sigma''}{(mk\text{-}While(test,body),\sigma) \xrightarrow{st} \sigma''}$$

$$\frac{eval(rhs,\sigma) \xrightarrow{ex} v}{(mk\text{-}Assign(lhs,rhs),\sigma) \xrightarrow{st} \sigma \dagger \{lhs \mapsto v\}}$$

Fig. 3.4 SOS of the statements in *SimpleProgram*

$$\frac{(e,\{fn \mapsto 1, n \mapsto 0\}) \xrightarrow{ex} \mathsf{false}}{(mk\text{-}While(e,b),\{fn \mapsto 1, n \mapsto 0\}) \xrightarrow{st} \{fn \mapsto 1, n \mapsto 0\}}$$

$$\frac{(e,\{fn \mapsto 1, n \mapsto 1\}) \xrightarrow{ex} \mathsf{true}}{(b,\{fn \mapsto 1, n \mapsto 1\}) \xrightarrow{st} \{fn \mapsto 1, n \mapsto 0\}}$$
$$\frac{(mk\text{-}While(e,b),\{fn \mapsto 1, n \mapsto 0\}) \xrightarrow{st} \{fn \mapsto 1, n \mapsto 0\}}{(mk\text{-}While(e,b),\{fn \mapsto 1, n \mapsto 1\}) \xrightarrow{st} \{fn \mapsto 1, n \mapsto 0\}}$$

where:

$e = mk\text{-}RelExpr(n, \text{NOTEQUALS}, 0)$
$b = [mk\text{-}Assign(fn, mk\text{-}BinArithExpr(fn, \text{TIMES}, n)),$
$\qquad mk\text{-}Assign(n, mk\text{-}BinArithExpr(n, \text{MINUS}, 1))]$

Fig. 3.5 Two traces of inferences from the SOS in Figure 3.4

actually wrong to define *eval* as a function. With the inference rules, there is simply no rule whose hypotheses are all dischargeable. In this case, the computation is undefined.

It is also worth repeating the point that, so far, expression evaluation cannot change the state and this is made clear by the form of the semantic relation:

$$\xrightarrow{ex}: \mathscr{P}((Expr \times \Sigma) \times \mathbb{N})$$

This situation changes with the inclusion of functions in a language[8] — see Section 6.5.

3.2.3 Non-deterministic iteration

The idea in *NonDeterministicProgram* above of just executing a set of statements in arbitrary order is somewhat artificial. This section introduces and describes formally a more plausible construct for non-deterministic iteration. (Although the different instances of the body are executed separately here, this construct is developed further in Chapter 8 to exhibit concurrency.)

Because assignments change the store, the left-to-right order of statement evaluation is part of the essence of imperative programming languages. There is, however, a subtle danger of writing programs that are unnecessarily ordered. Although formal description of arrays is tackled in Section 4.3.2, the reader should readily spot that an initialisation such as:

```
for i := 1 to 100 do
    A(i) := 0
od
```

does not need to be executed in any particular order. A non-deterministic iteration such as:

```
for all i ∈ {1, .., 100} do
    A(i) := 0
od
```

would leave a compiler freedom to choose an optimal order or even make it easier to spot that some form of bulk write would be much more efficient. Furthermore, because multiplication is commutative, the factorial example could be written:

```
fn := 1;
for all i ∈ {1, .., n} do
    fn := fn * n
od
```

---

[8] Also by allowing pseudo-expressions such as $x++$ or $++x$.

The above examples actually determine a unique final state but:

```
for all i ∈ {1,.., 10} do
    result := i
od
```

is certainly non-deterministic.

An abstract syntax for such a non-deterministic looping construct could be:

$$ND\text{-}For :: \begin{array}{ll} control & : Id \\ low & : ArithExpr \\ high & : ArithExpr \\ body & : Stmt^* \end{array}$$

The semantics could be fixed by the following SOS rules:[9]

$$\frac{(low,\sigma) \xrightarrow{ex} lv \\ (high,\sigma) \xrightarrow{ex} hv \\ (mk\text{-}Repeat(c,\{i \in \mathbb{N} \mid lv \leq i \leq hv\}, body),\sigma) \xrightarrow{st} \sigma'}{(mk\text{-}ND\text{-}For(c,low,high,body),\sigma) \xrightarrow{st} \sigma'}$$

$$\frac{set = \{\}}{(mk\text{-}Repeat(c,set,body),\sigma) \xrightarrow{st} \sigma}$$

$$\frac{v \in set \\ (body,\sigma \dagger \{c \mapsto v\}) \xrightarrow{stl} \sigma' \\ (mk\text{-}Repeat(c,set - \{v\},body),\sigma') \xrightarrow{st} \sigma''}{(mk\text{-}Repeat(c,set,body),\sigma) \xrightarrow{st} \sigma''}$$

3.3 Further material

Projects

Semantics can now be tackled for all of the enumerated syntactic projects listed in Section 2.3.[10] The final unnumbered challenge of looking at a whole language is likely to present the challenges discussed in subsequent chapters and thus should be postponed until description techniques for handling these challenges have been understood.

---

[9] This way of recording the semantics requires that *Repeat* is an acceptable first element of the pairs in the $\xrightarrow{st}$ relation. An alternative would be to define a separate relation $\xrightarrow{iter}$.

[10] There is an interesting interaction between for loops and declarations in that some languages treat the control variable as being "bound" within the loop — this aspect is picked up in Section 5.5. An alternative adopted in ALGOL 60 is to say that the value of the control variable is undefined on termination of the loop.

Alternatives

The semantics given so far are often referred to as "big-step" (or "natural" semantics). The applicability of this term is seen in the rule for statement sequences:

$$\frac{\begin{array}{l}(s,\sigma) \xrightarrow{st} \sigma' \\ (rest,\sigma') \xrightarrow{stl} \sigma''\end{array}}{([s] \curvearrowright rest,\sigma) \xrightarrow{stl} \sigma''}$$

where the conclusion of the SOS rule gives the relation for the whole sequence. (It is shown in Chapter 8 that describing the merging of threads in concurrency requires a "small-step" semantics. In a small-step semantics, a "configuration" keeps track of the activity remaining in each thread and a step makes an atomic transition of one thread at a time; SOS rules both show the state change and update the text remaining to be executed. Such a semantics is necessarily non-deterministic.)

An important issue arises with big-step semantics and termination. Consider the rule given for while statements:

$$\frac{\begin{array}{l}(test,\sigma) \xrightarrow{ex} \text{true} \\ (body,\sigma) \xrightarrow{stl} \sigma' \\ (mk\text{-}While(test,body),\sigma') \xrightarrow{st} \sigma''\end{array}}{(mk\text{-}While(test,body),\sigma) \xrightarrow{st} \sigma''}$$

For a non-terminating loop (in the extreme, while true do $x := x + 1$ od) it will never be possible to discharge the third hypothesis of the rule. Thus non-termination in the program is modelled by non-termination in the semantics.[11]

This fits with the notion that an operational semantics is providing an abstract interpreter. There is, of course, no way in general that the semantics could solve the "halting problem".[12]

The situation is even more complicated with non-deterministic programs where –from the same state– a program might either diverge or converge. A yet further issue involves "fairness" — see [Fra86, vGH15].

There are many ways of recording the relations between (program + initial state) and final state. An obvious candidate is to write the program as though it is a relation symbol (as could be done for permutations; $[A,A,B,B]$ permutes $[A,B,B,A]$); thus $\sigma[\![S]\!]\sigma'$ — this does not however extend cleanly to "small-step" semantics (see Chapter 8) because the text of the program has to be updated as well as the state.

Other options for recording the semantic relation include writing the program text on the relation arrow — see also Peter Mosses' "Modular SOS" [Mos04, Mos09]

---

[11] A more mathematically pleasing treatment is possible with denotational semantics and this is discussed in Section 7.1.

[12] Although the "Halting Problem" is often associated with Alan Turing's name, the undecidability result in [Tur36] is different because it concerns infinite number representations and Turing's programs were not in general intended to terminate. The impossibility of constructing a program that will determine whether an arbitrary machine will halt is given in [Dav65a]. Useful historical notes are [Pet08, pp.328–329] and further discussion by Post and Davis is in [Dav65b].

and [HC12] from Rob Colin and Ian Hayes. What is common to these presentations is the necessity of using relations and the convenience of defining such relations by inference rules.

It is worth noting that the advantages of mathematical abstractions like objects, functions and relations do not guarantee ease of implementation. This point becomes clearer when more advanced object language features like "heap storage" and the consequent need for "garbage collection" are considered in Chapter 6. One point that can be made here is that mathematical abstractions such as natural numbers cannot be implemented — for example, the non-terminating program given above is bound to overflow on any actual computer.

Further reading

There are a number of books that treat operational semantics including [RNN92, Hen90]. They could be said to go deeper into the theory whereas the current book aims to show how to apply the ideas of operational semantics to realistic programming languages. (References to books on other semantic approaches are given in Chapter 6.)

Historical notes

As far as tackling the semantic description of typical imperative programming languages, John McCarthy's "Micro-ALGOL" description in [McC66] is a key historical reference. In the talk given at the famous *Formal Language Description Languages* working conference in 1964, he both introduces a form of abstract syntax and gives an operational semantics using a function. McCarthy's choice of language constructs is interesting: he could have made his life easier by doing as Edsger Dijkstra later did and selecting only the structured language features described here in Appendix A. In fact, Micro-ALGOL has no while loop but does have a goto statement. The reader should avoid jumping to the conclusion that this was a mistake that would not have been made had Dijkstra's goto letter [Dij68b] been written earlier. It is at least plausible that McCarthy made a deliberate choice to include labelled statements and it certainly had a significant impact on work that followed. The state of McCarthy's semantics had to include the full text of the program and a program counter; the semantics of a goto changed the program counter.

That same working conference was held at Baden bei Wien and its proceedings [Ste66] are an invaluable source because all of the formal discussions were recorded and transcribed. Professor Heinz Zemanek became the leader of the IBM Laboratory in Vienna and made sure that many of his colleagues took part in the process of capturing this valuable material.[13] The relevance of this is that the IBM Vienna Laboratory went on to produce operational semantic descriptions of the PL/I language. This was a huge undertaking: PL/I had most of the features found in any of FORTRAN, COBOL and ALGOL (sadly without the elegance and the taste of the last of those three). Not only did the Vienna group have to find ways of modelling all of the features of ALGOL omitted from McCarthy's Micro-ALGOL, they also had to model features such as the concurrency that came with "tasking" in PL/I, "exceptions" and under-determined storage mapping.

The PL/I formal descriptions were labelled "ULD-III" which stood for "Uniform Language Description" — the Roman numbering three gave absolute precedence to IBM's official natural-language document that claimed to describe the language and the existence of a semi-formal ULD-II written by the IBM UK Lab in Hursley. There were three complete versions of ULD-III.[14] Probably the most useful first-hand account is [LW69]. J.A.N. Lee coined the name "Vienna Definition Language" (VDL is not to be confused with VDM, which came later — see [Jon01]) for the description method.

As is so often the case, hindsight provides rather unfair judgements but it is true that the VDL description method had unfortunate properties that complicated its use. The Vienna group acknowledged their main influences as:

- John McCarthy — including [McC66],
- Cal Elgot — especially [ER64] and
- Peter Landin — [Lan66b], which was also presented at the Baden bei Wien IFIP Working Conference.

Perhaps the most troublesome features of VDL descriptions can be grouped under McCarthy's term of "grand-state" descriptions:[15]

1. The full text of a PL/I program is included in the ULD-III state because of abnormal sequencing (whether from goto statements or exceptions). This decision is a magnified version of the program counter in McCarthy's [McC66] — but the magnification makes a monster of the original.
2. The state of VDL descriptions included a stack of "environments" (see Section 5.2). This fits with Landin's SECD machine idea but –as explained in Section 5.5– is a definite impediment to proofs about VDL descriptions.

McCarthy's phrase pinpoints the fact that there are serious disadvantages in putting things in the state that are not changed by executing (normal) statements of the program.

In passing, it is worth noting how ALGOL 60 became a testbed for semantic description techniques — in [JA16, AJ18] four more-or-less complete descriptions

---

[13] More is said on this meeting in [AJ18] and at greater length in [Ast19].

[14] These have all been scanned and, along with key working documents, are available from my web site: http://homepages.cs.ncl.ac.uk/cliff.jones/semantics-library/

[15] McCarthy used this term in several discussions — an early reference is in an exchange at an IFIP Working Group discussion [Wal69, p.33] — but it is also clear that the concern is behind Strachey's comment on McCarthy's talk at the 1964 Working Conference (see [McC66, p.11]).

of that language are described along with references to other attempts. The earliest of these ([Lau68]) was undertaken by Peter Lauer because Heinz Zemanek wanted evidence to show that the criticism levelled at the ULD descriptions of PL/I had far more to do with the chosen object language than being a valid objection to the VDL meta-language. (The problem referred to as having a grand state did however also dog Lauer's ALGOL description.)

The comment in Section 1.5 about a language description being used as a criterion for compiler correctness can now be expressed formally. If a compiler *comp* maps source programs to the language of some machine whose semantics is described by $\xrightarrow{mc}$, that compiler is correct with respect to the language semantics $\xrightarrow{st}$ providing:[16]

$$\forall s \in Stmt \cdot$$
$$\forall \sigma, \sigma' \cdot (comp(s), \sigma) \xrightarrow{mc} \sigma' \;\Rightarrow\; (s, \sigma) \xrightarrow{st} \sigma'$$

Notice that this is not an equivalence (i.e. the reverse implication is not required) because the language semantics can be non-deterministic and describe a range of permissible results.

Two of the earliest publications on using a formal description in compiler correctness proofs are [MP66, Pai67]. Details of the IBM Vienna Lab work on developing compilers from formal language descriptions (particularly that on the "block concept" such as [Luc68, JL70]) are given in Section 5.5; a useful overview is contained in [Jon82a] and extensive work on Ada in [BO80b, BO80a]. The work on the Texas "stack" is published in [Moo19].

Unhappiness with gratuitous difficulties in basing reasoning about compiler designs on such (grand-state operational) definitions led the Vienna group to move to denotational semantic descriptions (see Sections 7.1–7.2). Again, ALGOL was used as a demonstration [HJ78, HJ82] and among other object languages, Pascal [AH82] and Modula-II [AGLP88] have been described using VDM (see Chapter 11).

Using the denotational approach certainly prompts the use of "small-state semantics". Gordon Plotkin had made significant contributions to the *domain theory* that underlies the denotational approach when he took a sabbatical (from Edinburgh) to Aarhus University. There he taught an operational approach and his course notes [Plo81] provide the foundation of *Structural Operational Semantics*. These notes were widely circulated and eventually republished as [Plo04b]; the accompanying [Plo04a] provides a fascinating commentary on this period.

---

[16] This is a slight simplification in that –in reality– the states of the machine will differ from those of the language description. Expanding this is not difficult but does show the interesting need to relate the run-time state to the abstraction (see [Jon76] for further details).

Chapter 4
Constraining types

In early versions of FORTRAN, the type of a variable was determined by the first letter of its identifier. This chapter shows how to describe an object language that expands on the idea of listing the permissible names of variables and looks at the advantages of declaring a specific *type* for each variable. This makes it possible to detect –before a program is executed– some mistakes that a programmer might make. More generally, all forms of context dependancy offer ways of avoiding an attempt to give semantics to meaningless programs. There is nothing in formal semantic approaches that requires that object languages be *strongly typed*. Methods for describing languages at various points on the strength-of-typing spectrum are presented in Section 4.1.

Language issue 6: Type declarations

Fixing the types of variables in declarations makes it possible to detect programming errors statically (before execution). Maximising the idea of types results in a "strongly typed" language. The availability of static type information can also make it easier for a compiler to generate efficient code for the statements in the language. This is an extension of the redundancy concept addressed in Issue 5.

A meta-objective of this and subsequent chapters is to show that the metalanguage introduced in Chapters 2 and 3 copes easily with new features in the object language. In fact, the semantic tools in SOS do not need to change at all in this chapter; it is the idea of using "context conditions" to define the context dependancies of a language which is new (Section 4.2). Section 4.3 goes on to explore the key role of state descriptions. As in other chapters, a concluding section on further material (Section 4.4) is included.

© Springer Nature Switzerland AG 2020
C. B. Jones, *Understanding Programming Languages*,
https://doi.org/10.1007/978-3-030-59257-8_4

4.1 Static vs. dynamic error detection

There are many things that can be wrong with a program. In general, they cannot all be detected by any algorithm. There are, however, some aspects of languages for which it can be said that certain programs make no sense.

In fact, the language descriptions in Chapters 2 and 3 have not so far excluded *SimplePrograms* that use identifiers in statements that are not listed in the *vars* list. This can be checked statically for a *SimpleProgram*: all uses of *Id* in expressions or on the left-hand side of assignments must have been declared in the *vars* list. This is a simplified case of the more general context dependancies considered in Section 4.2.

There is a related issue that requires a dynamic –or run-time– check and that is the danger that a program attempts to access a variable before any assignment has been made to it. Of course, one way of avoiding this problem is for the language designer to arrange that all declared variables are given initial values at the start of execution. This is however a design choice. If a language does not decree that such initialisation occurs, there needs to be a check on variable access such as the second hypothesis in the following SOS rule:

$$e \in Id$$
$$e \in \mathsf{dom}\,\sigma$$
$$\overline{(e,\sigma) \xrightarrow{ex} \sigma(e)}$$

The description in Section 3.2.2 of reading SOS descriptions as inference rules indicates that, if no rule can be found whose hypotheses are fulfilled, the execution is undefined and thus the program is erroneous. It might, of course, be desirable in a full language to include some form of exception-raising and -handling mechanism but this topic is deferred to Chapter 10.

Language issue 7: Initial values

Programming languages that require all variables to be initialised avoid some programming errors (or, alternatively, obviate the need for run-time checks). There is however a trade-off here because a careful programmer who always makes sure that variables are set before use is paying for the redundant initialisation. Note that checking for initialisation by (meaningful) assignment requires flow tracing.

Language issue 8: Initial expressions

An alternative language design decision is to allow programmers to write initial expressions as part of variable declarations. Notice that until there are nested blocks (see Chapter 5) such expressions can only yield constant initial values.

4.2 Context conditions

A prime example of context dependancy concerns the use of variables in ways which do not correspond to their intended types. Language designers can choose to make compile-time detection of such errors possible by recording rules that are statically checkable. For example, a language might rule out adding a character string to a number. If variables are untyped and can be assigned any values, the consequences of such violations can only be detected at run-time. In contrast, if variables are typed, it is possible for a compiler to flag any program which applies an arithmetic operator to a character string operand.

There are, of course, cases where operators are intended to be *polymorphic* in the sense that the same operator can be applied to operands of different types. For example, the plus symbol might be overloaded and –as well as being applied to numbers– used in a programming language to mean concatenation of strings. A language can also be designed to be permissive in the sense that some type differences in operands to a binary operator are resolved by coercing the type of one operand to that of the other. Thus an arithmetic operator with operands that are integers or reals could convert an integer operand to a floating-point number before applying the operator.

Language issue 9: Type information

The designer of a language must decide the extent to which type information is required in programs. Type information provides redundancy and makes it possible to detect some program errors from the static text of a program. The availability of type information can also facilitate generation of more efficient code than is possible if no information is available about the intended roles of different variables.

In order to introduce the alternative description techniques, a rather coarse distinction is made in this chapter between static and dynamic checking. This degree of difference can be demonstrated by allowing variables in *BaseProgram*s to take values that are either integers ($\mathbb{Z}$) or Booleans ($\mathbb{B}$). The full description of *BaseProgram* is contained in Appendix B; the text of this chapter picks out the main decisions; after understanding these points, the reader should have no difficulty in reading the description in the appendix.

Note that some distinctions from the abstract syntax of *SimpleProgram* of Chapter 2 have been dropped in that the *test* parts of both *If* and *While* here appear to allow any *Expr* — the checking on types is now done in the context conditions.

Given that there are two types of variables, meaningless programs can arise in a number of ways — for example:

- the *test* expression in an *If* or *While* statement might be an arithmetic expression;
- an arithmetic operator might be applied to expressions (*RelExpr*) that yield a Boolean result.

If there were no type indications in programs, it would be possible to say that the type of a variable was determined by the first assignment to its name. In this case, it would not be possible –in general– to detect type errors statically. It is true that egregious cases of these errors such as:

if 42 then $n := 1$ else $n := 2$ fi
$n := \text{true} + 7$

could be detected statically but, since assignments to variables can depend on the flow of control, types cannot –in general– be determined statically. The checking would then have to be made in the SOS rules as in Section 4.1 above.

Because both BNF and the basic description of objects can essentially only cope with context-free languages, the challenge faced by those describing –or designing– a programming language is:

> **Challenge V: Context dependancy**
> A convenient notation is required to cut down the objects defined by the abstract syntax of a language to the "meaningful" texts (i.e. those which are in accord with any type restrictions that the language imposes on valid programs).

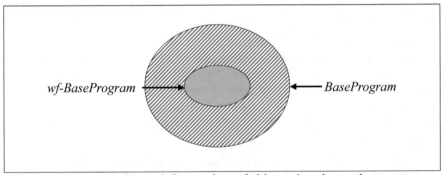

Fig. 4.1 Context conditions define a subset of objects given by an abstract syntax

Defining the subset of objects (satisfying an abstract syntax) to which meaning will be given is pictured in Figure 4.1. There are several ways in which the class of *well-formed* objects can be defined. Here a predicate is written:

$wf\text{-}BaseProgram: BaseProgram \rightarrow \mathbb{B}$

Only objects of *BaseProgram* for which *wf-BaseProgram* yields true are considered in the semantic description. This test can be defined in terms of three recursive predicates that check statements and expressions. These predicates require an extra argument that carries down the type information from *BaseProgram*:

$TypeMap = Id \xrightarrow{m} ScalarType$

The signatures of the two statement-level predicates are:

$wf\text{-}StmtList: Stmt^* \times TypeMap \rightarrow \mathbb{B}$
$wf\text{-}Stmt: Stmt \times TypeMap \rightarrow \mathbb{B}$

The first of these is trivial, just requiring that all elements of the list of statements are well formed (with respect to the same type map):

$wf\text{-}StmtList : Stmt^* \times TypeMap \to \mathbb{B}$

$wf\text{-}StmtList(sl, tpm) \quad \triangle \quad \forall i \in \text{inds } sl \cdot wf\text{-}Stmt(sl(i), tpm)$

The well-formedness of an assignment statement depends on two things:

- that the expression forming its right-hand side is well formed — a function such as:

$wf\text{-}Expr : Expr \times TypeMap \to \mathbb{B}$

could be used to determine this;
- a type match between the *lhs* and *rhs* components of the statement.

Because it is a single identifier in this simple language, the type of *lhs* is simply $tpm(lhs)$. To complete the check of matching, there is an obvious need for a function that determines the type of an expression but there are also expressions that are in themselves obviously inconsistent. Rather than define two separate functions for checking the well-formedness of an expression (*wf-Expr*) and for computing its type, a single function can be defined that performs both tasks (with the result ERROR indicating non-well-formed expressions):

$c\text{-}type : Expr \times TypeMap \to (\text{INTTP} \mid \text{BOOLTP} \mid \text{ERROR})$

With this, it is straightforward to define:

$wf\text{-}Stmt(mk\text{-}Assign(lhs, rhs), tpm) \quad \triangle$
$\qquad lhs \in \text{dom } tpm \land$
$\qquad c\text{-}type(rhs, tpm) = tpm(lhs)$

The test for well-formed *If* and *While* in Appendix B should be obvious and the full definition of *c-type* is easy to read.

Finally, it has to be shown how the type information in a *BaseProgram* provides the *TypeMap*:[1]

$wf\text{-}BaseProgram : BaseProgram \to \mathbb{B}$

$wf\text{-}BaseProgram(mk\text{-}BaseProgram(types, body)) \quad \triangle$
$\qquad wf\text{-}StmtList(body, types)$

---

[1] In languages with nested blocks/procedures (see Chapter 5) or classes and methods (see Chapter 9), the *TypeMap* has to be updated with declaration information that is contained in nested texts.

Because semantics are only given for well-formed texts (see Figure 4.1), the appropriate *wf* predicate can be thought of as an extra hypothesis for any SOS rule. The elision of such lines fits with the position in VDM that data type invariants restrict types.

It is useful to think of the context conditions in relation to the type checking done in a compiler. Just as with the diagnostics in a compiler, it is not always obvious how far such checks should extend. For example, a while statement whose test is true will definitely loop forever — but so would one that looked for a counterexample to Fermat's last theorem. An indication of what is reasonable to check in context conditions is whether the test depends only on symbols (such as operators) rather than their meaning.

Language issue 10: Types as assertions

Type definitions are essentially a form of assertion: they constrain what can be done to variables declared to be of a particular type. Whereas general assertions (see Section 7.3.1) require proof of their consistency, typing declarations are checkable by simple static rules.

Language issue 11: Stong type systems

Type systems can be much richer than that used in this chapter. For example, variables might be declared to hold values that are intended to represent lengths or areas so that it is valid to multiply two lengths to compute an area but incorrect to add a length to an area. Such types provide extra compile-time checking even though both types might use the same machine representations of numbers at run-time.

Furthermore, types can be restricted by predicates. A trivial example is that values representing minutes might be limited to be integers between 0 and 59; once records are introduced (see Section 4.3.3), predicates can use a value in one field to restrict the range of admissible values in another.

A reader who has followed the semantics in Section 3.2 will have no difficulty in reading the semantics of *BaseProgram* in Appendix B. In that description, the class of *Id* has not been divided; a completely equivalent description of the language could be written separating, say, *IntId/BoolId*. This point becomes more pressing when identifiers for procedures (or classes and methods) are present in a language. The decision on sub-dividing the class of identifiers is really a matter of taste. The position adopted here is that, if the written forms of the identifiers are not distinguished, the work of defining their use should be done in the context conditions and a single class of *Id* used in the abstract syntax.

It is an important property that –for elements of *BaseProgram* that satisfy *wf-BaseProgram*– there will be no run-time type errors. This type safety property is useful because it shows that type information is not needed in the run-time state.[2]

---

[2] There were a number of technical reports written around the VDM description of PL/I [BBH+74] that addressed the use of the formal description of a language as a basis for compiler design. One that relates to the current topic is [Izb75], in which Herbert Izbicki proves that –because of checks

> **Language issue 12: Writeability versus readability**
> There are situations where un-typed scripting languages can be justified for pro-
> ductivity but, if such programs are to be used for a long time, the cost of main-
> tenance is likely to increase because changes cannot benefit from a record of the
> intentions of the original designer.

4.3 Semantic objects

In the introductory languages of Chapter 3 and Appendix B, the states (Σ) are simple
mappings that associate values with identifier names. Even there the notion of the
state as the objects underlying the semantic description is informative but the role
of semantic objects is even clearer with richer languages.

In fact, the notion of the abstract state space used in a description of a language
tells a skilled reader an enormous amount about the language. This is extremely
valuable because the description of the semantic objects –even for a large language–
is likely to be rather short (e.g. the VDM description of PL/I [BBH$^+$74] comprises
over 100 pages of formulae but the definition of the semantic objects is less than two
pages long). More importantly, returning to the *Leitmotiv* of this book, states are a
crucial starting point for the designer of a programming language.

This section outlines the way in which semantic objects are enriched for several
modest extensions to the language of Appendix B; more ambitious languages are
modelled in Chapters 5–10.

4.3.1 Input/output

The key characteristic of imperative languages is that their core statements change
something. That something could be a database, a projection of some virtual reality or the position of a robot arm. In the languages considered above, assignment
statements can change the values of variables. In order to illustrate how other sorts
of state can be manipulated, *BasePrograms* can be extended to include input/output
(I/O) by adding *Read* and *Write* statements. This can be illustrated by rather simple
forms of I/O but extensions to multiple named files etc. are considered below.

The syntax and semantics of *While* and *If* statements are unchanged — they
continue to play the role of orchestrating which core (state-changing) statements
are executed and in what order.

The simple message here is that, if the core statements of a language can change
something, the state (Σ) must contain fields in which the current values are stored.
Adding a simple *Write* as an option to the abstract syntax for *Stmt* is trivial:

---

that have been made in the context conditions– no run-time type mismatch errors can occur. Such
"type soundness" arguments are also discussed in [Sym99].

Stmt = $\cdots$ | *Write*

Write :: *value* : *Expr*

The semantics needs to arrange that the value of the expression is appended to a state component that records all such values written. Thus the underlying semantic objects need to be:

Σ :: *store* : *Id* $\xrightarrow{m}$ $\mathbb{N}$
       output : $\mathbb{N}^*$

Notice that, in addition to the new *output* field, the values of variables are still in the *store* component of the state.

An SOS rule for *Write* is:

$$\frac{(e, store) \xrightarrow{ex} v}{(mk\text{-}Write(e), mk\text{-}\Sigma(store, out)) \xrightarrow{st} mk\text{-}\Sigma(store, out \frown [v])}$$

Notice that executing a *Write* statement does not change the *store*.

The SOS rules for accessing values from identifiers and changing them by assignments need straightforward revision:[3]

$$\frac{(rhs, store) \xrightarrow{ex} v}{(mk\text{-}Assign(lhs, rhs), mk\text{-}\Sigma(store, out)) \xrightarrow{st} mk\text{-}\Sigma(store \dagger \{lhs \mapsto v\}, out)}$$

Again, what does not change is important: executing an assignment does not change the output file.

Adding an input statement poses only one extra question — the syntax is straightforward:

Stmt = $\cdots$ | *Read*

Read :: *lhs* : *Id*

Of course, the *Read* identifies a place where the next input value should be placed and thus the *lhs* field is an identifier rather than an *Expr* as in *Write*.

The extension of the semantic objects is also obvious:

Σ :: *store* : *Id* $\xrightarrow{m}$ *ScalarValue*
       output : $\mathbb{N}^*$
       input : $\mathbb{N}^*$

The additional consideration is that, presumably, a *Read* from an empty *input* should fail — see the discussion on run-time errors in Section 4.1. So the SOS rule might be:

$$\frac{in \neq []}{\begin{array}{c}(mk\text{-}Read(lhs), mk\text{-}\Sigma(store, out, in)) \xrightarrow{st} \\ mk\text{-}\Sigma(store \dagger \{lhs \mapsto \mathsf{hd}\,in\}, out, \mathsf{tl}\,in)\end{array}}$$

---

[3] Peter Mosses' M-SOS is discussed in Section 4.4: his approach attempts to record semantic rules in a way which enhances their re-usability in different contexts.

To return to the point about the extent to which semantic objects can contribute disproportionally to understanding a language, consider the semantic object:

$$\Sigma \ :: \ store \ : \ Id \xrightarrow{\ m\ } ScalarValue$$
$$files \ : \ FileId \xrightarrow{\ m\ } \mathbb{N}^*$$

This would immediately prompt a reader to think about a language in which I/O statements can create and access any number of named files. Furthermore, an extension to:

$$\Sigma \ :: \ store \ : \ Id \xrightarrow{\ m\ } ScalarValue$$
$$files \ : \ FileId \xrightarrow{\ m\ } File$$

$$File \ :: \ contents \ : \ ScalarValue^*$$
$$index \ \ \ \ \ \ : \ \mathbb{N}$$

would support a language with statements that operate at indexed points within files. Further extensions might include ownership and (read/write) permissions as in Unix.

Language issue 13: What are the underlying objects of a language?
The designer of a programming language must decide what can be changed by the core statements of the language; a description of the chosen language must use semantic objects that reflect what can be changed.

4.3.2 Arrays

The simple languages considered so far have manipulated only *ScalarValues*. The message about semantic objects being helpful in grasping what can –and cannot– be done in a programming language is reinforced when composite values such as arrays and records are considered.

The ability to manipulate some form of array value is present in most programming languages.

Language issue 14: The role of arrays
Arrays are fundamental to many mathematical and engineering problems. Their inclusion in the first versions of FORTRAN was probably key to its adoption and APL [Ive62] pushed array handling to its limit. Interestingly, few programming languages support classical matrix algebra support — instead the most common approach is to offer minimal ways of grouping elements into arrays and to provide statements such as for loops with which a programmer can define algorithms over array values by manipulating their elements.
Hardware index registers make it possible to generate efficient code for referencing array elements. Compilers can further improve code by using techniques such as "strength reduction" [GvRB+12].

A simple form of an array is a one-dimensional vector that can be modelled with:

$$Vector = ScalarValue^*$$

Arrays can then be defined as vectors of things that could either be scalar or array:

$$Array = (ScalarValue \cup Array)^*$$

But this has the disadvantage that it would appear to allow a form of "ragged array" in which different indexes at the outermost level select sub-objects of varying dimensionality.[4] A better basic model might be:

$$Array = \mathbb{N}^* \xrightarrow{m} ScalarValue$$

For simplicity, this assumes that the indexing of any dimension starts at one but it is easy to change this so that, for example, defining array dimensions $A(5:15, -10:20)$ is permitted.

Language issue 15: Dynamically defining array bounds

Without some outer context, array bounds can only be constants. Blocks are covered in Chapter 5 and they make it possible –as in ALGOL 60– to declare arrays in inner blocks whose bounds are defined by variables (or expressions that use such variables) from outer blocks.

Furthermore, array parameters can be declared whose bounds are determined by the size of a passed argument array.

Normal arrays might have a denseness requirement that all valid index lists are in the domain of the array model but there are also applications for "sparse arrays" that allow gaps.

Language issue 16: Mapping arrays

A multi-dimensional array has to be mapped onto the linear addresses of the target computer and this requires that either "row major" or "column major" order is adopted. This can have significant impact on the concept of accessing "slices" of an array; this issue becomes more interesting when combined with parameter passing and is left to Chapter 5. There is, however, a clear question for the language designer of whether to prescribe the layout of an array as part of a language description.

FORTRAN's COMMON storage made it possible to declare a two-dimensional array in one sub-program and to view it as a one-dimensional vector in another sub-program that actually shares the same storage.

4.3.3 Records

Viewed abstractly, there are two differences between records (known as "structures" in PL/I) and arrays. Firstly, array elements are homogenous in the sense that all elements are of the same type, whereas the fields of a structure can be of different types. Secondly, array elements are accessed by numerical indexing whilst the fields of a structure are identified by identifiers. In a sense,

---

[4] APL [Ive62] did actually allow such raggedness.

A: array(3) of $\mathbb{N}$

and

S: struct
      one: $\mathbb{N}$
      two: $\mathbb{N}$
      three: $\mathbb{N}$

could serve the same purpose.

Language issue 17: Supporting records
Many programming languages offer the ability to define records (or structures). Furthermore, the fields of such records –as well as being scalar values– can be arrays and the elements of arrays can be records.
There are issues around declaring record types that are addressed in Section 6.3.

It should come as no surprise that a model of the store can be built around:[5]

$$Store = Id \xrightarrow{m} Value$$

$$Value = ScalarValue \mid ArrayValue \mid RecordValue$$

$$ArrayValue = \mathbb{N}^* \xrightarrow{m} Value$$

$$RecordValue = Id \xrightarrow{m} Value$$

But there is a potential difficulty beyond the two obvious differences between records and arrays, and this points to a more general warning.

Language issue 18: Storage mapping of records
Given that the fields of a record are inhomogeneous, there can be short fields followed by ones that take more machine store; the latter are likely to need alignment on store boundaries (be they bytes, words or double words) — this provides flexibility in projecting the abstract record onto the linear machine addresses. This language issue was present in PL/I structures and led to the need to implicitly define the storage mapping in the formal description — this is described in [BW71] by Hans Bekič and Kurt Walk.

The generic warning here is that mathematical abstractions do not necessarily expose all of the problems faced in implementations. It is, however, true that difficulty in finding a clean mathematical model is a clear indication that it will also be difficult to implement a feature (or interaction between several language features). One of the advantages in constructing a formal model of a language is that it is much less time-consuming than building a full implementation; ironing out problems with a formal description can save much wasted effort. The message of this subsection is that thinking carefully about the semantic objects of a language description is extremely cost-effective.

---

[5] Pascal has an intriguing with construct that "opens up" the names of a record — this is discussed in Section 5.5.

4.4 Further material

Projects

Interesting extensions to the language in Appendix B include:

1. Adding a string type to the language with a set of appropriate operators including ones that take, say, strings and integers as operands (basing the semantic description on an abstract syntax separates out the issue of defining the concrete syntax).
2. Assignment statements that have multiple left-hand sides and the same number of expressions on the right-hand side were allowed in, for example, CPL [BBHS63]. They can be used, for example, to switch the values of two variables as in:

$x, y := y, x$

Notice that, for this to have the desired effect, the above is not the same as two assignments:

$x := y; \; y := x$

3. A fairly ambitious project is to add proper array expressions and assignments to the given language description.
4. An even more ambitious –but very interesting– language extension is to add relational database features to the language — there are many other decisions to be made: a "tuple" can be represented as a vector and a relation is a set of tuples — an alternative is to bring field names into play and model a tuple as a mapping. The role of types and field names in defining "join" requires thought. Relational division is a fun exercise. (Related reports are [Dat82, Han76, Owl79].)[6]

Further reading

Despite the emphasis put here on the distinction between problems that can be detected statically (compile-time) and dynamically (run-time), many formal semantic descriptions (e.g. [Lau68, Mos74]) handle them together. This has the unfortunate result that the semantic description is further complicated by errors that are manifest in the source text alone.

Furthermore, what is here referred to as "context conditions" is sometimes called "static semantics" (and what is here just "semantics" is termed "dynamic semantics"). These terms are avoided in the current book. The term "context conditions" probably made its first appearance in [vWMPK69]. Aad van Wijngaarden's own approach involved "two-level grammars" (see [Sin67, vWMPK69]) but any comparison is complicated by the fact that, although such grammars could clearly describe context conditions, Van Wijngaarden chose, in the description of ALGOL 68 to minimise the distinction between syntax and semantics [vWSM+76, LvdM80, Lin93].

---

[6] The major issues would concern concurrency control — this point is picked up in Section 8.6.

Another approach is the "dynamic syntax" idea of [HJ73], in which the process of parsing declarations dynamically creates appropriate syntax rules for parsing statements.

It is also worth noting that well-formedness could be expressed using inference rules such as:

$$lhs \in Id$$
$$rhs \in Expr$$
$$\frac{c\text{-}type(rhs, tpm) = tpm(lhs)}{mk\text{-}Assign(lhs, rhs) \in Assign}$$

The subject of types has its own wide literature — see for example [Pie02].

A valuable approach that is not covered here is "type inference", in which as much type information as can be deduced from use of identifiers etc. is used to determine a sensible typing for the whole text — see [Mil78b].

Chapter 5
Block structure

Section 4.3 emphasises the important role that semantic objects can play in understanding or, indeed, designing a programming language. This point becomes more obvious as the language challenges increase. This chapter examines ideas used to model the way in which blocks can be used to define different scopes for names of variables and a variety of parameter passing modes for procedures.

It is again the case that the meta-languages introduced for simple languages cope with describing the new language features.

5.1 Blocks

> **Language issue 19: Scoping**
> Most programming languages offer ways to define different "scopes" for variables so that the same name can be used to refer to different variables in various contexts.

ALGOL 60 employed *blocks* to define different scopes and the block concept is present in a wide variety of languages that appeared subsequently. Figure 5.1 presents an example program (in a simple but arbitrary concrete syntax) in which the name *a* in the inner block denotes a different variable than the *a* in the outer block — the example emphasises this by giving the two variables different types. The outer block also introduces *i* and *j*, which remain visible in the inner block because these names are not redeclared; the inner block also declares *b*, which name is only visible in that inner block. A full description of a small language that includes blocks and procedures is contained in Appendix C. The text of this chapter brings out only the main modelling points.

One possible abstract syntax for *BlocksProgram* is:

BlocksProgram :: *body* : *Stmt*

As well as assignments, conditionals etc., *Block* is now an option for *Stmt*:

Stmt = ··· | *Block*

© Springer Nature Switzerland AG 2020
C. B. Jones, *Understanding Programming Languages*,
https://doi.org/10.1007/978-3-030-59257-8_5

```
                    program
                      begin
                      bool a; int i int j;
                      a := true; i := 1; j := 2;
                        begin
                        int a; int b;
                        a := 1; j := 3; b := 7
                        end;
                      if i = j then a := false fi
                      end
                    end
```

Fig. 5.1 An example with blocks defining scopes of variables

Thus any sequence of statements can contain blocks and blocks can be nested to any depth the programmer chooses.

In an initial abstract syntax for *Block*, only the local variable declarations are considered (in Section 5.3 the ellipses are replaced by procedure declarations):[1]

$$Block :: var\text{-}types : Id \xrightarrow{m} ScalarType$$
$$\cdots$$
$$body \qquad : Stmt^*$$

As in Section 4.2, a *TypeMap* is needed to define the context conditions — this is also extended in Section 5.3 to cover procedures — but, as far as the scalars are concerned, it suffices to have:

$$TypeMap = Id \xrightarrow{m} (ScalarType \mid \cdots)$$

The interesting context condition shows how the local type information overwrites that of the context in which the block is located:[2]

$$wf\text{-}Stmt(mk\text{-}Block(vm, \cdots, body), tpm) \quad \triangleq$$
$$\cdots$$
$$wf\text{-}Stmt\text{-}List(body, tpm \dagger vm)$$

At the outermost (*BlocksProgram*) level, there are no variables declared.

$$wf\text{-}BlocksProgram : BlocksProgram \to \mathbb{B}$$
$$wf\text{-}BlocksProgram(mk\text{-}BlocksProgram(b)) \quad \triangleq \quad wf\text{-}Stmt(b, \{\mapsto\})$$

---

[1] Again, there are alternative ways of defining the same language content. It might for example be sensible to insist that the *Stmt* in the *body* of *BlocksProgram* is always a *Block*. In contrast to earlier chapters, a *Compound* statement is introduced in Appendix C — as becomes clear, this is the same as a *Block* with no local declarations. Such choices have only minor influence on the semantics.

[2] Remember that the VDM map overwrite operator gives precedence to pairs from its second operand.

> **Language issue 20: Pre-defined constants**
> A language could include pre-defined constants such as (an approximation to) π; such names would be installed in the initial type map.

It is possible to couch the semantics in terms of the state from Appendix B:

$$\Sigma = Id \xrightarrow{m} ScalarValue$$

The important semantic point that must be fixed is that the block structure dictates a "nesting" discipline on the variables; for this reason, they are often called "stack variables". Thus the *body* of the *Block* is executed (see σ_i in the SOS rule below) with local variables even if the names were known in the encompassing list of statements; once that *body* has been executed, values are taken from σ_i' for those identifiers that remained visible from the outer block and the values that were hidden are recovered from σ:

$$\sigma_i = \sigma \dagger (\{id \mapsto 0 \mid id \in \operatorname{dom} vm \wedge vm(id) = \textsc{IntTp}\} \cup$$
$$\{id \mapsto \mathsf{true} \mid id \in \operatorname{dom} vm \wedge vm(id) = \textsc{BoolTp}\})$$
$$\frac{(body, \sigma_i) \xrightarrow{stl} \sigma_i'}{(mk\text{-}Block(vm, body), \sigma) \xrightarrow{st} ((\operatorname{dom} vm) \triangleleft \sigma_i') \cup ((\operatorname{dom} vm) \triangleleft \sigma)}$$

Figure 5.2 provides an annotated version of Figure 5.1 showing the states at key points.

```
program
  begin
  bool a; int i int j;
  a := true; i := 1; j := 2;
                        σ = {a ↦ true, i ↦ 1, j ↦ 2}
    begin
    int a; int b;
    a := 1; j := 3; b := 7
                        σᵢ' = {a ↦ 1, i ↦ 1, j ↦ 3, b ↦ 7}
    end;
                        σ' = {a ↦ true, i ↦ 1, j ↦ 3}
  if i = j then a := false fi
  end
end
```

Fig. 5.2 The example of Figure 5.1 annotated with states

A way of simplifying this description is given in Section 5.2 but, before that is done, the useful VDM map operators $\triangleleft/\triangleleft$ are explored.

The state resulting from a block is defined in the SOS rule above to be the union of two mappings (of type $Id \xrightarrow{m} ScalarValue$). Looking firstly at the left operand of the union, assume for the moment that:

$$\operatorname{dom} \sigma_i' = \operatorname{dom} \sigma_i$$

Installing the initial values in σ_i gives:

dom σ_i = dom $\sigma \cup$ dom vm

The definition of $\triangleleft$ expands to give:

$(\text{dom } vm) \triangleleft \sigma_i' = \{id \mapsto \sigma_i'(id) \mid id \in \text{dom } \sigma_i' \wedge id \notin \text{dom } vm\}$

Then it follows that:

dom σ_i' = dom σ_i = (dom $\sigma \cup$ dom vm) $\Rightarrow$
$\qquad (\text{dom } vm) \triangleleft \sigma_i' = \{id \mapsto \sigma_i'(id) \mid id \in \text{dom } \sigma \wedge id \notin \text{dom } vm\}$

Turning to the second operand of the union:

$(\text{dom } vm) \triangleleft \sigma = \{id \mapsto \sigma(id) \mid id \in \text{dom } \sigma \wedge id \in \text{dom } vm\}$

Combining the results shows that the initial assumption:

dom σ' = dom σ

holds.

Moreover, if all variables from the outer context are redeclared in the inner block:

dom $\sigma \subseteq vm$

then (writing σ' for the right-hand side of $\xrightarrow{st}$ in the SOS rule):[3]

$\sigma' = \sigma$

Language issue 21: Arrays whose size depends on data
There are many language features modelled in this book but different chapters try to focus on one feature at a time. Extensions such as adding I/O or arrays can be applied to most languages so formal descriptions are only written out where the combination is non-obvious. It is, however, worth making a point on arrays here. There are obviously many applications where a programmer would want to create arrays whose bounds depend on input data. Section 4.3.2 points out that this is not possible in the outermost scope of a program. Inner blocks offer an easy way to define the bounds of arrays in terms of variables whose values are computed in embracing contexts.

5.2 Abstract locations

The preceding section addresses the language issues around the same name referring to different variables (in different scopes); this section moves towards a more delicate feature of many programming languages. Section 5.4.1 shows how to model

---

[3] Of course, this throws doubt on the perceivable effect of such a block. In fact, if the *body* of a *BlocksProgram* is a *Block*, the conclusion has to be that executing the program has no effect. It would, however, be straightforward to add some form of I/O to this language as described in Section 4.3.1.

one way in which different identifiers can refer to the same variable. (Different parameter passing modes for the example program in Figure 5.6 are discussed along with Issue 25. Other ways of explicitly manipulating addresses include "heap variables" — see Section 6.4.)

> **Challenge VI: Modelling sharing**
> How is a language description to model sharing? In the case in hand, multiple identifiers sharing access to the same variable (and the pattern of sharing varying over time). This sharing problem is in fact far more general and crops up again with objects in Chapter 9 and would, for example, play a role in the description of a Unix-style file system.

Two important modelling points can be extracted before "by reference" parameter passing is tackled:

- *locations* serve as an abstraction of machine addresses; and
- the fact that the relationship between identifiers and locations can be held in an *environment* that changes less often than the store (Σ).

Both of these points can also be used to provide a clearer model of the semantics of *Block* than is given in the preceding section. The set *ScalarLoc* is an infinite set of objects about which nothing is known other than the ability to test them for equality. The modelling decision is to split the mapping from identifiers to their values into two mappings:

$$Env = Id \xrightarrow{m} ScalarLoc$$

$$\Sigma = ScalarLoc \xrightarrow{m} ScalarValue$$

The semantic relation $\xrightarrow{st}$ now has the type:

$$\xrightarrow{st}: \mathscr{P}((Stmt \times Env \times \Sigma) \times \Sigma)$$

This makes clear that the environment (*Env*) cannot be changed by executing a statement (*Stmt*): the $i+1^{th}$ statement in a list is executed in the same environment as the ith statement even if the ith statement is a *Block*.[4] (Moreover, sharing can be modelled as in Figure 5.3, where two different identifiers can be mapped (in an *Env*) to the same location.)

The abstract syntax of *Assign* is unchanged from that in Appendix B:

$$Assign :: lhs : Id$$
$$\qquad\quad rhs : Expr$$

but its semantics now has to obtain the location corresponding to the identifier (*lhs*); the state (σ) is updated at the appropriate location:

$$\frac{(rhs, env, \sigma) \xrightarrow{ex} v}{(mk\text{-}Assign(lhs, rhs), env, \sigma) \xrightarrow{st} \sigma \dagger \{env(lhs) \mapsto v\}}$$

---

[4] As discussed in Section 5.5, *not* making this clear was a serious disadvantage of the form of operational semantics used in the early Vienna Lab formalisation of PL/I.

Similarly, the option that a simple form of expression can be just an identifier is unchanged in the abstract syntax:

$$Expr = \cdots \mid Id$$

but the type of the $\xrightarrow{ex}$ relation becomes:

$$\xrightarrow{ex} : \mathscr{P}((Expr \times Env \times \Sigma) \times ScalarValue)$$

and the SOS rule has to obtain the location (from env) before it can use the location to access the value (from σ):

$$\frac{e \in Id}{(e, env, \sigma) \xrightarrow{ex} \sigma(env(e))}$$

Christopher Strachey –who made many wise observations about programming languages– referred to $env(id)$ as the left-hand value and $\sigma(env(id))$ as the right-hand value of id. These terms obviously derive from assignment statements but are useful in discussing differing evaluation modes in other contexts including parameter passing (see Section 5.4).

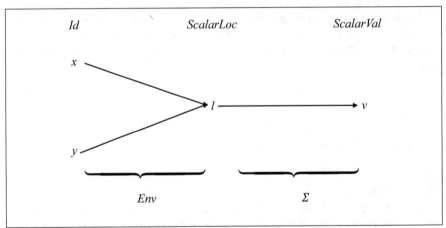

Fig. 5.3 Identifiers sharing a location

The following SOS rule shows that *newlocs* is a one:one mapping[5] whose domain is exactly the set of identifiers for local variables of the *Block* and whose range is disjoint from any locations in use in the current σ. After executing the *body* of a block, the state that results from executing the whole *Block* is found simply by restricting σ' to the set of locations that existed before the *Block* was executed. There is less to do than in the model above because identifiers from the context of the block that were redeclared within the block had different locations under which their values were stored:

$$newlocs \in (Id \xleftarrow{m} ScalarLoc)$$
$$\text{dom } newlocs = \text{dom } vm$$
$$\text{rng } newlocs \cap \text{dom } \sigma = \{\}$$
$$env' = env \dagger newlocs \dagger \cdots$$
$$\sigma_i = \sigma \dagger (\{env(id) \mapsto 0 \mid id \in \text{dom } vm \wedge vm(id) = \text{INTTP}\} \cup$$
$$\{env(id) \mapsto \text{true} \mid id \in \text{dom } vm \wedge vm(id) = \text{BOOLTP}\})$$
$$\frac{(body, env', \sigma_i) \xrightarrow{stl} \sigma_i'}{(mk\text{-}Block(vm, pm, body), env, \sigma) \xrightarrow{st} \text{dom } \sigma \lhd \sigma_i'}$$

The definition of *env'* is completed below when procedures are added to the language.

Figure 5.4 provides an annotated version of Figure 5.1 showing the environments and states at key points. As predicted in Section 5.1, deriving (from σ_i') the state that results from the whole block is easier in the presence of *env* because the locations form the appropriate bridge (notice that, in Figure 5.4, σ_i' retains the value for *la* but that this location is not in *env'*).

It is important that *ScalarLoc* is a set of unanalysed tokens. Were it, for example, to be made equal to some form of number ($\mathbb{N}$) it would be unclear whether a program could perform address arithmetic. Whilst there are programming languages that allow such manipulation, this is not the intention here and the constraint is again made completely clear by the choice of semantic objects.

The choice of new locations in the SOS rule for blocks is non-deterministic but, given the preceding point about the set *ScalarLoc* being just tokens, there is no program that can be influenced by the choice. Furthermore, there is no difference in the resulting state after the execution of the block terminates, whatever choice is made

---

[5] A one:one mapping $Id \xleftarrow{m} ScalarLoc$ is employed in preference to a normal many:one mapping $Id \xrightarrow{m} ScalarLoc$, which would require a data type invariant:

$$one\text{-}one: (X \xrightarrow{m} Y) \to \mathbb{B}$$

$$one\text{-}one(m) \triangleq \text{card rng } (m) = \text{card dom } m$$

or:

$$one\text{-}one(m) \triangleq \forall a, b \in \text{dom } m \cdot m(a) = m(b) \Rightarrow a = b$$

```
            program
              begin
              bool a; int i int j;
              a := true; i := 1; j := 2;
```
$$env = \{a \mapsto la, i \mapsto li, j \mapsto lj\}$$
$$\sigma = \{la \mapsto \text{true}, li \mapsto 1, lj \mapsto 2\}$$
```
                begin
                int a; int b;
                a := 1; j := 3; b := 7
```
$$env' = \{a \mapsto ln, i \mapsto li, j \mapsto lj, b \mapsto lb\}$$
$$\sigma'_i = \{la \mapsto \text{true}, ln \mapsto 1, li \mapsto 1, lj \mapsto 3, lb \mapsto 7\}$$
```
                end;
```
$$env = \{a \mapsto la, i \mapsto li, j \mapsto lj\}$$
$$\sigma' = \{la \mapsto \text{true}, li \mapsto 1, lj \mapsto 3\}$$
```
              if i = j then a := false fi
              end
            end
```

Fig. 5.4 The example of Figure 5.1 annotated with environments and states

for rng *newlocs*. Interestingly, there is a strong technical reason for showing the non-determinism. The obvious way to compile blocks is to reflect the stack structure of blocks[6] and to allocate the next n machine addresses for the local variables of any block; on exit from the block, the stack pointer is simply set back to the machine address on block entry and a sibling block would reuse the same addresses for its local variables. But this is not the only possibility: a compiler could compute different addresses for all blocks contained in one scope (this would create space for all contained blocks regardless of the fact that sibling blocks cannot be active at the same time). It is straightforward to show that this is an allowable implementation of the non-deterministic choice of locations; a much messier equivalence proof would be required if natural numbers were used for locations and the description essentially "bolted in" the stack implementation.

As observed, careful choice of abstractions such as tokens for *ScalarLoc* makes properties of a language description manifest without needing to draw out consequences from detailed sequences of state transitions.

---

[6] Stack variables (in blocks and procedures) can be contrasted to "heap" variables, which are discussed in Section 6.4.

5.3 Procedures

> **Language issue 22: Procedures and functions**
> The idea of separating out portions of a program that can be invoked at different
> points in a program has been around since the time of Alan Turing (Gauthier
> van den Hove [vdH19] discusses Turing's use of *bury*/*disinter* and shows need
> for "modifying programs" (or indirect jump)).
> In languages with nested scopes, this idea becomes more interesting and care-
> ful models fix essential issues about the binding of variables. Procedures are
> normally invoked using some form of call statement (being invoked in a state-
> ment context, procedures do not normally return values); functions are used in
> expression contexts and normally return at least one result value.
> Not only does the use of procedures and functions make it easier for a reader
> to understand a program, they also ensure that subsequent modifications are
> applied to all uses.

Procedures are considered first — functions are discussed in Section 6.5. Procedures are named and their definitions (*ProcDef*) are local to a block:

$$Block :: \; var\text{-}types \; : \; Id \xrightarrow{\;m\;} ScalarType$$
$$proc\text{-}defs \; : \; Id \xrightarrow{\;m\;} ProcDef$$
$$body \qquad : \; Stmt^*$$

In the same way as variable names are local to the block in which they are declared,
any procedures declared in a block are only known within their declaring block. As
in Section 4.2, no attempt is made to subdivide the class of *Id*; since their written
forms are taken to be the same, checking for disjointness of variable and procedure
names is left to the context conditions.

A possible abstract syntax for procedure definitions lists the names of parameters
and separates their types.[7] The *body* of a procedure is shown as a *Stmt*:

$$ProcDef :: \; params \qquad : \; Id^*$$
$$paramtypes \; : \; ScalarType^*$$
$$body \qquad : \; Stmt$$

The *TypeMap* needed for the context conditions can now be completed (from that
in Section 5.1):

$$TypeMap = Id \xrightarrow{\;m\;} (ScalarType \mid ProcType)$$

$$ProcType :: \; paramtypes \; : \; ScalarType^*$$

Notice that only the types of parameters are needed to type check calls. The completed (formal) context condition for blocks is contained in Appendix C — it essentially:

---

[7] This is another place where there is not one single abstract syntax that works well for all purposes:
for instance, there are advantages and disadvantages in separating the parameter types from their
names.

- checks that names of variables and procedures are disjoint;[8]
- checks each *ProcDef* is well formed with respect to a type map containing both the variables known in the context and the local parameter names;
- checks that the *body* of the *Block* is well formed with respect to a type map containing the local variables and procedures (this includes checking that the argument lists in call statements match the types of the respective parameters).

So far –and as in Appendix C– procedures cannot be called recursively. The neatest way of modelling recursion needs the concept of "fixed points" (see Section 7.1) over environments. (There is a messy alternative with labelling environments that is not pursued here.)

It was noted above that the association between identifiers and locations should be kept in an environment (*Env*) because it cannot be changed by assignments. The same train of thought makes it sensible to place procedure denotations (*ProcDen*) in the environment:

$$Env = Id \xrightarrow{m} Den$$

$$Den = ScalarLoc \mid ProcDen$$

$$ProcDen :: params : Id^*$$
$$ body : Stmt$$
$$ context : Env$$

There is an important and profound language issue in the binding of non-local names in procedure definitions. Consider the procedure p in the block depicted in Figure 5.5: the (parameterless) procedure p has a reference to the non-local identifier i; nearly all programming languages are defined so that this is taken to refer to the declaration in the closest embracing block. To emphasise this point, notice that p is called from an inner block that declares a separate variable i. The reference to i in the procedure definition has no connection with this new variable.[9]

Language issue 23: Bindings of variables in procedures

A language designer must take a position on static (lexicographic) versus dynamic (call chain) semantics. ALGOL 60 chose lexicographic binding and most subsequent languages adopted this convention. Early versions of Lisp implemented dynamic binding in spite of the fact that McCarthy was motivated by the lambda calculus (which he frankly confessed that he did not fully understand at the time). Later versions of Lisp and Scheme support static binding.

Turning to the *Call* statements, which invoke procedures:

$$Stmt = \cdots \mid Call$$

---

[8] Notice the decision to forbid variables and procedures having the same name: this restriction is not essential and is shown solely as an illustration.

[9] Informal (and even some formal) descriptions of procedure call semantics with lexicographic binding of non-local identifiers often use a "copy rule" that replaces the procedure call with a copy of its definition. This poses a serious danger of getting the wrong binding and the danger is only avoided by a rather complicated (and oft-times imprecise) renaming of clashing variable names.

```
begin
  int i;
  proc p() ···; i:=1; ··· end
  ⋮
  begin
    int i;
    ⋮
    call p()
    ⋮
  end
  ⋮
end
```

Fig. 5.5 Lexicographic binding of non-local names in procedures

For now, arguments are restricted to be identifiers:[10]

$$\begin{array}{lll} Call :: & procedure & : Id \\ & arguments & : Id^* \end{array}$$

Well-formedness is checked by:

$$\begin{array}{l} wf\text{-}Stmt(mk\text{-}Call(proc, args), tpm) \quad \triangleq \\ \quad proc \in \mathsf{dom}\, tpm \wedge \\ \quad tpm(proc) \in ProcType \wedge \\ \quad \left(\begin{array}{l} \mathsf{let}\ mk\text{-}ProcType(ptl) = tpm(proc)\ \mathsf{in} \\ \mathsf{len}\, args = \mathsf{len}\, ptl \wedge \\ \forall i \in \mathsf{inds}\, args \cdot tpm(args(i)) = ptl(i) \end{array}\right) \end{array}$$

The semantic rules for different parameter passing modes are discussed in the remainder of this chapter and the two predominant modes are described in Appendix C. What is common to the two rules for a call to a procedure, say p, is that its denotation is retrieved from the environment in which the call is written; that procedure denotation includes the environment of the context where the procedure was declared; the denotation also contains the list of parameter names and the body of the procedure. A local environment is generated (differently in the two parameter passing modes) and the state extended in the case of call-by-value parameter passing. The body of the block is then executed using this environment and state.

Notice that type information is not required in the procedure denotations because the body of the procedure has been type checked against the information about the types of the parameters.

[10] Restriction to identifiers means that the same syntax can be used for call by reference (see Section 5.4.1) and call by value (see Section 5.4.2); the latter case can use general expressions as arguments.

Language issue 24: Array arguments

 Issue 21 explains how nested blocks can declare arrays whose bounds are defined in terms of variables whose values are set in outer blocks. Arrays can be passed as arguments to procedures so that the bounds of the argument determine those of the parameter (see Section 5.5).

Although not the main topic of the current book, there are points at which it is worth drawing attention to the challenges of implementing features in high-level programming languages. As pointed out in [vdH19], finding a way of keeping track of the accessible stack variables in a language (ALGOL 60) with nested blocks and recursive procedures required the invention of Dijkstra's "display" mechanism. This idea became a key test bed for the justification of implementation ideas with respect to formal language descriptions — see [JL71, HJ70, HJ71].

5.4 Parameter passing

There are many modes in which arguments can be passed to procedures.[11] The two most widely used of these are to pass the address of the argument or to pass its value; these are modelled in Sections 5.4.1 and 5.4.2 respectively. Further alternative parameter passing modes are discussed in Section 5.5.

The outline program in Figure 5.6 provides a basis for comparing parameter passing modes.

```
program
  begin
  int i,j;
  proc p(int x,  int y)
      i:=i+1; x:=x+1; y:=y+1
    end
    ⋮
    i:=1; j:=2;
    call p(i,j);
    write(i,j);
    call p(i,i);
    write(i,j)
    end
  end
```

Fig. 5.6 Parameter passing modes to procedures

---

[11] The terminology used here is: "arguments" are what occur in the call statement (or function reference); "parameters" are the names used within the header of the procedure or function definition. ALGOL 60 uses the terms "actual parameter" and "formal parameter".

> **Language issue 25: Parameters in object-oriented languages**
> Language designers normally select one or two different parameter passing
> modes to be available to programmers (see Issue 27 on how to distinguish the
> passing mode of each parameter if there is more than one mode).
> This issue is somewhat different in object-oriented languages — see Chapter 9.

5.4.1 Passing "by reference"

One option for parameter passing is to pass the address of the argument — at least
for scalar values, this is a very simple idea. Different languages employ the terms
"by reference" or "by location" for this mode of parameter passing.[12]

There are several reasons why languages allow some form of "by reference"
parameter passing:

- it avoids copying values (this point is more important when considering arrays
  etc. — see below);
- it makes it possible, for example, to switch the values of arguments;[13]
- it provides a way of returning more than one result (effect) of a procedure invocation.

```
    program
      begin
      int i,j;
                        cenv = {i ↦ li, j ↦ lj}
      proc p(int x,  int y)
                        lenv = {i ↦ li, x ↦ li, j ↦ lj, y ↦ lj}
                        σ = {li ↦ 1, lj ↦ 2}
        i := i + 1;  x := x + 1;  y := y + 1
                        σ' = {li ↦ 3, lj ↦ 3}
      end
        ⋮
      i := 1;  j := 2;
                        cenv = {i ↦ li, j ↦ lj}
                        σ = {li ↦ 1, lj ↦ 2}
      call p(i,j)
                        σ' = {li ↦ 3, lj ↦ 3}
      end
    end
```

Fig. 5.7 Parameter modes: pass by reference

---

[12] This is also a restricted form of ALGOL 60's "by name" parameter passing mode — see Section 5.5.

[13] This is known as "Jensen's device".

The program in Figure 5.7 is decorated with the environment (*env*) and state (σ) at key points in the execution. The invocation of $p(i,j)$ passes the location of the outer variables i and j to x and y respectively; within this invocation of p, references to x are effectively the same as references to i (and the same is true of y/j). Therefore after the execution of $p(i,j)$ the values of i and j are both 3.

A subsequent invocation of $p(i,i)$ would essentially equate all of the addresses of i, x and y and the resulting value of i would be 6.

The SOS rule for *Call* in the case of "by location" parameter passing is actually simpler than that in Section 5.4.2 because the left-hand value of an identifier can be obtained with $env(args(i))$. Thus:

$$\frac{\begin{array}{l} \textit{mk-ProcDen}(parms, body, cenv) = env(p) \\ lenv = cenv \dagger \{parms(i) \mapsto env(args(i)) \mid i \in \text{inds}\,parms\} \\ (body, lenv, \sigma) \xrightarrow{st} \sigma' \end{array}}{(\textit{mk-Call}(p, args), env, \sigma) \xrightarrow{st} \sigma'}$$

It should be noted that there is a serious complication with this mode of parameter passing in that a reader of a program cannot assume that different identifiers denote distinct variables; someone reading a program (even its original author after some elapsed time) might miss quite subtle errors deriving from an assumption of separation.

It is useful now to see how clean ideas can be combined. If the model of arrays discussed in Section 4.3.2 is changed so that:

$$Env = Id \xrightarrow{m} Den$$

$$Den = ScalarLoc \mid ArrayDen \mid ProcDen$$

$$ArrayDen = \mathbb{N}^* \xrightarrow{m} ScalarLoc$$

then it is trivial to change the semantics for *Call* so that elements of arrays can be passed as arguments in the "by reference" mode. Such generalisations become mandatory for clear presentations of algorithms such as those that manipulate "B-trees" (see [Knu73, §6.2.4]) where B-tree nodes need to be passed by reference (or by value-return) to achieve efficient updates.

Language issue 26: Array slices

It is, in fact, possible to go much further. PL/I allows, for example, a "slice" of a two-dimensional array to be passed as an argument to a parameter that is declared to be a (one-dimensional) vector. This facility can be completely general: arbitrary dimensions can be sliced to access arrays of any lesser dimension.

The preceding language issue indicates another place where it is easy to define things on a mathematical abstraction that are non-trivial to implement. To take the two-dimensional case, an $n \times m$ array must be mapped onto the linear addresses of the hardware either in row-dimensional or column-dimensional order. Whichever mapping order is chosen, a slice on one dimension will be in contiguous store but the other will be fragmented. By-reference passing of fragmented slices requires considerable ingenuity on the part of the compiler writer.

The meta-point here is that failure to find a neat mathematical abstraction is almost certainly an indication that user comprehension and/or the ability to compile a language feature will be compromised; successful mathematical abstractions might still be challenging to map onto an unforgiving von Neumann architecture.

5.4.2 Passing "by value"

Parameter passing "by value" does just what its name suggests. To use Strachey's terminology (see Section 5.2) it is the right-hand value that is passed to the called procedure. The semantics of *Call* essentially creates a local block introducing new locations for the arguments; the values of the arguments from the call are then installed as the initial values of these new locations. In contrast to call by reference, assignment to a named parameter has no effect outside the block. (However, assignments to non-local variables can cause side effects and this point becomes important when considering functions — see Section 6.5.) Just as in a block written by the programmer, the local variables disappear on exit from the called procedure.

The semantics for this form of call are included in Appendix C, and Figure 5.8 indicates the values of env/σ for the specific program under call-by-name parameter passing. In the semantics of *Call*, the value of a single identifier can be obtained by $\sigma(env(args(i)))$ for each argument. Figure 5.6 has used simple identifiers as arguments so that the contrast with passing "by location" from Section 5.4.1 can be made, but there is, in fact, no reason with "by value" why the arguments should not be general expressions. In this case, the semantics would have to construct a list of values using $(args(i), env, \sigma) \xrightarrow{ex} vl(i)$.

Language issue 27: Marking parameter passing modes

In a programming language that offers more than one way of passing arguments to parameters, there must be a way of marking which mode is to be selected. Interestingly, ALGOL 60 makes "by name" parameter passing the default and any parameter names that are to be passed by value must be explicitly listed in the ⟨value-part⟩. Pascal uses "by value" as its default and requires that by reference parameters are marked var in the parameter list.

PL/I takes a different path: the mode of parameter passing is determined by the form of the argument: an expression argument is passed by value whereas a simple identifier is passed by reference.

```
        program
          begin
          int i,j;
                            cenv = {i ↦ li, j ↦ lj}
        proc p(int x, int y)
                            lenv = {i ↦ li, j ↦ lj, x ↦ lx, y ↦ ly}
                            σ = {li ↦ 1, lj ↦ 2, lx ↦ 1, ly ↦ 2}
          i:=i+1; x:=x+1; y:=y+1
                            σ = {li ↦ 2, lj ↦ 2, lx ↦ 2, ly ↦ 3}
        end
          ⋮
        i:=1; j:=2;
                            cenv = {i ↦ li, j ↦ lj}
                            σ = {li ↦ 1, lj ↦ 2}
        call p(i,j)
                            σ = {li ↦ 2, lj ↦ 2}
        end
      end
```

Fig. 5.8 Parameter modes: pass by value

5.5 Further material

Projects

Because the languages being considered are themselves getting interesting, there are many projects that the reader could now enjoy. For example:

1. The syntax of iterative for loops is a suggested project in Section 2.3; the semantics of the option to bind the control variable as local to the statement could now be fully explored.
2. It is relatively straightforward to write out the semantics of parameter passing "by value/return" because it works like a combination of "by value" parameter passing and the creation of a new block (but remember that a value must be passed back at the end of the procedure execution). There is a need for a context condition to avoid two different values being passed back to the same variable.
3. ALGOL 60's full by name parameter passing is slightly trickier and requires that there is a check that the argument is only a single identifier if the parameter is used in a "left-hand" context.
4. Modify the description in Appendix C to allow arrays to be passed as by location arguments. A slightly more ambitious version of this project would include the ability to pass "slices" of arrays (the reader might also want to think about the attendant need for functions that make it possible to determine the lower and higher bounds of a dimension *lbound/hbound*).
5. Thinking about "separate compilation" is interesting because it focuses on what information is needed in descriptions of the interface.

6. Pascal offers an intriguing with statement that unfolds the names of the fields in a record.

Further reading

It was indicated in Section 3.3 that there are various ways of recording a semantic relation (between pairs of *Program*$/\Sigma$ and Σ); now that environments (*Env*) are involved it would also be possible to emphasise their relative constancy by writing them separately from the main relation — e.g.

$$env \vdash \frac{(rhs, \sigma) \xrightarrow{ex} v}{(mk\text{-}Assign(lhs, rhs), \sigma) \xrightarrow{st} \sigma \dagger \{lhs \mapsto v\}}$$

The clear separation of the environment (*Env*) from the state (Σ) is important and has an interesting history. The early operational semantics work in the IBM Vienna Lab focussed on the PL/I language. This was a huge undertaking; an outline of the effort is given in [AJ18, §3] and a first-hand account in [LW69]; further connections are also traced in Chapter 11. Jan Lee introduced the term *Vienna Definition Language* (VDL) [Lee72] (which is not to be confused with VDM).

The state of the VDL operational descriptions of PL/I was huge and among other things included a stack of environments for all contexts that had been entered but not completed. This had unforeseen consequences when it came to basing proofs on VDL semantics: the property alluded to above that the environment is the same after any statement as it was before that statement required a messy argument because of the presence of the stack of *Env*s. Peter Lucas wrote the first such "twin machine" proof [Luc68] but even the more developed [JL71] spent more space on this lemma than on the real core of the design.

These difficulties were identified as shortcomings of the operational approach and contributed to the move to denotational semantics (see Section 7.1), where the separation of the environment from the state was almost mandatory. Subsequent to the Vienna group moving to the denotational approach [BBH$^+$74] (see [Jon01] for more details), Gordon Plotkin proposed *Structural Operational Semantics* (SOS), where the separation of environment from store is also clear [Plo81].

Chapter 6
Further issues in sequential languages

As made clear at the beginning of this book, it is not the aim to cover all possible language challenges. This chapter mentions some interesting extensions to languages and either sketches an approach to their models or provides references to where such models are developed. The material here concerns only sequential features of languages — mainly in the ALGOL or Pascal families; material on concurrency in the spirit of Eiffel [Mey88], Go [DK15] or even Java [GJSB00] (i.e. concurrency in an object-oriented context) is deferred to Chapter 9.

Here again, an important message is that the meta-language introduced to cope with the semantics of languages as simple as that in Chapter 3 suffices to describe programming languages that have been –or are still– used to build significant computer applications.

6.1 Own variables

There is an obvious issue of making the effect of executing a program visible beyond its execution.

Language issue 28: Effects of a program
There are many ways in which programs can have an influence beyond their execution — for example:

- Input and output are discussed in Section 4.3.1;
- Updating databases is touched on in Section 4.4 and further discussion is in Section 9.7;
- Object-oriented programs can be linked to object stores (see Chapter 9).

Within a program, there is a related issue of how to retain the values of block-local variables beyond an execution of a *Block*. Note that, in Chapter 5, even the locations of local variables are discarded at block exit.

© Springer Nature Switzerland AG 2020
C. B. Jones, *Understanding Programming Languages*,
https://doi.org/10.1007/978-3-030-59257-8_6

> **Language issue 29: Retaining values of block-local variables**
> It is sometimes useful to arrange that the value of a variable on entry to a block
> is influenced by the value associated with that name from the previous execution
> of that block.

The *own variable* feature of ALGOL 60 proved to be one of its most contentious
(see, for example, [Knu67]). The intention is clear: a programmer can add the qualification own to a declaration and such variables do, precisely, retain their values
between block executions. Nor, in the simple cases, is there any difficulty in providing a model: all that is necessary is to retain the location of the variable in the
store and find a way of recording that location in a place where it can be retrieved
at block entry. In fact, some descriptions of ALGOL 60 (see [AJ18]) simply add a
fictitious outermost block containing the whole program and generate the locations
of own variables in that encompassing block. This trick neatly finesses some of the
"trouble spots" relating to own variables.

Recall however that inner blocks in ALGOL can declare array dimensions that
depend on the values of non-local variables. If an own array variable has such dynamic bounds, there is no obvious way in which the value of the array can be re-
tained between block executions.

This is a case where attempting to write a formal description of a language could
have readily located an issue that needed resolving by its designers.

6.2 Objects and methods

The idea of "object-oriented" languages has become a major topic of programming
language theory and practice. The reason that such languages are important in this
book is the role they play with concurrency and, after that general issue is tackled in
Chapter 8, Chapter 9 is devoted to a concurrent object-oriented language. It is, however, useful to build links between the material in Chapter 5 and object-orientation
independently of the topic of concurrency and that is done in this section.

Looking at what might be loosely called members of the ALGOL family of languages, blocks are effectively executed in the same way as other statements in that,
when execution reaches the begin bracket of the block, the whole block is executed
to its end bracket[1] at which point the block is complete. During the execution of the
block, any local variables are created (on the stack) but they disappear on completion of the block. The situation with procedure calling is slightly more complicated
but in essence similar. On encountering a *Call*, the appropriate procedure body is
located and (after parameter installation) executed to its end at which point all trace
of any variables within the procedure is expunged.

---

[1] This ignores the possibility of abnormal exit: this issue is tackled in Chapter 10 but it is both true
and important that it does not change the discussion here.

This forgetting of variables from blocks or procedures is made clear by the fact that the statement after a block or a call uses the environment that sets the context prior to that action.

Objects were first implemented in the Simula language [DMN68]. As its name hints, the application was writing simulation programs. The specific challenge was writing Monte Carlo simulations of ships docking at piers. Faced with the challenge of writing programs that represented arbitrary numbers of physical-world objects, the designers of SIMULA (Ole-Johan Dahl and Kristen Nygaard) realised that blocks could have multiple instantiations to stand for such things as the boats in their simulations.

Thus blocks can be thought of as defining *classes*, whose instances are *objects*. Furthermore, procedures associated with a block provide a guide to what become the *methods* of the class. But there are three essential differences to normal blocks:

- Firstly, for the intended purpose, objects must retain their values between uses. (It is perhaps worth comparing this with the idea of own variables in ALGOL 60 which are discussed in Section 6.1.) This means that the semantic objects for a language like Simula need at least a mapping from object *Reference*s to a VDM record that has as one component a mapping from (local) variable names to their values.
- Secondly, since objects do not have the same ephemeral existence as *Block*s, there will need to be a way of *garbage collecting* objects that can no longer be used.
- Thirdly and, perhaps most interestingly, the scope of method names is deliberately external to the objects (in contrast to procedures in ALGOL-like languages, which methods otherwise resemble).

A full description of such a sequential object-oriented language is straightforward to construct but, as is made clear above, the real interest here is to use object-oriented concepts in tandem with concurrency (see Chapter 9). A major problem with concurrency is "data races" and it turns out that the localisation of state in OOLs helps ameliorate this problem.

It is worth observing one further advantage of OOLs: the aim of *abstract data types* is to insulate users from the representation of complicated data types. The fact that data is internal to objects and that the only interface is through the methods ensures that the representation details are hidden from users of the class and they can be changed without affecting users of the class.

6.3 Pascal variant records

Pascal is a well-designed and clean language from one of the world's greatest designers of programming languages: Niklaus Wirth and Tony Hoare provided key insights for ALGOL W [WH66, BBG$^+$68] and Wirth was the major designer of

both the Modula series [CDG$^+$89] and the Oberon series [Fra00] of languages.[2]
The Pascal feature of *variant records* has however some messy consequences and it
is interesting to look at how a formal description pinpoints the problems.

Language issue 30: Variant records

It is sometimes useful to declare a record type that, as well as some common
fields, indicates that there are variants of the type; these variants can have different numbers of fields with distinct sets of names and their types (and thus sizes)
do not need to match.

An example declaration of a variant record might be:

```
var r: record
        f:Type1;
        case b:{OPTION1,OPTION2} of
            OPTION1:{x:Type2}
            OPTION2:{y:Type3}
        end
```

(Here *Type2* and *Type3* could themselves be complicated records — even variant
records.)

There are both implementation efficiency and program clarity arguments for
some form of variant record feature. One of Wirth's strengths as a language designer is that he always appears to have a clear idea of how a language feature can
be implemented and one of the initial arguments for variant records was that there
was a way of saving store by overlaying different record types. With ever-cheaper
store, the more enduring argument is that a programmer's intentions are clearer with
a variant record than with two separate record declarations that a reader has to compare line by line to spot what is common and where the differences are located.

The form of variant record in the example above is a *tagged variant record*. It is
correct to write statements such as:

```
r.b:=OPTION2;
r.y:=···;
```

But this shows that the model of records envisaged in Section 4.3.3 is no longer
adequate. Changing the model is not entirely trivial. The deeper problem is that the
distinction that says that environments are fixed at the block level no longer holds:
the first assignment above changes the identifiers and their respective locations. Furthermore, an assignment:

```
r.x:=···;
```

implicitly changes the tag. If this were not enough complications, *untagged variant
records* are allowed where there is no explicit tag field within the record. Coupled
with the ability to pass values of such types by say a value/return parameter mechanism, this collection of decisions greatly complicates the model of Pascal in [AH82]

---

[2] Perhaps he would prefer to have Euler [WW66] forgotten because one of its key design objectives
was rather limiting.

and re-reading pages 180–186 of that reference brings out the pain that Derek Andrews and Wolfgang Henhapl experienced in having to model the interaction of such a collection of features.

6.4 Heap variables

Tackling applications related to artificial intelligence (AI) in general and machine-assisted reasoning in particular prompted Herb Simon and Allen Newell to develop the IPL-V language [New63, SN86] and John McCarthy to design Lisp 1.5 [ML65], which are both languages that support *list processing*.

In contrast to arrays (or records), lists are seen as dynamic data structures where individual data items are linked. Such links have to be in close correspondence with machine addresses.[3] In fact, Lisp used the terms car/cdr to stand for "contents of address register" and "contents of decrement register" which directly reflected the structure of the IBM 7xx machine that was used for the initial implementation.

Language issue 31: Dynamic data topology
Computer applications that are best implemented with arbitrary and dynamic graphs of elements indicate a need for programming languages that directly support list processing.

Variables declared in *Block*s are accessed via their names and are referred to as *stack variables* because their lifetime is governed by entering and completing blocks, which means that they can be allocated on a (last-in-first-out) *stack*. In contrast, dynamically created values are referred to as *heap variables*.

Lisp-like languages organise everything in lists.[4] Pascal supports both stack and heap variables. A natural programming style is to have records whose values can contain both application data and pointers to other instances of records.

In the meta-language being used in this book (VDM), records can be nested:

$$R :: v : \mathbb{N}$$
$$n : [R]$$

In a programming language, a pointer to the record is used (that pointer can of course be nil).

Language issue 32: Declaring and using pointer types
Languages with both stack and heap data need a way to distinguish a variable that contains a value of a given type from a variable that contains the address of a value of that type. Similarly there need to be ways of distinguishing the use of an identifier to access the value of a pointer variable in contrast to using it as a pointer to another element.

---

[3] It is of course possible to simulate list processing with arrays using the array index as a surrogate for machine addresses, but the same difficulties recur.

[4] This includes programs themselves, which makes it possible for AI applications to change programs dynamically.

In Pascal, the dynamic creation of a data element of some type is achieved by executing a new statement. At the implementation level, this implies the existence of a free-storage manager that tracks unused storage and allocates free space on each call.

There are a number of related programming pitfalls associated with list processing. An obvious difficulty is that the free-storage manager cannot create arbitrary numbers of new addresses because any machine has a finite store and address space. This problem is particularly acute for programs that execute for a long period of time.

One way of ameliorating this problem is to offer a dispose statement that a programmer should use to return surplus addresses to the free-storage manager. But this approach has its own dangers. A program might be designed to create a complicated graph-like data structure where pointers are copied and can occur in many places. It should be a programming error to dispose of an address that can still be accessed via another path: such *dangling pointers* can result in unpredictable behaviour that –especially in the presence of concurrency– can be extremely difficult to debug.

An alternative way forward is to make the implementation responsible for recognising when elements of data can no longer be reached. So-called *concurrent garbage collectors* are highly delicate pieces of code whose requirement is that they should not affect the semantics of the program they are meant to assist (see for example [JL96]).

Given that the idea of having a surrogate for machine addresses has been introduced in Section 5.2, it is not difficult to devise a semantic model of a language that includes heap variables. The key is to recognise that the set of *Values* must include *Locs*. Such a definition is not written out in the current book because most of the issues (including garbage collection) are discussed in the context of object-oriented languages in Chapter 9.

It is worth mentioning that garbage collection is one of the places where it is not difficult to write a mathematical description but its implementation can be rather expensive (in both running time and programmer ingenuity).

There is a variety of language features relating to heap storage. For example PL/I has a notion of *regions*, which are disjoint spaces that can be managed as whole collections. PL/I also includes the unwise decision that programmers can obtain the addresses of stack variables.

This last point emphasises that making machine addresses data items that programmers can manipulate is extremely dangerous because a program can access or change storage that is completely outside its own collection of variables. Reading or changing data that belongs to the operating system has probably cost more money than any other feature of programming languages. Introducing a proper type structure that forbids any modification of addresses is one useful step but it does not prevent malicious code being written in a language like C. Running all programs on top of a *virtual machine* can provide a level of security but hardware implementation of something like *capabilities* [Lev84] is the only really safe solution.

6.5 Functions

In most respects, the issues around modelling functions are the same as those addressed in Chapter 5 for procedures but there are some additional points that are
of interest for models of languages. One important distinction is that, whereas procedures are invoked in a statement context, functions are activated as expressions.
As such, functions should obviously be given a return type in a language which is
strongly typed.

Language issue 33: Pre-defined functions
ALGOL 60 defined some functions (at a notional outermost scope) that can be
used anywhere within a program. This can be modelled as an encompassing
block.

An abstract syntax for programmer-defined functions can be given as a simple
extension of the language in Chapter 5:

$$FunDef :: type \qquad : ScalarType$$
$$params \quad : Id^*$$
$$paramtypes : ScalarType^*$$
$$body \qquad : Stmt$$

There is no difficulty in extending this to return non-scalar values. Some care with
regard to matching dimensions is required if array values can be returned.

6.5.1 Marking the return value

A related question is how the portion of the program that defines the function (its
body) should identify the value to be returned:

- A language can require that an explicit return statement identifies the value to be
  returned; the programmer would write something like:

  function $f(\cdots)$
  $\cdots$
  return(e);
  $\cdots$
  end

  As well as causing evaluation of e to yield the value to be returned to the calling
  context, executing the return terminates execution of the *body*.
- In some languages (including ALGOL 60) the return value is indicated by an
  assignment to the name of the function as in:

```
function f(···)
      ···
   f := ···
      ···
end
```

The value returned is that of the last assignment executed before the *body* completes (i.e. the assignment does not cause execution of the *body* to terminate).

- In languages where statements have values, the value of the function can be the value of its defining *body*.

In languages that have an explicit return statement, that statement can be placed inside other phrases such as loops, blocks etc. Modelling abnormal termination is itself a problem whose discussion is postponed to Chapter 10.

6.5.2 Side effects

Both procedures and functions can, in most procedural languages, give rise to *side effects* in that statements to be executed in their *body* part can assign to variables that are non-local to that *body* or even perform input/output.

Procedure calls in a sequential language are executed in a clearly defined order. Function calls are initiated in expression contexts such as:

$$x := f(x) + g(y)$$

This can open up a form of non-determinacy that must be faced in a semantic description. A –possibly unexpected– feature interaction is with the fact that language designers do not typically constrain the order in which sub-expressions are evaluated. There are good reasons for this:

- compiler writers are normally faced with a limited set of fast registers and will want to optimise their use — this can result in evaluating sub-expressions in non-obvious orders;
- an even more extreme optimisation is that a compiler might be written to evaluate "common sub-expressions" only once.

Thus the fact that function calls occur within expressions gives rise to some messy questions about non-determinacy (because of side effects).

> **Language issue 34: Contrast with pure mathematical functions**
> If a language allows side effects and does not fix the exact order in which terms in expressions are to be evaluated, expressions that look as though they use mathematical functions can give rise to non-determinacy.

Pascal is a rather clean language but has a most unpleasant surprise for the writer of its formal description. The compiler writer is given permission to re-order how sub-expressions are evaluated because the Pascal documentation says that any program that gives different results depending on the order of evaluation is deemed to be erroneous. A faithful formal description of Pascal must therefore be at pains[5] to specify all possible results and then check that the set of such results has exactly one element.

Language issue 35: Side effects from shorthands

As well as bringing assignment-statement-like side effects into expressions, shorthands such as $x + +/ + +x$ introduce similar problems to function calls.

6.5.3 Recursion

Most of the topics in this sub-section could be discussed in the context of procedures but they are issues which really beg resolution for functions. In particular, recursive procedures can be useful but recursion is almost ubiquitous for functions.

Amending the context conditions for *BlocksProgram* in Appendix C to allow recursion is straightforward: it is only necessary to add the local *proc-tpm* to the updated environment used in:

$$\forall p \in \operatorname{dom} pm \cdot \textit{wf-ProcDef}\,(pm(p), tpm' \dagger \textit{proc-tpm})$$

Changing the semantics for *Block* is more difficult because of the need to store the environment of the procedures (or functions) within their denotations. One way of solving this is to have a separate labelled collection of environments and to store the label of the environment rather than the object itself. A more elegant solution is to accept the recursive definition of environments and to define the value as the relevant fixed point. This idea is explained in Section 7.1.

6.5.4 Passing functions as parameters [*]

A useful way of achieving generic programs is to write functions that accept arguments that are functions. For example, a function that returns a sequence that results from applying its functional argument to every element of an argument sequence might be:

$$apply : (X \to Y) \times X^* \to Y^*$$

$$apply(f,s) \quad \triangleq \quad \text{if } s = [\,]$$
$$\text{then } [\,]$$
$$\text{else } [f(\operatorname{hd} s)] \frown apply(f, \operatorname{tl} s)$$
$$\text{fi}$$

---

[5] This would require a "small-step" semantics — see Chapter 8.

The type of *apply* shows that its first argument is itself a function. The function *apply* could be used for many different purposes (e.g. doubling every number in a list or reversing every string in a list of sequences of characters).

Language issue 36: Higher order programming
Higher-order functions are a key to achieving generic programs in purely functional languages.

With care on the part of programmers, higher-order functions can also be used in imperative programming languages but indisciplined use of imperative features such as side effects can subvert any advantages that might otherwise be gained by this style of programming. Models of full-blown passing of functions and procedures are given in the ALGOL 60 descriptions cited in [AJ18].

Language issue 37: Function types
In order to write (a finite form of) a type for a function that can take itself as an argument, it is necessary to have a way of separating out the naming of the function type.

Procedure variables/results

In geometry, orthogonal lines are at right angles; more generally, orthogonality has to do with independence. The term is sometimes used in programming language design to argue that values of various types must be subject to the same rules.

Language issue 38: First-class objects
It can be argued that since –for example– variables can contain integers, integers can be passed as arguments and expressions can yield integers, values of any type should enjoy the same "first-class" status.

Earlier projects have indicated that there is virtue in saying that a concept like conditional statements invites consideration of conditional expressions and even conditional references (see Section 2.3). ALGOL 60 extended this argument to labels: since there were constant labels, there should be switch variables to which labels could be assigned and such switch variables could be used in goto statements. The designers of ALGOL 68 went further and argued that there should be variables that could take procedures as values.

It is worth examining this plausible-sounding argument in terms of formal models. As Hans Bekič showed in [Bek73], such variables can result in violations of the normal scoping rules. While it is true that passing procedures or functions as arguments to other procedures or functions can only result in them being called whist their context is still active, procedure variables can be assigned values that exist longer than their context. The same problem can arise with returning procedure values from functions.

6.6 Further material

Projects

1. It is interesting to look at functions that, instead of returning a single value, can return a tuple of results. Ways of passing multiple values from a function include side effects and using parameters that are passed either by name or value/return but there is no reason why function types cannot be extended so that a call could be written as:

   $(x, y) := f2(\cdots)$

2. Looking in detail at the semantics of allowing side-effect-inducing expressions like $x++$ in C is instructive.
3. The semantics of the sequential OOL envisaged in Section 6.2 are not difficult to write.

   In its simplest form, run-time exception handling can be viewed as a form of procedure call. But exception handlers can be programmed so as to not return to the source of the exception and are thus better discussed in Chapter 10.

Chapter 7
Other semantic approaches

The main focus in this book is on the operational approach to documenting the semantics of programming languages. There are however other approaches and understanding them is both instructive in itself and also throws light on operational semantics by clarifying their relationship thereto.

A broad distinction between semantic methods can be made:

- "Model-oriented" methods are built around an explicit notion of an (abstract) state of a machine underlying the semantics.
- "Property-oriented" approaches attempt to define the semantics in terms of properties of texts in the language.

Operational semantics is clearly model oriented in that meaning is given to texts in a language $\mathcal{L}$ by defining how those texts transform an underlying abstract state.

Denotational semantics makes an important step of abstraction by fixing the semantics of $\mathcal{L}$ by mapping its constructs into functions from states to states. It turns out that the states in operational and denotational approaches can be identical for simple languages and this supports viewing both of these approaches as model oriented.

Early in attempts to capture the semantics of programming languages, researchers investigated fixing key aspects of semantics by characterising equivalencies between texts (e.g. [Bek64]). This is certainly one way to define semantics by properties and relates to recent research on "algebraic semantics" (see Section 7.5). More prominent in the property-oriented semantics world is the research on "axiomatic semantics", in which logics are provided for deducing properties of programs written in a language $\mathcal{L}$. Denotational semantics is outlined in Sections 7.1 and 7.2; Sections 7.3 and 7.4 discuss axiomatic semantics. A full study of these approaches would require far more than this short chapter and fortunately good texts exist already — a selection of these are cited in Sections 7.2 and 7.4.

© Springer Nature Switzerland AG 2020
C. B. Jones, *Understanding Programming Languages*,
https://doi.org/10.1007/978-3-030-59257-8_7

7.1 Denotational semantics

The step from operational to denotational semantics can be compared to that from interpreters to translators. An operational semantics provides an abstract interpreter that takes a program and a starting state and –for a deterministic language– computes the final state. (The extension to use relations to final states for non-deterministic languages is introduced in Section 3.2.) Denotational semantics maps a deterministic program to a function from states to states. Just as operational approaches provide abstract interpreters that avoid the details required in a machine-code interpreter, the functions that serve as denotations of programs are more abstract than a machine-code program generated by a translator for the language.

As is shown below, the abstract states used in denotational semantics are, in simple cases, the same as would be used in an operational description. The denotational description is more abstract than an operational description because the former abstracts away from the initial state required by the operational description. There is however a cost associated with this abstraction: denotational semantics needs some more sophisticated mathematical concepts than underlie operational descriptions.[1] This section only outlines the main objectives of the denotational approach and mentions the mathematical challenges.

Starting with the observation made in earlier chapters that the effective statements in an imperative programming language are those that change the state, a way of creating a function from states to states is required — for example a meaning function $\mathcal{M}$ applied to *Assign* statements should yield a function:[2]

$$\mathcal{M}[\![mk\text{-}Assign(lhs,rhs)]\!] \triangleq \cdots$$

For a simple language such as that in Chapter 3, the type of this meaning function $\mathcal{M}$ is:

$$\mathcal{M}[\![\_]\!]: Stmt \to (\Sigma \to \Sigma)$$

The ($\mathcal{M}$) semantics for assignment statements could be written with the state (σ) made explicit:

$$\mathcal{M}[\![mk\text{-}Assign(lhs,rhs)]\!](\sigma) \triangleq \sigma \dagger \{lhs \mapsto eval(rhs,\sigma)\}$$

The discussion that follows about the need to have a uniform way of defining $\mathcal{M}$ as having the type $Stmt \to (\Sigma \to \Sigma)$ for any statement argues for having a direct way of defining $\mathcal{M}[\![mk\text{-}Assign(lhs,rhs)]\!]$ without applying it to the state argument. Fortunately Alonzo Church's *Lambda notation* (see for example [Han04]) provides a way of writing unnamed functions. For example, the identity function can be defined in the Lambda notation as:

$$Id = \lambda\sigma \cdot \sigma$$

---

[1] During the development by Strachey, Scott and colleagues at the University of Oxford, the term "mathematical semantics" was used; use of the adjective "denotational" came later — see [Sto77].
[2] The use of "Strachey brackets" ($[\![\ ]\!]$) is a convention that has no deep meaning.

A Lambda expression follows the Greek letter λ with a list (in this case one) of parameter names with the definition of the function after a dot.

The Lambda calculus is more than a notation — its semantics is fixed by a *theory of equality* given by a small collection of equality rules between Lambda expressions. Lambda functions can have type decorations — a specific identity function could be defined:

$$Id = \lambda\sigma{:}\Sigma \cdot \sigma$$

and this point becomes important below. Although it was clear that the typed Lambda calculus had models, until Dana Scott's ground-breaking research in Oxford, no one had succeeded in showing that there were underlying models of the untyped Lambda calculus. Unfortunately, features of programming languages like ALGOL 60 relied on the untyped calculus.

Using Lambda notation:

$$\lambda\sigma \cdot \sigma \dagger \{lhs \mapsto eval(rhs, \sigma)\}$$

is a function from states to states and can be used to avoid writing the σ on the left of the defining $\triangle$ above:

$$\mathscr{M}[\![mk\text{-}Assign(lhs, rhs)]\!] \triangle \lambda\sigma \cdot \sigma \dagger \{lhs \mapsto eval(rhs, \sigma)\}$$

A key goal of denotational semantics is to express the meaning (denotation) of compound statements in terms of the meaning of the components of the compound object. Technically, this notion is that $\mathscr{M}$ is a *homomorphic mapping* from syntactic objects to their denotations.

For simple compounds, this works nicely with mathematical composition of two functions defined as:[3]

$$f_1 \circ f_2 \triangle \lambda x \cdot f_2(f_1(x))$$

Fixing the meaning of compound statements simply composes the meanings of the two statements:

$$\mathscr{M}[\![S1; S2]\!] \triangle \mathscr{M}[\![S1]\!] \circ \mathscr{M}[\![S2]\!]$$

The mathematical challenge begins to increase with the denotation of while statements. With the identity function (*Id*) as above and using an obvious notation for conditionals,[4] the denotation of *While* can be written:

$$\mathscr{M}[\![mk\text{-}While(test, body)]\!] \triangle$$
$$\mathscr{M}[\![test]\!] \to \mathscr{M}[\![mk\text{-}While(test, body)]\!] \circ \mathscr{M}(body) \ \square$$
$$Id$$

The fact that the left-hand side of the definition (i.e. $\mathscr{M}[\![mk\text{-}While(test, body)]\!]$) also appears on the right of the definition symbol requires some clarification. Given

---

[3] Mathematicians are divided about which order defines composition — the choice makes no essential difference to the rest of the discussion.

[4] The conditional can be encoded as a Lambda function but this detail is not germane to what follows.

certain conditions, such definitions can be considered to define *fixed points*. Fixed points of recursive definitions can be built up — consider:

$WH = $ while $i \neq 0$ do $i := i - 1$ od

Where the test is false, the recursive branch of the definition given above is not needed and the whole function is defined to be the identity function. Therefore the pair $(0,0) \in \mathcal{M}[\![WH]\!]$. But once that base element is in $\mathcal{M}[\![WH]\!]$, so must be the pair $(1,0) \in \mathcal{M}[\![WH]\!]$. Iterating this process requires that at least:

$\{(i,0) \mid i \in \mathbb{N}\} \subseteq \mathcal{M}[\![WH]\!]$

The set $\{(i,0) \mid i \in \mathbb{N}\}$ is a fixed point of $\mathcal{M}[\![WH]\!]$ because the recursive definition does not force the addition of any further pairs. It is in fact the *least fixed point* because arbitrarily adding, say, $(-7,0)$ results in further values. But the least fixed point is the denotation that makes sense for *While*.

Since the least-fixed-point construction creates infinite objects in general, it does not actually offer a useful tool for calculation. But it is the underlying semantics and in terms of that semantics the useful proof rule of *fixed-point induction* can be justified.

It is useful to return to the comparison between operational semantics as offering an (abstract) interpreter and denotational semantics as defining a translation. The mapping provided in the latter case is really an expression of the Lambda notation. This is what Peter Landin envisioned in his important papers [Lan65a, Lan65b]. It must be understood, however, that obtaining an expression for say the application of the meaning function $\mathcal{M}$ to a program for factorial does not immediately yield the mathematical function:

$\{(i,i!) \mid i \in \mathbb{N}\}$

To prove this requires properties of the factorial operator. But given such properties, there is a mathematical rule for such proofs.

In contrast, using an operational semantics needs not only the properties of the factorial function but any proof has to be an induction over the steps of the computation. This means that there are proofs that are more elegant when based on denotational semantic descriptions than if they were based on operational semantics. Typical cases where denotational semantics shine are to show that composition is associative or that unwrapping a while loop with a conditional preserves the original meaning.

The advantages of abstracting denotations become clearer for languages that are modelled with environments:

$\mathcal{M}[\![\_]\!]: Stmt \rightarrow (Env \rightarrow (\Sigma \rightarrow \Sigma))$

Firstly, there is an expression for

$\mathcal{M}[\![mk\text{-}Assign(\cdots)]\!]: Env \rightarrow (\Sigma \rightarrow \Sigma)$

The environment has been bundled into the definition. Furthermore, the formula:

$\mathcal{M}[\![S1;S2]\!] \triangleq \mathcal{M}[\![S1]\!] \circ \mathcal{M}[\![S2]\!]$

still provides a homomorphic mapping to the richer denotations.

Environments are also encapsulated in procedure definitions so that there is an obvious comparison between call by value:

$$Pden = ScalarValue^* \rightarrow (\Sigma \rightarrow \Sigma)$$

and call by reference:

$$Pden = ScalarLoc^* \rightarrow (\Sigma \rightarrow \Sigma)$$

Unfortunately, this is precisely the point at which the mathematical underpinning becomes more questionable. If there were a strict hierarchy of procedures, types could be associated with each denotation and the typed Lambda calculus would have sufficed for the space of denotations. But, for languages in which procedures can accept arbitrary procedures as arguments, no such ordering could be defined. Strachey and Landin had rather naively continued to use an *untyped Lambda calculus* as a way of expressing the semantics of languages like ALGOL 60 and CPL [BBHS63], where self application was allowed.

Scott raised the alarm and was for a time convinced that there were no models for the untyped Lambda calculus [Sco69].[5] Scott, however, went on to provide precisely such a model and, in a series of monographs from the Oxford Programming Research Group in 1969, established what is now known as *domain theory*. The essence of Scott's insight was that restricting denotations to monotone and continuous functions provides a sufficient foundation.

Although Scott's models for the untyped Lambda calculus had resolved a key issue in the foundations of mathematics, this did not mean that finding denotations for programming constructs would always be straightforward. The maligned *GoTo* statement is an example of exceptional sequencing in that a goto can force the closure of an arbitrary collection of dynamic contexts. Even the concept of a *Return* statement from within a function can have a similar effect and exception handlers present the same sort of challenge. The homomorphic rule suggests that the denotation of any statement should be constructed from the denotations of its components but it is not obvious how to apply this dictum in the case of exceptional sequencing. One solution is to use *continuations* and this approach is described in Chapter 10.

As explained in Chapter 8, non-determinacy is inherent in modelling concurrency and this posed further challenges for denotational semantics.

7.2 Further material

Chris Hankin's [Han04] is more than adequate to provide the necessary background on the Lambda notation.[6]

---

[5] Just as Cantor had shown that there are more reals than rational numbers by an enumeration argument, it appeared that a cardinality contradiction existed for functions that could take themselves as arguments.

[6] Church's [Chu41] is the original source and includes the wonderfully clear description:

The history of the evolution of denotational semantics is addressed in several places:

- Joe Stoy's excellent book [Sto77] is still an invaluable source (the Foreword by Dana Scott is extremely useful).
- A masterly general biographical article on Strachey from Martin Campbell-Kelly is [CK85].
- Shortly before Christopher Strachey's untimely death, he wrote jointly with Robert Milne [MS74], which was a submission for the (Cambridge University) Adams Prize. They did not win the award but, after Strachey "shuffled off this mortal coil", Milne revised the work into a rather challenging two-volume book [MS76]. Both a formal description of *Sal* and a proof of correctness of a compiler are covered.
- The group at the IBM Lab in Vienna adopted a denotational approach when in 1973 they had the opportunity to tackle developing a compiler from a formal description of PL/I. The areas of VDM that relate to language semantics adopt a denotational approach albeit with differences from the Oxford style — see Chapter 10. This story is told in some detail in [AJ18]. Troy Astarte's thesis [Ast19] expands on the historical context of these events.
- The current author taught denotational semantics at Manchester University up to 1996 but on returning to academia in 1999 switched to teaching SOS at Newcastle University. The argument being –as presented by the current book– that a carefully constructed operational semantics is the perfect tool for thinking about the design of a programming language.
- The hundredth anniversary of Strachey's birth was marked by a conference in Oxford and video recordings of the talks are available.[7] Two gems among them are Stoy's talk and the panel discussion where Roger Penrose describes his attempt to interest Strachey in the Lambda calculus and his delayed acceptance.
- The origin of the series of theorem proving assistants from HOL [Gor86] through Isabelle [Nip09] was actually LCF from Robin Milner and colleagues [GMW79]. The "Logic of Computable Functions" was motivated by Scott's work. The LCF implementation was also notable for being the genesis of the original ML ("Meta-Language") programming language, which evolved into Standard ML [MTHM97].

The topic of basing compiler designs on denotational descriptions warrants some expansion. The Sal language tackled in [MS76] is certainly substantial. The 1973–76 efforts at the IBM Lab in Vienna tackled PL/I: a denotational semantics for the ECMA/ANSI subset of PL/I is given in [BBH⁺74]; specific details of the work are in Technical Reports [Wei75, Izb75, BIJW75]; and a summary of the approach

---

A function is a rule of correspondence by which when anything is given (as an argument) another thing (the value of the function for that argument) may be obtained. That is, a function is an operation which may be applied on one thing (the argument) to yield another thing (the value of the function).

[7] http://podcasts.ox.ac.uk/series/strachey-100-oxford-computing-pioneer

is in [Jon76]. Key aspects of the approach include viewing the run-time state of execution as a representation of the abstract states (see Section 7.3.5) and relating programs that satisfy the concrete syntax to the abstract syntax of the language description.

As described in more detail in [AJ18, JA18], the work was terminated when IBM cancelled the machine for which the compiler was being constructed. First as an LNCS [BJ78] –and later as [BJ82]– the aspects of VDM relating to language description eventually received wider publication. Chapter 11 mentions other uses of VDM as a basis for compiler development including the Danish Ada compiler [BO80a].

7.3 The axiomatic approach

If program specifications are presented as pre and post conditions:[8]

$$pre: \Sigma \to \mathbb{B}$$
$$post: \Sigma \times \Sigma \to \mathbb{B}$$

it is possible to reason about program correctness in terms of an operational semantics as follows:

$$\forall \sigma, \sigma' \in \Sigma \cdot pre(\sigma) \wedge (s, \sigma) \xrightarrow{st} \sigma' \Rightarrow post(\sigma, \sigma')$$

But such proofs can become cumbersome. The term "axiomatic semantics" comes from Tony Hoare's seminal 1969 paper [Hoa69] entitled "An axiomatic basis for computer programming". This approach offers a far more natural way to reason about program correctness and, moreover, lends itself to support a development method for programs. This section gives enough of an overview of the approach to relate it to operational semantics.

7.3.1 Assertions on states

It is both useful and historically relevant to begin with the idea of recording assertions about the state of a computation on a flowchart. A key reference that had a significant influence on subsequent research is Bob Floyd's "Assigning meanings to programs": in [Flo67] a program is presented by its "flowchart" but, as well as the instructions and tests being written in rectangles and ovals, logical assertions are associated with the arcs between boxes.

---

[8] The case is made below that post conditions should be relations between initial and final states; Sections 7.3.1 and 7.3.2 follow the historical development where even post conditions were originally taken to be predicates of a single state.

Figure 7.1 contains a version of Floyd's annotated flowchart for an algorithm that computes integer division by successive subtraction. The algorithm is straightforward: x is to be divided by y computing the quotient in q and leaving any remainder in r.[9] Looking at the decorating assertions, the overall required effect is associated with the exit from the program (just before the oval marked **HALT**) as:

$0 \leq r < y$
$x \geq 0$
$x = r + q * y$

The initial conditions are marked on the arc after the oval marked **START** as:

$x \geq 0$
$y > 0$

Some of the assertions can be shown to be mechanically derivable from others but the assertion within the loop is crucial to establishing correctness:

$r \geq y > 0$
$x \geq 0$
$q \geq 0$
$x = r + q * y$

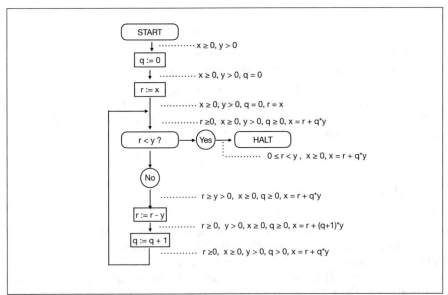

Fig. 7.1 Integer division example from Floyd's [Flo67]

<hr />

[9] Notice that this fits with the idea that programs extend the instruction set of a machine: Floyd assumed that there was a subtract instruction but not one for integer division.

Clearly, the annotating assertions need to be consistent with the program on which they are placed and rules for checking this are provided in [Flo67].[10] While it is true that adding assertions to a program (in Floyd's case, on its flowchart) requires extra effort from the programmer, their presence makes it possible to prove that the program satisfies its specification (under a clear set of assumptions).

In fact, Floyd's rules provide a way of deriving some assertions from the code plus a minimal set of assertions. Annotations must at least be provided for the final arc and one to mark some point within any loop. The first of these is anyway the specification of what the program should do and an assertion within the loop captures the intention of the loop.[11]

Floyd's paper was circulated privately in 1967 and discussed at the 1968 IBM Yorktown conference on the "Mathematical Theory of Computation". A copy of Floyd's original hand-drawn figure is given in Figure 7.2. Apart from the trivial difference between lower- and upper-case identifiers, the obvious addition to Figure 7.1 is that Floyd has two lines on each assertion. The second line of Floyd's annotations provides an argument for termination of the loop and is not examined in detail here because Hoare chose not to include them in his system. Suffice it to say that the termination argument relies of finding a reducing quantity that is bounded from below (a well-founded ordering) — in Figure 7.2, Floyd uses a lexicographic pair.

Section 7.4 mentions that even earlier than Floyd, Alan Turing used the idea of adding annotations to a flowchart in [Tur49]. Turing also saw the need to reason about termination and has the lovely comment:

> Finally the checker has to verify that the process comes to an end. Here again he should be assisted by the programmer giving a further definite assertion to be verified. This may take the form of a quantity which is asserted to decrease continually and vanish when the machine stops. To the pure mathematician it is natural to give an ordinal number. ... A less highbrow form of the same thing would be to give the integer ...

The final ellipses contain an expression in terms of two to the power of the word size of the machine!

7.3.2 Hoare's axioms

Tony Hoare's paper [Hoa69] includes a generous acknowledgement of the influence of Floyd's paper but takes a crucial step beyond the idea of assertions as annotations. The key innovation is that a logical system can be created for reasoning about programs and consistent assertions. What are now known as "Hoare triples" con-

---

[10] The paper includes many other interesting technical ideas — some of which are mentioned in Section 7.4.

[11] Such loop-cutting assertions become "loop invariants" in Hoare's approach — see Section 7.3.2. They can also be thought of as local "data type invariants" that are like context conditions.

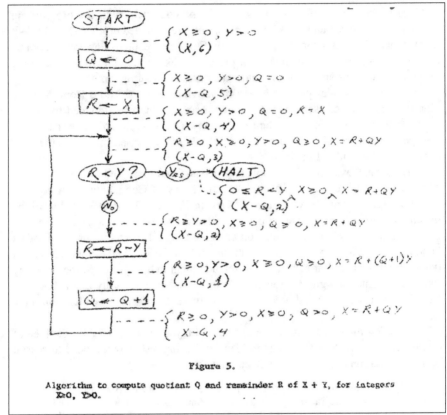

Figure 5.

Algorithm to compute quotient Q and remainder R of X ÷ Y, for integers
X≥0, Y>0.

Fig. 7.2 Floyd's original version of Figure 7.1

tain two logical assertions (predicates) surrounding a program text — they are now
written:[12]

$$\{P\}\ S\ \{Q\}$$

and are to be read as asserting that, if program S is started in a state that satisfies
predicate P, any final state will satisfy predicate Q. The predicate P is referred to as
the pre condition and Q as the post condition of S. One of Hoare's claims was that
it was not necessary to pin down more details of the domain of these predicates. It
facilitates the comparison with operational semantics to assume that they are predicates on the state of the computation, and this is certainly the way in which Hoare
triples are most commonly used.

An inference system can be defined for deducing valid judgements that are
recorded as Hoare triples. "Axioms" (or rules of inference) for the simple language
of Chapter 3 are given in Figure 7.3. The use of inference rules is of course famil-

---

[12] In fact, Hoare originally (in [Hoa69]) chose to present the triples bracketed as $P\ \{S\}\ Q$.

$$\fbox{;}\frac{\begin{array}{l}\{P\}\ S_1\ \{Q\}\\ \{Q\}\ S_2\ \{R\}\end{array}}{\{P\}\ S_1;\ S_2\ \{R\}}$$

$$\fbox{if}\frac{\begin{array}{l}\{P\wedge b\}\ S_1\ \{Q\}\\ \{P\wedge\neg b\}\ S_2\ \{Q\}\end{array}}{\{P\}\ \text{if}\ b\ \text{then}\ S_1\ \text{else}\ S_2\ \text{fi}\ \{Q\}}$$

$$\fbox{while}\frac{\{P\wedge b\}\ S\ \{P\}}{\{P\}\ \text{while}\ b\ \text{do}\ S\ \text{od}\ \{P\wedge\neg b\}}$$

$$\fbox{:=}\frac{}{\{P[e/x]\}\ x:=e\ \{P\}}$$

$$\fbox{consequence}\frac{\begin{array}{l}P'\Rightarrow P\\ Q\Rightarrow Q'\\ \{P\}\ S\ \{Q\}\end{array}}{\{P'\}\ S\ \{Q'\}}$$

Fig. 7.3 Hoare's axioms

iar from SOS (see discussion in Section 3.2.2) and –as with SOS rules– those in Figure 7.3 are generic in the sense that any valid substitution is taken to be allowed.

The first rule in Figure 7.3 is for the *composition* of two statements and identifies the predicate that characterises the post state of S_1 with the pre condition for S_2. An example inference that corresponds to the body of the loop in Figure 7.1 would be:

$$\frac{\begin{array}{l}\{x=r+q*y\}\ r:=r-y\ \{x=r+(q+1)*y\}\\ \{x=r+(q+1)*y\}\ q:=q+1\ \{x=r+q*y\}\end{array}}{\{x=r+q*y\}\ r:=r-y;\ q:=q+1\ \{x=r+q*y\}}$$

The two hypotheses of that example can both be justified using the fourth rule in Figure 7.3, which is for assignment statements. That *assignment rule* uses a notion of substitution of an expression for an identifier: $P[e/x]$ is the predicate expression P with all occurrences of x replaced by e. The axiom (with no hypotheses) says that $P[e/x]$ is a valid pre condition for the assignment $x:=e$ to achieve a post state that satisfies P. Thus the first hypothesis of the argument above about the body of the loop follows from:

$$\{x=(r-y)+(q+1)*y\}\ r:=r-y\ \{x=r+(q+1)*y\}$$

The most interesting of the rules in Figure 7.3 is the one (while) that addresses loops because it brings in the important notion of a *loop invariant*. Ignoring the occurrences of b for the moment, the rule states that, if P is a predicate whose truth is preserved by S, then it follows that any number (including zero) of iterations of S will preserve P. The actual rule makes discharging the hypothesis easier to do by noting that S will only be executed in situations where b holds. Furthermore, the conclusion can be strengthened by noting that, when the loop terminates, b cannot hold.

A key property of the loop in Figure 7.1 could be justified by the following instance of this rule (which uses the result established above for the body of the loop):

$$\frac{\begin{Bmatrix} x=r+q*y \\ r\geq y \end{Bmatrix} \begin{array}{l} r:=r-y; \\ q:=q+1 \end{array} \{x=r+q*y\}}{\{x=r+q*y\} \begin{array}{l} \text{while } r\geq y \text{ do} \\ r:=r-y; \\ q:=q+1 \\ \text{od} \end{array} \begin{Bmatrix} x=r+q*y \\ r<y \end{Bmatrix}}$$

The overall pre/post for Figure 7.1 would be:

$$\{x\geq y\wedge y>0\}\ DIV\ \{0\leq r<y\wedge x\geq 0\wedge x=r+q*y\}$$

which follows from:

- simple instances of the assignment and composition axioms to verify the initialisation; and
- a composition of that initialisation with the result about the loop.

The rule for conditional statements (the second in Figure 7.3) should be obvious. The *consequence* rule notes that, given $\{P\}\ S\ \{Q\}$ has been established, a triple with a stronger pre condition and/or a weaker post condition must also hold.

Note that the rules as given in Figure 7.3 do not offer a way of establishing termination — this and other comments on the method itself are given in Section 7.4. The conditional result is that a program will satisfy its specification if it terminates; this is sometimes referred to as "partial correctness" but the term is not used further in this book.

It is interesting to observe that checking programs which contain assertions does not fit the strict distinction between static context conditions and run-time errors. The idea of program verification is certainly that it should be conducted prior to execution on the static text of a program but checking assertions is not –in general– a decidable process because it requires theorem proving.

Of more interest for now is that there are two senses in which axiomatic semantics can be viewed as complementary to model-oriented approaches such as SOS:

- It should be possible to reason in a natural way about the correctness of programs written in a language $\mathscr{L}$. An axiomatic semantics for $\mathscr{L}$ has formal rules for such reasoning and it is possible to mechanise the checking of such rules in a theorem proving system such as Isabelle [NPW02]. Beyond the question of whether formal proofs will be written for programs in $\mathscr{L}$, it should be realised that difficulties in constructing an axiomatic semantics is a warning that even informal reasoning might be error prone. One obvious example is that the proof rule given for assignments in Figure 7.3 does not hold for a language that permits parameter passing by location because an assignment to one identifier could affect the value of what appears to be a distinct variable.
- There are well-known dangers in writing "axioms". In particular, it is difficult with extended sets of rules to be certain that they are "consistent" in the sense that

inferences cannot yield contradictions. The standard way of establishing "consistency" is to show that a model of the axioms exists, and with programming languages this can be done by showing that the axioms are true of some model-oriented semantics. This task has been undertaken in [Lau71b, HL74, Don76].

There is also the question of the *completeness* of a set of axioms. For a system such as Hoare's, this asks whether all true statements about programs can be deduced from the axioms. This question becomes rather technical because of concerns about the expressiveness of predicates and the inevitable undecidability of the predicate calculus over arithmetic. An insightful description of the completeness issue is given in [AO19].

7.3.3 Specification as statements

Assertions on states as in the style of Floyd are certainly useful in proving that a given program satisfies a stated specification. With some care, such assertions can also be used in program development. But Hoare-style axioms make it much easier to see how a *development process* can be based on formalism. The idea is to start with a formal specification[13] of the program and to use the inference rules to decompose the task. Thus an overall specification can be realised by a decomposition that introduces putative components that are –at that point– only given as specifications. Such decomposition steps are repeated until all of the specifications have been developed to code. The final executable program is the collection of these expansions.

This idea has prompted various authors (e.g. Andrzej Blikle [Bli81], Carroll Morgan [Mor88, Mor90] and Ralph Back [BvW98]) to include a "specification statement" in a programming language and for *contracts* to be included in the Eiffel language [Mey88]. Morgan uses:

frame: $[P, R]$

where *frame* lists the names of variables that can be changed, P is a predicate of one state as the pre condition and R is a relation over two states that is the post condition.[14]

It is interesting to see how easy it is to extend the language description in Chapter 3 to allow specification statements embedded in a program; such a specification will contain a pre condition (a predicate of a single state) and a post condition (a relation over two states). The differences between Morgan-style specification statements, Eiffel-style contracts or some two-dimensional layout (with keywords distinguishing the predicates) are just concrete syntax details.

Thus, extending *Stmt* in *SimpleProgram* of Chapter 3:

---

[13] This does not, of course, answer the question of how a formal specification of a complex system is obtained. Research in this area is contained for example in [Jac00] and given a more formal basis in [JHJ07, BHJ20].

[14] The move to relational post conditions is discussed in Section 7.4.

$Stmt = \cdots \mid Spec$

$Spec \; :: \; frame \; : \; Id\text{-set}$
$\qquad\qquad pre \quad : \; LogExpr$
$\qquad\qquad post \quad : \; LogExpr$

The semantics of *Spec* is both partial and non-deterministic so the hypotheses of the SOS rule for *Spec* require that the pre condition P is true and that the relational post condition holds for the pair of states σ, σ':[15]

$$\frac{\begin{array}{l} P(\sigma) \\ frame \lhd \sigma' = frame \lhd \sigma \\ Q(\sigma, \sigma') \end{array}}{(mk\text{-}Spec(frame, P, Q), \sigma) \stackrel{st}{\longrightarrow} \sigma'}$$

So, for example:

$$mk\text{-}Spec(\{y\}, \text{true}, x \leq y' \leq (x+2), \sigma_1) \stackrel{st}{\longrightarrow} \sigma_2$$

non-deterministically allows:

$$\sigma_1 = \{x \mapsto 1, y \mapsto 0\}$$
$$\sigma_2 \in \left\{ \begin{array}{l} \{x \mapsto 1, y \mapsto 1\} \\ \{x \mapsto 1, y \mapsto 2\} \\ \{x \mapsto 1, y \mapsto 3\} \end{array} \right\}$$

There is a danger with specifications that they ask for something infeasible such as finding the largest prime number; the immediately preceding specification can be made unrealisable by changing its frame:

$$\{\,\}\text{:}[\text{true}, x \leq y' \leq (x+2)]$$

which would only be achievable if the initial value of y already satisfied the post condition whereas the pre condition specifies that an implementation should work for any state.

7.3.4 Formal development

After Hoare's 1969 paper, it was realised that there was an even more important use for the axioms than reasoning about finished programs: the stepwise development of programs from their specifications could be formalised using the same rules of inference. Hoare published a stepwise development of his famous Quicksort algorithm [Hoa61] in [Hoa71b, FH71] and a variety of formal development approaches followed. These include the program development aspects of VDM from the early 1970s that were eventually published as a book [Jon80].

The reason that having a formal basis for design decisions is important in that their validity can be checked as they are made — long before all of the code is developed: under the assumption that subsequent steps will find valid implementations

---

[15] Detailed syntax and semantics for *LogExpr* are omitted here.

of the precisely specified sub-components, a proof that the higher-level component is correct can be constructed and reviewed. This topic moves away slightly from language description but is sufficiently important to warrant the diversion and anyway connects with the development of compilers from semantic descriptions of their source languages.

Specifications are then an abstraction of the code that can be developed from them. They record what any user of that code needs to know. (The reader might want to look back at the comments about specifications of factorial and sorting in Section 1.5.) As in the artificial example in Section 7.3.3, and in general, such specifications can be non-deterministic. They are frequently also "partial" in the sense that they record assumptions about the initial state. This is important because programs can rarely achieve their post conditions from arbitrary initial states. For states where the pre condition does not hold, the code is unconstrained. It is thus the responsibility of the programmer to ensure that the context of the specified code establishes the pre condition.

Carroll Morgan's *Refinement Calculus* works nicely with small examples and has the advantage (over the rules in Figure 7.3) that its post conditions are relations between initial and final states.[16]

A specification of multiplication might be written as a specification statement:[17]

$$\{r,i,j\}\colon [0 \leq i,\ r' = i*j]$$

meaning that any program that satisfies this specification is allowed to change the values of the variables r,i,j and must ensure that the final value of r (thus r') is the product of the initial values of i and j. It is essential that the specification uses the initial values of i,j because otherwise the post condition could be satisfied by:

$$r := 0;\ i := 0$$

So-called *wide-spectrum languages* allow specifications and code to be mixed so that it is possible to record a first mini-step of design as:

$$r := 0;\ \{r,i,j\}\colon [0 \leq i,\ r' = r + i*j]$$

Motivated by Hoare's rules, an inference system can be defined for judgements that one such mixed expression satisfies another:

$$S1 \ \textbf{satby} \ S2$$

An obvious substitution for the assignment shows that:

$$\{r,i,j\}\colon [0 \leq i,\ r' = i*j] \ \textbf{satby}$$
$$r := 0;\ \{r,i,j\}\colon [0 \leq i,\ r' = r + i*j]$$

---

[16] Technically the rule for while loops used below differs from Morgan's in its handling of termination; the reason for using the VDM termination argument is given below.

[17] To provide a compact example, it assumed that the language does not offer a multiplication operator. Here again, there is an echo of the role of programs as providing the route to extending the expressive power of a language.

The specification statement on the right can be developed (with no need to modify j) to:

$\{r,i\}: [0 \le i,\ r' = r + i * j]$ **satby**
    while $i \ne 0$ do $\{r,i\}: [0 < i,\ r' + i' * j' = r + i * j \wedge 0 \le i' < i]$ od

And the specification of the body of the loop:

$\{r,i\}: [0 < i,\ r' + i' * j' = r + i * j \wedge 0 \le i' < i]$ **satby**
    $r := r + j;\ i := i - 1$

This gives an algorithm that takes time linear in the initial value of j but it is possible to get a logarithmic performance by taking advantage of the ability to change j:

$\{r,i,j\}: [0 < i,\ r' + i' * j' = r + i * j \wedge 0 \le i' < i]$ **satby**
    $\{r,i,j\}: [0 < i,\ r' + i' * j' = r + i * j \wedge 0 \le i' \le i \wedge \neg\text{is-even}(i)];$
    $r := r + j;\ i := i - 1$

and use shifts to multiply/divide by two:

$\{r,i,j\}: [0 < i,\ r' + i' * j' = r + i * j \wedge 0 \le i' \le i]$ **satby**
    while $\text{is-even}(i)$ do $i := i/2;\ j := j * 2$ od

There is a crucial property of the **satby** ordering. The technical expression is that the constructs of the programming language are *monotonic* in this order. Simply put this says that if a program fragment C has been shown to satisfy a specification S — and C contains a component that is given by a specification s_{comp} — then a development of C where s_{comp} is replaced by anything that satisfies the specification s_{comp} will also satisfy S.

So, for example:

$[P, Q]$ **satby** while b do $[P_c, Q_c]$ od $\wedge$
    $[P_c, Q_c]$ **satby** $C \Rightarrow$
        $[P, Q]$ **satby** while b do C od

This justifies collecting the steps above to justify that the program:

$r := 0;$
while $i \ne 0$ do
    while $\text{is-even}(i)$ do
        $i := i/2;$
        $j := j * 2$
    od
    $r := r + j;$
    $i := i - 1$
od

satisfies the specification $\{r,i,j\}: [0 \le i,\ r' = i * j]$.

In the multiplication example above, the specification:

$\{r,i,j\}: [0 < i,\ r' + i' * j' = r + i * j \wedge 0 \le i' < i]$

is non-deterministic in that it does not say by how much the value of i should be reduced. This flexibility is used to develop both the linear algorithm in which the reduction is by one per execution of the loop body and the faster algorithm in which i is halved as long as its value remains even.

The rules for VDM differ from those for the refinement calculus only in the way that termination is proved. There is also a difference in concrete syntax because VDM specifications have tended to be used on applications where long pre and post conditions do not fit conveniently into a single-line specification statement. VDM specifications are usually displayed vertically with keywords marking the pre/post conditions (see [Jon90]):

Mult

ext wr r, i : $\mathbb{Z}$
   rd j : $\mathbb{Z}$
pre $0 \leq i$
post $r' = i * j$

The VDM rule for sequential composition can be written:

$$;\text{-}1 \quad \frac{\{pre\} \ S_1 \ \{interface \wedge rel_1\}}{\{interface\} \ S_2 \ \{rel_2\}}{\{pre_1\} \ S_1; S_2 \ \{rel_1; rel_2\}}$$

Where $rel_1; rel_2$ denotes composition of relations.

The decision to write *interface* (rather than pre_2) serves to emphasise that the decomposition should actively divorce the sub-components from each other. A small example of such *active decomposition* can be extracted from the *Mult* development. While it would not result in incorrect code, a specification of

$$\{r, i\} : [0 \leq i \wedge r = 0, \ r' = i * j]$$

fails to separate the sub-components as well as:

$$\{r, i\} : [0 \leq i, \ r' = r + i * j]$$

This point is echoed in Section 7.4 on a more interesting example.

The issue of termination is, as always, of interest (and more is said about it in Section 7.4). Morgan follows precedent in giving an argument about a reducing value; Dijkstra calls this a *variant function* that maps single states to a set like the integers. Given that VDM uses relational post conditions, it is more natural to establish termination by saying that the body of the loop should be specified by a well-founded relation (*rel*) and use the rule:[18]

$$while\text{-}1 \quad \frac{\{inv \wedge B\} \ S \ \{inv \wedge rel\}}{\{inv\} \ \text{while } B \text{ do } S \text{ od } \{inv \wedge \neg B \wedge rel^*\}}$$

A summary of a VDM development of *Mult* can be written out as in Figure 7.4.

---

[18] The relation rel^* is the reflexive closure of *rel*.

```
pre 0 ≤ i
  r := 0;
  pre 0 ≤ i
    while i ≠ 0 do
    inv 0 ≤ i
    rel r' + i' * j = r + i * j ∧ i' < i
      while is-even(i) do
      inv 0 ≤ i
      rel r' + i' * j = r + i * j ∧ i' < i
        i := i/2;
        j := j * 2
      od;
      r := r + j;
      i := i - 1
    od
    post r' + i' * j = r + i * j ∧ i' = 0
  post r' = i * j
```

Fig. 7.4 Annotated version of the multiplication program.

Developments of larger applications show more clearly the importance of employing non-deterministic specifications. For example, the development of a system that needs a free-storage manager might rely on only outline properties such as never being allocated the same address twice. These properties can be recorded and the main application developed on the assumption that an appropriate free-storage manager will be developed. This effectively delays (or separates the task of) making design choices about the specific organisation of free chains etc.

7.3.5 Data abstraction and reification

The material on axiomatic descriptions of constructs of imperative programming languages fits most naturally into the material in the current book. But experience has shown [Jon80, Jon90] that the topic of *data reification*[19] is actually more important in specifying and formally developing programs. There is also a link with language description that is explained at the end of this section.

An important part of designing any program is choosing data structures that make algorithms efficient. The details of, for example, doubly linked lists have however no place in a specification; they are neither the first issues to be clarified as to what a program should do nor are they of concern to a user of the program who only wants to understand its functionality. It is therefore wise to describe a program in terms of abstract data objects that fit the concepts being specified and to defer the design of data structures that admit efficient algorithms.

---

[19] Most authors use the term *data refinement*.

Two examples are:

- The *Sieve of Eratosthenes* is an algorithm for finding all prime numbers up to some given n by sieving out all of the composite numbers. A program that implements the algorithm will almost certainly use a vector of bits where the ith bit being 1 indicates –in the final state– that i is a prime number. But this is one possible representation and introduces messy implementation details that have no place in a specification. A much more perspicuous specification can be written in terms of sets of numbers. Furthermore, the example lends itself to implementations using concurrency (see Section 8.4) and important early steps of the development can be made and verified with the more abstract data representation.
- An application sometimes referred to as *union/find* provides a way of recording equivalence relations. The specification is clearly and briefly described in [Jon90, Chap. 11] in terms of a partition of some arbitrary set X. There is an algorithm due to Michael Fisher and Bernie Galler that uses an ingenious tree representation of equivalence classes. The taste and efficiency of the representation does not justify its incursion into the specification.

The process of choosing appropriate representations (or "reifications") of abstractions has similar monotonic properties to the rules related to **satby** and thus fits into a natural formal development process. Despite its importance, even programming languages that allow assertions do not support documentation of data abstractions. The closest approximation is the use of libraries as in Java's *Standard Template Library* but this is only for a fixed repertoire of abstractions.

The links to semantic language description are both general and specific. Generally, the message of using –for example in state descriptions– objects that are as abstract as possible has been emphasised in earlier chapters. Specifically, the choice of an abstract syntax is a clear attempt to avoid clouding a semantic description with the representation details necessary to support parsing. In the Vienna Lab compiler work, [Wei75] describes the connection between abstract and concrete syntax and its role in compiler development; [Jon76] describes how the relationship between the abstract state of the semantic types and the actual run-time state informs the compiler development.

7.4 Further material

The literature on program verification and/or formal development is extensive. One attempt to trace the evolution of the field is [Jon03]; an early assessment of Hoare's axiomatic approach is given in [Apt81], which has been considerably expanded to [AO19] (which was conveniently published 50 years after [Hoa69]). In view of these sources, only a few key steps are noted here together with additional references to those mentioned in Section 7.3:

- John von Neumann's decision to use a form of *assertion box* in what became [GvN47] has been pinpointed by Mark Priestley [Pri18] to a letter from

von Neumann to Herman Goldstine dated March 1947. It must be said that the
description in [GvN47] is far from clear.
- Alan Turing's "Checking a large routine" [Tur49] does have a clear programme
  of annotating a flowchart with assertions. This is a remarkable paper: in just three
  pages Turing gives an inspired motivation for assertions, a proof of a doubly
  nested program and an argument for its termination.

Sadly, neither of these papers had any significant effect on verification research: [GvN47] introduced the idea which became known as the *von Neumann
(computer) architecture* and was studied mainly by people who were designing
early digital computers; [Tur49][20] was not known to Floyd or Hoare until after their
key papers were published. As noted in [Jon03], van Wijngaarden was at the 1949
conference where Turing gave his talk but he failed (or refused) to link it to his
own [vW66a].

- Bob Floyd's paper [Flo67] (discussed above) certainly set the stage for many
  subsequent steps on program verification.[21] As published, it used a complicated
  "forward assignment rule" that requires an existential quantifier. The paper does
  include termination proofs of the two algorithms considered and gives properties that are required of sensible proof rules for programming constructs. (Dijkstra [Dij76] would later formalise such rules as *healthiness conditions* for his
  predicate transformers.)
- Jim King's Ph.D. [Kin69] was supervised at CMU by Floyd — King built the
  Effigy system [Kin71] that both attempted to check Floyd-style annotations to
  (PL/I) programs and deploy *symbolic execution* as an additional tool.[22]
- As well as acknowledging the influence of Floyd's paper, Hoare's [Hoa69] cites
  Aad van Wijngaarden's [vW66a], which tackles axioms for finite computer arithmetic, and Peter Naur's [Nau66], which uses *general snapshots* to record assertions but expressed more as comments than in a formal logical notation.
- Hoare (possibly prompted by Floyd's form of annotating assertions), Dijkstra and
  others used post conditions that were predicates of a single state. From early publications, VDM used relational post conditions. The consequent inference rules
  are bound to be somewhat more complicated but unfortunately those in [Jon80]
  were (to use Peter Aczel's understatement) "unmemorable". Aczel showed in an
  unpublished note [Acz82] that rules for post conditions of two states (a) were better and (b) could be presented clearly. These rules were then employed in [Jon86]
  and subsequent publications on VDM. Other specification languages such as
  Z [Hay87], B [Abr96] and Event-B [Abr10] also use relational post conditions.

---

[20] Not only are these proceedings somewhat inaccessible, Turing's short paper was printed with
many typographical errors that impaired understanding — it was "exhumed" and republished
in [MJ84].

[21] Floyd's paper was first available as a mimeographed copy in 1966 and can be seen at:
http://homepages.cs.ncl.ac.uk/cliff.jones/publications/MSs/Floyd67.pdf

[22] King moved to IBM Research and the current author used *Effigy* and showed (around 1976)
that it could be used to formally develop programs by using Prove/Assume commands to record
specifications of undeveloped sub-components.

- The *SIEVE* example mentioned above in connection with data reification provides a more compelling example of the desirability of "active decomposition". The post condition of the whole program specifies that the final state should contain only primes (up to some given n). A natural decomposition in the development of the Eratosthenes program is to have an initialisation phase that puts all natural numbers from $2..n$ into the state and a second phase that removes composites. Following a *weakest pre condition* method computes the pre condition of the sieving phase to be exactly the post condition of initialisation. But the sieving process functions perfectly well on any initial state: it will remove composites if there are any. It is for this reason that the ;-I rule of VDM shown above emphasises finding an interface predicate (*interface*) that the designer can use to separate the sub-components properly.

- Although static proofs about programs provide much more assurance than testing, even without such proofs, run-time evaluation of assertions provides a way of detecting errors much closer to their source than trying to trace back from a program crash resulting from corrupt data. This idea was proposed in Ed Satterthwaite's thesis [Sat75], is used in Eiffel [Mey88] and GCC[23] and is employed informally by many industrial groups.

- The topic of termination arguments has an interesting history. Turing and Floyd both used formal arguments about reducing quantities; Dijkstra [Dij76] confined himself to predicates of a single state so formalised the idea of reducing quantities with rules about *variant functions*; VDM uses the fact that termination follows directly if the relation for the loop is well founded.

- In addition to the problem of proving that loops do not run forever, there is a danger that they abort in some way such as division by zero or computer representations of numbers overflowing. (This was why van Wijngaarden looked at the axiomatisation of finite computer arithmetic in [vW66a].) Dick Sites in his beautiful thesis [Sit74] describes needing to prove *clean termination* — the same problem is tackled in [CH79].

- Since King's early *Effigy* system referred to above, huge strides have been made in providing software that supports the task of creating (machine-checked) proofs. General theorem provers include HOL-light [Har09], Isabelle [NPW02]. and Coq.[24] ACL-2 (the most recent development of the Texas work that began with [BM81]), KIV[25] and Dafny[26] are examples of tools more closely geared to software development.

Returning to the history of the ideas on axiomatic semantics, there is an interesting connection with the famous (1964) Baden bei Wien Working Conference. Hoare did not present a paper but expressed strongly the idea that a language description should be able to leave some things undefined (more in the tone of the current book, one might say "under-defined"). Hoare went on to produce at least two significant

---

[23] https://en.wikipedia.org/wiki/GNU_Compiler_Collection

[24] https://coq.inria.fr

[25] https://www.uni-augsburg.de/en/fakultaet/fai/isse/software/kiv/

[26] https://en.wikipedia.org/wiki/Dafny

drafts of an approach that attempted to be more axiomatic than say McCarthy's operational semantics. Floyd's paper was sent to Hoare by Peter Lucas because the Vienna group had been studying it; Hoare saw that Floyd's assertions provided a key idea that resolved issues with his earlier attempts and quickly wrote the definitive [Hoa69]. Hoare has reflected on this experience in [HJ89] and talked about how he might have done things differently in an ACM recorded interview.[27]

Hoare and colleagues went on to tackle various other programming constructs including [Hoa71a, CH72] but the attempt to provide an axiomatisation of Pascal [HW73] is incomplete. The only full language description in the axiomatic style appears to be the Turing language [HMRC87]. A more promising avenue that is pursued in SPARK-Ada [Bar06] and "featherweight Java" [IPW01] is to identify subsets of complicated languages that can be axiomatised.

7.5 Roles for semantic approaches

Given the range of semantic approaches, it is worth indicating where this author considers their respective contributions are most likely to be effective.

Authors of early operational semantic descriptions tended to put too many things into a monolithic "grand" state. This had the effect of making it hard to establish properties of such definitions. Plotkin's "Structural Operational Semantics" essentially resolved this issue and, for example, the split between environments and states made in denotational descriptions can be mirrored in operational descriptions. The consistent argument throughout this book is that SOS descriptions provide a very productive tool for both language understanding and design. With little need for sophisticated mathematical concepts, features of modern programming languages can be written and read. The argument is often made that compiler designers should base their developments on denotational descriptions but this author would also use an operational description as a basis for compiler design.

An unassailable point is that programming languages have a sequential aspect that can be difficult to express in approaches that might look more mathematically elegant. Model-oriented approaches use an explicit notion of the state of a computation; this affords a way of coping with the fact that so-called variables change their values during a computation. Operational descriptions make this explicit; denotational descriptions do have a neat mathematical model of composing functions from states to states. But concurrent threads updating a shared state (as discussed in Chapter 8) are much harder to cope with denotationally precisely because this sort of interference is inherently operational. A further challenge comes with exceptional ordering (as discussed in Chapter 10).

The above praise of operational semantics is in no way intended to deny the advantages of denotational semantics for looking at deeper properties of programming languages. One important example is the way that denotational semantics provides

---

[27] https://www.acm.org/turing-award-50/turing-laureate-interviews

an understanding of termination: partial functions (from states to states) neatly capture what it means for a while loop to fail to terminate on some inputs. The fact that an operational semantic description will itself yield no result for a non-terminating program is one manifestation of the fact that proofs based on operational descriptions tend to be inductions over the computation.

It is also worth noting that there are other spaces of mathematically tractable denotations than functions over states: several authors have used Robin Milner's π-calculus [SW01] as a target for mapping concurrent object-oriented languages; and "game semantics" has been used for example in [A+97].

Moving on to property-oriented descriptions, that considered in Section 7.3 is axiomatic semantics. Although it is possible to base proofs about programs in some language $\mathcal{L}$, something like Hoare's axioms –or a variant such as the refinement calculus– provide by far the most natural way to verify or develop programs. It is noted above that there are few languages that have a complete axiomatic semantics but a practical way forward is to identify subsets of larger languages about which an axiomatic style of reasoning is practical. Furthermore, designers of languages are well advised to understand where their design decisions make it difficult to provide proof obligations because such features are likely to present challenges even for informal understanding of programs in the putative language.

An example of an issue that might be motivated by considering the axiom of assignment given in Figure 7.3 is that this axiom is not valid for languages that permit parameter passing by location (see Section 5.4) because an assignment to the left-hand-side value of one identifier can affect the right-hand values of other identifiers. This might prompt a language designer to consider incorporating parameter passing by value/return. This latter mode does not however offer avoidance of copying data during procedure or function calls.

Similar comments can be made about "algebraic semantics" [Koz97, HvS12, HCM+16, DHMS12]: such properties –or their absence– can inform language designs. Investigating algebraic properties of concurrency has proved both challenging and revealing.

Tony Hoare and colleagues have looked at "unifying theories" in [HH98] — a useful introduction to the "UTP" approach is [WC04]. In particular, UTP can be used to provide insights into the relationships between semantic approaches.

Chapter 8
Shared-variable concurrency

This chapter moves beyond issues present in sequential languages typified by AL-GOL descendants. The topic of concurrency is important and challenging in many ways.

There are several reasons why programs need to exploit parallelism.

- applications such as those that support many simultaneous users are inherently parallel;
- using fast processor cycles when some threads of execution are held up waiting for slower external devices;
- as circuits approach atomic limits, hardware speed increase and miniaturisation are unlikely to continue to follow Moore's law and provide the speedup on which society has relied for decades — fortunately, it is now practical to put many cores on a wafer — but this potential parallelism has to be exploitable via software.

8.1 Interference

In some cases, programs can achieve rapid execution using parallel threads with disjoint data.[1] However, as soon as there is a need for threads to access and change shared data, the resulting concurrent threads become extremely difficult to design:

- The number of paths through a sequential program is exponential with respect to the number of branch points; with concurrency, the number of effective paths explodes because of interference from state changes made by concurrent threads.
- It is notoriously difficult to debug concurrent programs since executions starting in identical states can progress differently because of interference from concurrent processes.
- One particularly unpleasant consequence of the preceding point is that a programmer who is trying to locate the source of erroneous behaviour can add trac-

---

[1] Often referred to as "Single Instruction Multiple Data" (SIMD) parallelism.

© Springer Nature Switzerland AG 2020
C. B. Jones, *Understanding Programming Languages*,
https://doi.org/10.1007/978-3-030-59257-8_8

ing statements that change the timing behaviour in a way that hides the error (this gives rise to the term "Heisenbugs").

Language issue 39: Concurrency

There are actually many issues in concurrency: they include interference and its control for mutual exclusion, synchronisation, the transfer of information and deadlock detection/avoidance.

Typically, hardware provides low-level concurrency primitives (e.g. a "compare and swap" instruction) for synchronisation. Programming language designers have devised a range of ideas in an attempt to make the design and justification of concurrent programs somewhat tractable. Dijkstra's semaphore idea (using p/v) is one of the earliest.[2] More structured language extensions followed including:

- Conditional critical sections [Hoa72]
- Monitors [BH73, Hoa74a]
- software transactional memory
- designers of *process algebras* [Hoa85, Mil89, Bae90] attempted to eschew the notion of shared state but communication-based concurrency does not, in fact, slay the dragon of interference.[3]

Modelling such constructs is an interesting challenge which is addressed in this chapter. The specific target in Chapter 9 is to show how to use object-oriented ideas as a way of structuring concurrency but the modelling ideas are generic over most concurrency constructs.

Describing concurrent programming languages poses some of the same challenges as face the programmer using such languages: the interaction between threads makes it difficult to describe aspects of a language in a structured way. The good news is that there is no need to extend the meta-language developed in earlier chapters. The challenge is to express interference in a reasonably structured way.

Challenge VII: Modelling concurrency

How can shared-variable concurrency –and the inherent interference that manifests itself by state changes that give rise to massive non-determinacy– be described using SOS?

Section 8.2 explains the essential development of the operational semantic descriptions that is required to model concurrent shared-variable threads; a small (and clearly artificial) language is used to explain the core idea with a minimum of distractions. Section 8.3 extends the discussion on granularity; Sections 8.4 and 8.5 pick up the topic of reasoning about programs written in the object languages.

The topic of object-oriented languages (initiated in Section 6.2) is resumed in Chapter 9 because such languages can provide an extremely useful way of controlling concurrency and thus provide tractable languages for programmers.

---

[2] It is interesting that Gary Peterson [Pet81] found a way of programming the p and v operations without hardware support.

[3] The focus in this book is on shared-variable concurrency — some discussion of process algebras is in Section 8.6.

8.2 Small-step semantics

The first issue to get clear is the way in which (shared-variable) concurrency gives rise to non-determinacy. With two threads (S_1, S_2), (S_3, S_4) running in parallel,

$$(S_1; S_2) \parallel (S_3, S_4)$$

there are six possible orders in which the statements can be executed even if statements are considered to execute atomically[4] — the set of sequences is:

$$\left\{ \begin{array}{l} [S_1; S_2; S_3; S_4] \\ [S_1; S_3; S_2; S_4] \\ [S_1; S_3; S_4; S_2] \\ [S_3; S_4; S_1; S_2] \\ [S_3; S_1; S_4; S_2] \\ [S_3; S_1; S_2; S_4] \end{array} \right\}$$

To see how this affects the results, consider the following instances of the S_i:

$$(x := 1; \ x := x + 3) \parallel (x := 2; x := x * 2)$$

Again, for the moment, assuming that assignment statements execute atomically, the final value of x is in the set $\{4, 5, 7, 8, 10\}$. It is the task of the language description to say that all of these outcomes are allowed — and to make clear that no others are considered to be correct.

The point is made in Section 3.2 that SOS rules provide a natural way of describing non-determinacy and they are therefore ideal for concurrency. What has to be recognised, in an operational framework, is that there needs to be a way to record the statements that are still to be executed in each thread. In previous chapters, the SOS rules are written so that they discard executed statements. The most obvious case is the left-to-right evaluation of a list of statements, where the head of the list is executed and the rest of the computation is only affected by the tail of the list.

With concurrent threads, there is essentially a tree of putative next steps. In the early Vienna Lab (VDL) operational descriptions, this control tree was completely explicit as a state component. An advantage of SOS is that the selection of next steps is implicit in the selection of SOS rules. The same choices as were explicit in the VDL control tree have to be indicated but SOS succeeds in factoring the non-determinacy out of the state and into rule selection.

The key response to the challenge of describing concurrency is to define the semantic relation over *configurations* that pair the remaining text to be executed with the state.

To illustrate this, a part of an artificial programming language with two parallel threads is considered: threads contain only assignment statements (issues such as blocks and procedures are postponed):

Par :: *thrd1* : *Assign**
        thrd2 : *Assign**

---

[4] This unrealistic assumption is reconsidered in Section 8.3.

and the state is as in the simplest languages:

$$\Sigma = Id \xrightarrow{m} ScalarValue$$

Configurations are $Par \times \Sigma$ and the semantic relation becomes:

$$\xrightarrow{par} : \mathscr{P}((Par \times \Sigma) \times (Par \times \Sigma))$$

The rule that expresses what happens when a statement from thread $thrd1$ is executed uses $\xrightarrow{st}$ to reflect the state change of a single assignment statement and $\xrightarrow{par}$ shows the executed statement $s1$ being dropped from the configuration leaving the remaining list of statements ($rl1$) in the resulting configuration:

$$\frac{(s1,\sigma) \xrightarrow{st} \sigma'}{(mk\text{-}Par([s1] \frown rl1, sl2), \sigma) \xrightarrow{par} (mk\text{-}Par(rl1, sl2), \sigma')}$$

The obvious symmetrical rule for $thrd2$ is:

$$\frac{(s2,\sigma) \xrightarrow{st} \sigma'}{(mk\text{-}Par(sl1, [s2] \frown rl2), \sigma) \xrightarrow{par} (mk\text{-}Par(sl1, rl2), \sigma')}$$

If Par is added as an option to the types of $Stmt$:

$$Stmt = \cdots \mid Par$$

the effect of a whole Par as a statement requires executing all statements in both threads; this uses the notion of the *transitive closure* of a relation:

$$\frac{config \xrightarrow{par\ *} config' \qquad config' \xrightarrow{par} config''}{config \xrightarrow{par\ *} config''} \qquad \qquad \overline{config \xrightarrow{par\ *} config}$$

With this $\xrightarrow{par}$ can be linked back to $\xrightarrow{st}$ as follows:

$$\frac{(mk\text{-}par(thrd1, thrd2), \sigma) \xrightarrow{par\ *} (mk\text{-}Par([], []), \sigma')}{(mk\text{-}Par(thrd1, thrd2), \sigma) \xrightarrow{st} \sigma'}$$

To summarise:

- non-determinism is modelled by defining a relation because there can be more than one potential outcome of a program;
- small-step semantics have to use configurations that combine the program text that remains to be executed with the state of the variables;
- SOS rules provide a natural way of defining such a relation over configurations.

8.3 Granularity

It is straightforward to increase the size of language components that are executed atomically — that is, to have coarser granularity of merging concurrent threads. This is achieved by making large steps in the SOS rules. An extreme position is to prohibit any sharing of variables between parallel threads.[5] This certainly makes it easy to reason independently about the threads but the constraint is too extreme for many applications. There is a spectrum ranging from low-level system code that often results from intimate access to shared variables through to applications that revolve around large shared databases. Although the detailed language resolutions differ, the general need for ways to control access from separate threads to shared variables is something that must be modelled.

The serious challenge for semantic description is to move in the direction of finer granularity.

Language issue 40: Granularity

Fixing the granularity of interference in a shared-variable concurrent language is an important design issue. The ways in which the programmer can determine granularity must make it easy to understand programs. But it must also be possible to implement the language efficiently on realistic hardware.

The comment is made in Section 8.2 that the assumption that assignment statements can be executed atomically is unrealistic. This is because a compiler will typically expand a statement such as $x := x * 2$ into steps that place the (right-hand) value of the variable x into a register, then perform the multiplication before writing the computed result back into the location (left-hand value) for x. If another thread accesses and changes x between these steps, that update can be overwritten.[6] Thus the example threads at the beginning of Section 8.2 could –under the realistic assumption that only variable read and write are atomic– also give rise to the additional outcome that execution of the two threads would result in a final outcome with $x' = 2$. To see how this can come about, the following sequence of steps makes explicit the use of a temporary variable t — the two threads might interleave their steps as follows:

$$x := 2; x := 1; t := x; x := x + 3; x := t * 2$$

This is by no means an arcane detail: leaving aside for the moment that many crucial low-level programs have to be written in terms of such sequences of accesses, it is difficult to avoid similar problems at the level of transferring money between back accounts. This is a clear case against a language with such ill-constrained interference.

Although such low-level interference is undesirable, it is worth sketching how it can be modelled. The key to modelling finer-level thread merging is to modify configurations at the appropriate level. Thus a single SOS rule might be needed to show accessing one scalar value and replacing the identifier with the accessed value.

---

[5] Such a standpoint is adopted by many process algebras –see Section 8.6– as explained there, unfortunately this does not get around the problem of interference.

[6] One proposal to avoid this problem is known as "Reynolds' rule" (although John Reynolds told the current author that he had nothing to do with it!), which requires that only one shared variable occurs in any assignment. Unfortunately this fix does not resolve the real problem.

8.4 Rely/Guarantee reasoning [*]

This optional section picks up –from Section 7.3– the theme of providing ways of formally reasoning about –or formally developing– programs in an object language. Here, of course, the interest is in how to provide inference rules that support the introduction of concurrent threads whereas Chapter 7 addressed the story for sequential programming languages.

The rule for decomposing a specified task into two components that are to be executed sequentially shows that the second statement is initiated in the state that results from executing the first.[7] In contrast, parallel threads are initiated in identical states. Assuming that the two threads are specified as:

$$\{P_1\} \ S_1 \ \{Q_1\}$$
$$\{P_2\} \ S_2 \ \{Q_2\}$$

then, under rather strong assumptions, it would be true that their specifications can be combined as follows:

$$\{P_1 \wedge P_2\} \ S_1 \ || \ S_2 \ \{Q_1 \wedge Q_2\}$$

The key assumption is that there is no interference between the threads. This is a useful observation (and looks forward to the ideas in Section 8.5). Unfortunately, many interesting uses of concurrency have to cope with interference and the SOS rules covered in the earlier parts of this chapter are aimed at exactly characterising such interference.

This leaves the challenge of how a proof-oriented approach can deal with interference. This section outlines one approach that tackles interference head on and Section 8.5 outlines a line of attack that is predicated on avoiding interference.

The Rely/Guarantee (R/G) approach extends specification by pre/post conditions both to face interference and to provide ways of reasoning about it in program development. The fact that few programs can achieve their post relation in arbitrary starting states is recognised by recording pre conditions as part of a specification. Almost no useful post condition could be achieved by a program that experienced unconstrained interference on its variables so an R/G specification uses a *rely condition* that describes the interference that executions of the program must tolerate. Rely conditions are relations over two states; this fits naturally with VDM's relational post conditions and admits the view of a rely condition as the post condition of a potential interference step.

As emphasised by the colouring in Figure 8.1, both the pre and rely conditions are assumptions that the designer can make; ensuring that they are satisfied is a requirement on the context; in other words, the decomposition that introduces the specified components must show that the conditions pertain.

To this end, it is also necessary to document –for each component– its *guarantee condition* that expresses the maximum interference that it can inflict on sibling

---

[7] This holds in either the original Hoare rules as in Figure 7.3 or the VDM style that uses relational post conditions (see Section 7.4).

processes. Like post conditions, guarantee conditions are obligations on the running code.

Figure 8.1 indicates how the various predicates apply to the execution of the ongoing process and any other processes that can interfere with its variables. The contention is that rely and guarantee conditions offer a useful abstraction of interference. This claim is supported by evidence from a corpus of examples.

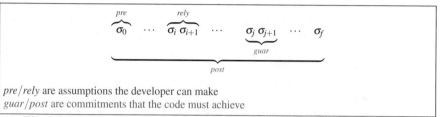

pre/rely are assumptions the developer can make
guar/post are commitments that the code must achieve

Fig. 8.1 A trace of states made by execution of a component and its context

An outline of one example of the use of R/G in development can be based on the "Sieve of Eratosthenes" mentioned in Section 7.4. The specification of the interesting part of the algorithm is to remove all composite numbers from a set. The following informal notes indicate how R/G rules are used (see [HJ18]) to formalise the development:

- A sequential program could execute $Rem(i)$ for values of i from 2 (to the square root of the maximum value in the set) whose role is to remove multiples of i. This was the core of Eratosthenes' inspired algorithm.
- For such a sequential implementation, the post condition of $Rem(i)$ could require that exactly the products (2 and above) of i should be removed from the set.
- If however the $Rem(i)$ procedures can execute concurrently, this exact equality cannot hold because interfering processes are also removing elements from the set.
- The post condition of $Rem(i)$ can be weakened to say that each instance is required to ensure that no multiples of i are present at termination of that instance. This is a lower bound on how $Rem(i)$ can affect the set.
- But the weakened post condition is not achievable with arbitrary interference on the set: $Rem(i)$ needs a rely condition that the set can only get smaller so the program can remove say $j * i$ and rely on the fact that it will not be re-inserted.
- Unfortunately, the weakening of the post condition would admit an implementation that removed elements (e.g. primes) that ought not to be removed — a guarantee condition on $Rem(i)$ can insist that it only removes multiples of i. This is the upper bound on its changes to the set.
- Finally, since the Rem processes must co-exist, each must guarantee to never put elements into the set.

The above conditions fit into the generic picture in Figure 8.1 and the appropriate proof rule can be used to justify this step of development. The pre, rely, guarantee and post conditions can be written as a quintuple wrapped around the program text that is to be executed: $\{P,R\}\, S\, \{G,Q\}$.[8] To indicate how the rely/guarantee rules relate to the non-interfering version of the parallel rule as at the beginning of this section, a slight simplification of the actual rule is:[9]

$$\boxed{\parallel \text{-}RG} \ \frac{\{P,R \vee G_2\}\, S_1\, \{G_1,Q_1\} \qquad \{P,R \vee G_1\}\, S_2\, \{G_2,Q_2\}}{\{P,R\}\, S_1 \parallel S_2\, \{G_1 \vee G_2, Q_1 \wedge Q_2 \wedge \cdots\}}$$

This rule shows that the pre and post conditions of the two parallel components can be combined providing the rely and guarantee conditions of the components agree.

The development of the parallel sieve in [HJ18] makes a subsequent data reification of the set into arrays of bits.

The "Sieve" example involves a collection of threads that (apart from their parameter) have identical specifications. Applications where the processes differ such as senders and receivers in "Asynchronous Communication Mechanisms" are more interesting (see [JH16]) and can be handled with the same proof rules.

R/G specifications can be written as five-tuples (pre, rely, program, guarantee, post) and proof rules given for justifying the introduction of concurrent processes (such a rule is given in [Jon00]).

Recent research has embraced the idea of specification statements and records rely and guarantee conditions as clauses to be wrapped around any specification. This way of presenting R/G thinking makes it possible to emphasise algebraic properties such as the distribution of rely conditions over decomposition [JHC15, HCM$^+$16].

Ian Hayes presented a tutorial in Chengdu (China) during 2018 and the proceedings [HJ18] include two worked examples (the tutorial itself additionally covered the Treiber stack). Further examples in the literature include: parallel "cleanup" operations for the *Fisher/Galler* algorithm [CJ00]; Simpson's "four-slot" implementation of *Asynchronous Communication Mechanisms* (ACMs) [JP11, JH16]; concurrent garbage collection [JVY17]; and Mergesort [JY15].

The origins of the R/G approach (in particular its relationship to the Owicki-Gries approach [Owi75, OG76]) are explored in [dRdBH$^+$01]. Examples of R/G developments clearly indicate a top-down design approach; finding a compositional approach to developing concurrent programs was a major objective of the research (again see [dRdBH$^+$01]).

8.5 Concurrent Separation Logic [*]

The key reference for Concurrent Separation Logic (CSL) is [O'H07]. In that paper Peter O'Hearn emphasises that CSL supports reasoning about (data) "race free-

---

[8] This quintuple version of rely-guarantee obviously follows Hoare triples (see Section 7.3.2).

[9] The simplification is that a stronger post condition can use information from the guarantee conditions.

dom" and contrasts this with the rely/guarantee approach, which tackles "racy programs". It is useful to again look at the idealised rule at the beginning of Section 8.4:
what this indicates is that a parallel combination can combine the pre and post
conditions of its sub-components providing there is no interference. Tony Hoare
in [Hoa72] could establish non-interference by looking at the alphabets of the two
parallel processes because only normal (i.e. stack) variables were being considered.
John Reynolds' "Separation Logic" [Rey02] tackles reasoning about heap variables
(i.e. dynamically allocated variables). This was in itself a bold and important step.
Concurrency adds to this the challenge that the ownership of dynamic addresses can
be exchanged between concurrent threads. The success of CSL is that it makes it
possible to reason about programs that achieve disjointness –and thus avoid data
races– even in the presence of such ownership exchanges.

The key CSL rule for reasoning about concurrent threads is:

$$\boxed{\parallel\text{-}SL}\frac{\{P1\}\ S1\ \{Q1\}}{\{P1*P2\}\ S1\parallel S2\ \{Q1*Q2\}}$$

This differs from the ideal rule at the head of Section 8.4 only in that logical conjunction has been replaced by "separating conjunction" (written as "*"). This operator requires that the addresses in the two operands do not overlap. It is important
to remember that both Reynolds' original Separation Logic and CSL address heap
variables.[10]

CSL owes its origins to detailed analysis of intricate pieces of code and tends to
be used in a bottom-up analysis of such programs rather than in top-down design.
That having been said and despite their different attitudes to data races, there are
many connections between CSL and R/G methods:

- RGSep [VP07, Vaf07] and SAGL [FFS07] offer explicit combinations of the
  approaches;
- Local R/G [Fen09] brings local reasoning and information hiding to concurrency
  verification;
- Deny/Guarantee [DFPV09] tackles fork/join concurrency, which is not obviously
  handled by the original phrase-structured R/G rules;
- research on "Views" [DYBG$^+$13] provides a common framework for justifying
  proof obligations.

A different sort of connection is exhibited in [JY15], where it is shown that separation can be viewed as yet another abstraction and a (top-down) development requirement is to show that the separation is preserved when mapping onto heap store
is undertaken.

---

[10] Another claim for separation logic is the use of a "frame rule" that provides a formal way of
promoting an assertion on one state to apply to a larger state. The claims for the uniqueness of this
rule tend to ignore that other methods have ways of defining frames. It is however true that VDM
and the refinement calculus handle stack –rather than heap– variables.

8.6 Further material

Projects

The technique of small-step SOS is exploited in the next chapter and any number of projects can be attempted there. The reader might like at this point to experiment with changing the semantics of the non-deterministic for loop from Section 3.2.3 so that all instances are executed concurrently.

Further reading

There are many interesting and useful books on the general topic of concurrency including [Sch97, MK99, BA06].

Even for operational semantics, there are further issues around concurrency that are left aside here. One that deserves at least a mention is *fairness* — consider:

$x := 0 \parallel$ while $x \neq 0$ do $i := 1 + 1$ od

There is clearly no *a priori* limit on the value of i but the question of whether the right-hand loop terminates depends on whether the scheduler is fair in the sense that it ensures the left-hand assignment does eventually execute. The standard reference on fairness is [Fra86]; Ian Hayes and Larissa Meinicke have also explored [HM18] the notion of "justness".

Because of its essentially operational nature, concurrency poses strong challenges for denotational semantics: Plotkin [Plo76] showed how to use power domains to handle concurrency; *resumptions* are described in [BA90]; other approaches include *game semantics* [Abr13].

A more radical approach to concurrency is to attempt to move away entirely from shared variables. Tony Hoare [Hoa78, Hoa85] and Robin Milner [Mil78a, Mil80] each developed *process algebras* in which communication was the main focus. Hoare's CSP is given a semantics in [BHR84] in terms of traces and refusals.

It is, however, worth emphasising that process algebras do not avoid the problem of *interference* as can be seen by the ease with which analogues of shared variables can be programmed in these notations. The question can then be asked whether traces and refusals offer a more convenient way of reasoning about interference than, say, R/G.

Further afield, many researchers prefer to reason about concurrent programs using *Temporal Logics*. Classic texts in this area include [MP95, Mos85] and a recent book is [Fis11]. An interesting combination of interval temporal logic and R/G is [STER11].

So-called *true concurrency* (as opposed to an interleaving model) has been studied via Petri nets — see [Rei12, Rei13].

The handling of concurrency in database management systems (DBMS) is interestingly different from the way that most HLLs embody the concept. Programming languages like Java put the onus on the programmer to acquire and release locks in a way that avoids data races. A database is a huge shared variable and a DBMS can run many concurrent transactions but here the detection of –and recovery from– clashing updates is handled entirely by the DBMS. So, although a project in Section 4.4 points out that it is not difficult to add relations as a value type, concurrency would be harder to model (see [BHG87, L$^+$94, WV01] and [HW90]).

Chapter 9
Concurrent OOLs

Although it is essential that specification methods are capable of describing languages –such as that outlined in Section 8.2– that permit unconstrained access to shared variables, it is more advantageous to use the description techniques to understand –and potentially design– languages that embody tractable concurrency.

The core ideas of object-oriented programming languages (OOLs) were first materialised in Simula [DMN68]; the concept proved to be extremely fruitful, offering advantages over say ALGOL.

- As its name suggests, "Simula" is a language for writing simulation programs. The ability to create arbitrary numbers of instances of classes made it easy to have one internal object per physical entity in a simulation.
- Objects provide a way of encapsulating "abstract data types", whose internal representation can be changed without affecting programs that use the prescribed interface.
- Because instance variables are local to objects, it is possible to limit data visibility between concurrent threads and thus control data races.
- Ideas around object-oriented databases followed from OOLs.

Objects can be seen as the culmination of earlier lines of evolution in programming languages. Objects themselves can be seen as multiply instantiated blocks; methods correspond to functions and procedures — albeit with non-ALGOL-like visibility rules; data races on instance variables within objects can be controlled; and the control of interference is governed by the programmer via the sharing of object references.

To expand on this last point, a class can be defined whose instances behave like shared variables; the instance variable of the class contains the current value; methods for say *read* and *write* can be defined. Although (for each instance of the class) only those methods can access that instance variable, any object that has a (shared) reference to the class would face essentially the same interference issues as are considered in Chapter 8. The control or reference sharing provides, however, a useful intuitive approach.

© Springer Nature Switzerland AG 2020
C. B. Jones, *Understanding Programming Languages*,
https://doi.org/10.1007/978-3-030-59257-8_9

Not only is it true that no new meta-language is required to describe concurrent OOLs, there are even no new language challenges. Preceding chapters have, for example, shown both how to introduce surrogates to model sharing and how concurrency is handled by choosing apposite "configurations". Challenges II–VII have provided the equipment to tackle the non-trivial combination of language features that are brought together in COOL.

Tackling concurrent OOLs in Sections 9.1–9.5 also affords the possibility to emphasise just how much the semantic objects can tell a skilled reader about a language. Returning to the message about the use of semantic descriptions in the design of languages, this of course argues for starting language design precisely with such semantic objects.

9.1 Objects for concurrency

A language that shows that object-oriented ideas can make concurrency tractable is Pierre America's POOL [Ame89]; the language COOL introduced in this section and fully described in Appendix D is inspired by POOL.

As mentioned in Section 6.2, a central idea in OOLs is that each object has its own copy of the instance variables of a class — this offers separation providing only the methods of the class are allowed to access the (instance) variables. At first sight, this might appear to go too far and make the activity in objects entirely disjoint. Such extreme isolation is overcome by allowing objects to communicate via method calls or invocations.

As explained in Section 6.2, to make this communication possible, it is necessary to ensure appropriate visibility of method names. In say ALGOL 60, procedure names declared within a block are visible only inside that block (see Section 5.3); in OOLs method names are visible to other classes. In fact, method invocation is precisely the means by which objects interact.

As also pointed out in Section 6.2, instance variables in OOLs preserve their values between method invocations.

A number of key questions remain about how to embed concurrency in a manageable OOL and options for COOL are investigated throughout this chapter.

9.1.1 An example program

In order to introduce COOL, consider the task of creating a "sorting ladder" that keeps a series of objects in ascending order of values of their v field as in Figure 9.1. Instances of the *Sort* class are linked via their l field (the final element in the ladder has a nil value in l). Thus the class description might declare variables:[1]

---

[1] Many years ago (in a *Heuriger* in Vienna) T.C. Chen outlined a potential use of "bubble memory" which could sort numbers in time (constant) one! The idea is to use parallel logic at each memory

Sort class
vars $v: \mathbb{N}; l: \mathsf{ref}(Sort); \cdots$

$\vdots$

By insisting that variables that contain references are declared to be specific to one class, it is possible to check statically that only known methods are invoked.[2]

Language issue 41: Strong typing in OOLs
The issue of static type checking (cf. Issue 6) in object-oriented languages can be extended to names of classes and their methods.

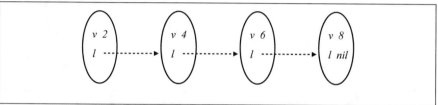

Fig. 9.1 Picture of a possible state of a sorting ladder

The intuition of COOL programs can be given by considering two methods.

- The *min* method simply returns the value of v in its instance.
- An *insert*(x) method either stores the value of the to-be-inserted parameter (x) or, if x is larger than the locally stored v, passes it to the next object in the ladder. The body of this method could contain a conditional (abbreviated below as *iif*):[3]

```
if v ≤ x
then {activate(l.insert(x))}
else {activate(l.insert(v)); v := x}
fi
```

This is embedded in a conditional that handles the end of the ladder (abbreviated below as *ins*):

```
if is-nil(l)
then {new (l); v := x; }
else {iif}
fi
```

---

cell so that inserted values trickle down to the appropriate place in the ladder; the smallest value can always be obtained from the first element of the ladder (followed by shuffling values up). This is effectively a concurrent algorithm — see Section 9.5.

[2] An alternative would be dynamic checking and, hopefully, some form of exception for unknown methods that could be trapped and also be handled dynamically.

[3] The full text of *Sort* is in Figure 9.9. The names *iif*/*ins* are used in Figure 9.3 to refer to these pieces of code (as though they were translated into abstract syntax form).

Suppose a client object –that has a variable l pointing to the first *Sorter* object in a ladder– executes:

activate($l.insert(7)$); activate($l.insert(3)$); activate($l.insert(9)$)

Then, providing each instance of the *Sort* class is executing as an independent thread, the three *insert* method calls can be handled concurrently as in Figure 9.2.

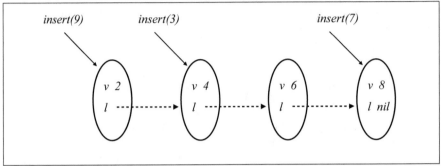

Fig. 9.2 Picture of activity in a concurrent sorting ladder

COOL's concurrency constructs are described in Section 9.5 and a number of alternatives are suggested in Section 9.7. Clearly, many details need to be pinned down but it is more interesting to look first at the objects that underpin the semantics of COOL. A full description of the language is given in Appendix D (this includes a list of abbreviations used to shorten the names of some records).

9.1.2 Semantic objects

The descriptions of the languages in earlier chapters have been followed by an indication of how informative their semantic objects can be. For COOL, the description here starts with the semantic objects in order to emphasise how much insight they convey about a language even before any detailed SOS rules are written.

Classes define the shape of objects including their instance variables; each object created for a class has local values for each of the instance variables. If each object is uniquely keyed by a *Reference*, a prime aspect of the state must be:

$ObjMap = Reference \xrightarrow{m} ObjInfo$

$ObjInfo :: \cdots$
$$\qquad\quad \sigma \;:\; VarStore$$
$\qquad\quad \cdots$

$VarStore = Id \xrightarrow{m} Val$

The values allowed include integers and Booleans; in addition values of type *Reference* can be stored (and nil used to mark an uninitialised variable of type *Reference*).

$$Val = \mathbb{Z} \mid \mathbb{B} \mid [Reference]$$

In the basic version of COOL, any object is created in a quiescent state being READY for a method call (this decision is reconsidered in Section 9.7). Objects can also be in an *Active* state and, as in the language sketch in Section 8.2, the *remaining code* of the method being executed is the other essential information for *Active* to function as a "configuration" (compare Section 8.2).

Furthermore:

- an active method records in *client* the identity of the object that gave rise to its activity;[4] and
- method activation requires that the body of a method can be located, so the *class* field of *ObjInfo* contains the name of the class.

Thus the key semantic objects are:[5]

$$
\begin{array}{lll}
ObjInfo :: & class & : Id \\
& \sigma & : VarStore \\
& mode & : \text{READY} \mid Active
\end{array}
$$

$$
\begin{array}{lll}
Active :: & rem & : Stmt^* \\
& client & : [Reference]
\end{array}
$$

The fact that the *rem* field has exactly one sequence of statements indicates the important decision in COOL that at most one method can be active in any object at any one time. An example of *ObjMap* that corresponds to Figure 9.1 is shown in Figure 9.3(b).

Language issue 42: OOLs: data races

The advantage that OOLs derive from instance variables only being accessed from methods within the class is that it removes the risk of simple data races. This advantage can be squandered if more than one method can be active in the same object at any time. A safe position is to require that only one method is active per object.

If (using a concrete syntax):

$$sl_0 = \text{activate}(l.insert(7)); \; \text{activate}(l.insert(3)); \; \text{activate}(l.insert(9))$$

were executed against the *ObjMap* in Figure 9.3(b), then the result depicted in Figure 9.3(c) would be the *ObjMap* in Figure 9.3(d)

An important property of many object-oriented languages is that the instance variables of any object (*ObjInfo*) can only be accessed and changed by the methods

---

[4] Details of when this value can be nil are contained in Section 9.5.

[5] Alternatively, an *Active* object could be distinguished from one that is quiescent (READY) by saying that an empty statement list marks the latter mode. However, the READY mode makes for clearer hypotheses to the SOS rules.

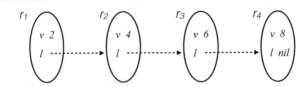

(a) Picture of a possible state of a sorting ladder.

$$\left\{ \begin{array}{l} r_0 \mapsto mk\text{-}ObjInfo(Client,\{sort \mapsto r_1\}, mk\text{-}Active(sl_o,k_0)), \\ r_1 \mapsto mk\text{-}ObjInfo(Sort,\{v \mapsto 2,l \mapsto r_2\}, \text{READY}), \\ r_2 \mapsto mk\text{-}ObjInfo(Sort,\{v \mapsto 4,l \mapsto r_3\}, \text{READY}), \\ r_3 \mapsto mk\text{-}ObjInfo(Sort,\{v \mapsto 6,l \mapsto r_4\}, \text{READY}), \\ r_4 \mapsto mk\text{-}ObjInfo(Sort,\{v \mapsto 8,l \mapsto \text{nil}\}, \text{READY}) \end{array} \right\}$$

(b) The *ObjMap* corresponding to the picture above with all objects quiescent.

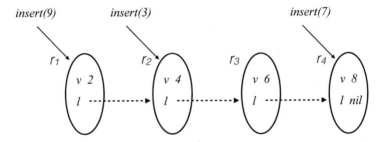

(c) Picture of activity in a concurrent sorting ladder.

$$\left\{ \begin{array}{l} r_0 \mapsto mk\text{-}ObjInfo(Client, \sigma_0, mk\text{-}Active([],k_0)), \\ r_1 \mapsto mk\text{-}ObjInfo(Sort,\{v \mapsto 2,l \mapsto r_2,x \mapsto 9\}, mk\text{-}Active(iif,r_0)), \\ r_2 \mapsto mk\text{-}ObjInfo(Sort,\{v \mapsto 4,l \mapsto r_3,x \mapsto 3\}, mk\text{-}Active(iif,r_1)), \\ r_3 \mapsto mk\text{-}ObjInfo(Sort,\{v \mapsto 6,l \mapsto r_4\}, \text{READY}), \\ r_4 \mapsto mk\text{-}ObjInfo(Sort,\{v \mapsto 8,l \mapsto \text{nil},x \mapsto 7\}, mk\text{-}Active(ins,r_3)) \end{array} \right\}$$

(d) A possible *ObjMap* during the three method activations in the picture above.

Fig. 9.3 Examples of *ObjMap*

of that object;[6] as observed above, this is what achieves encapsulation of data representations. Providing only one method can be active at any one time, the danger of data races on instance variables is eliminated. This cautious position is taken in the initial form of COOL. (An associated risk that comes from sharing references is discussed in Section 9.7.)

There remain two key further questions about adding concurrency to the language discussed in Section 6.2:

---

[6] Some languages (including Java) offer ways of exposing internal details of representations — an extension of this sort is considered in Section 9.7.

- how are the concurrent threads to be generated?
- what level of granularity of switching between threads is to be chosen?

Answers to both of these questions are interesting and could give rise to a variety of models which could be distinguished by studying their semantic objects. Here, a rather conservative view is considered initially — with some alternatives sketched in Section 9.7.

As with the configurations in Section 8.2, any active r_i can be selected to make the next small step in concurrent execution of the whole *ObjMap*. COOL sets the granularity of interference at the level of single statements: thus, switching between threads can occur after any *Stmt* is executed. For this reason, method activation is treated as a statement and cannot occur within expressions.

Language issue 43: Limiting interference in OOLs

The problems of non-determinacy and granularity that result from invoking functions within expressions are discussed in Section 6.5. In COOL, a conservative position is to require that methods can only by invoked at the statement level (i.e. not from within expressions).

Appendix D contains a full description of COOL including its abstract syntax and context conditions. It is however important to note how much of the capability of the language has been brought out by looking at the semantic objects before writing any SOS rules:

- *ObjInfo* clarifies what an object (instance of a *Class*) needs to contain.
- A newly created object is in the READY state.
- Knowledge of the variables (and later methods) of a class has to be obtained from the text of the *Classes*.
- The values of (instance) variables are local to each object and can only be accessed and changed by methods of that object.
- These values are preserved between method calls.
- An *ObjInfo* also records the *reference* of the client on whose behalf it is executing.
- The *rem*aining code to be executed in a method is stored in the *ObjInfo*.
- (Crucially) the granularity of interleaving between threads is set at the level of single statements.

9.2 Expressions

The syntax of COOL expressions given in Appendix D has only one extension from the languages considered in earlier chapters and that is the addition of a unary test as to whether a variable contains a nil reference:

Expr = $\cdots$ | *TestNil*

TestNil :: *object* : *Id*

The relevant change to the context conditions is to make *c-type* identify this form of expression as delivering a Boolean result.

To emphasise that the expression evaluation is deterministic, the semantics of COOL expressions is given as a function:

$$eval: Expr \times VarStore \rightarrow Val$$

and the relevant case is:

$$eval(mk\text{-}TestNil(id), \sigma) \quad \triangle \quad \sigma(id) = \mathsf{nil}$$

9.3 Simple statements

Moving on to the statements in COOL, the concurrency that is explained below requires that the semantic relation for statements is between two *ObjMap*s. Some constructs in COOL require additional information that is discussed below. For now the discussion is framed around:

$$\xrightarrow{st}: \mathscr{P}((\cdots \times ObjMap) \times ObjMap)$$

Most $\xrightarrow{st}$ transitions select one *Reference* that is *Active* and has the relevant statement type as the first element of *rem*.[7] Execution consists of making appropriate state changes and discarding the completed statement. The resulting object is stored under the original reference. Thus SOS rules for simple statements take the form:

$$robj = O(r)$$
$$mk\text{-}ObjInfo(cl, \sigma, mk\text{-}Active([mk\text{-}StatementType(\cdots)] \frown rl, k)) = robj$$
$$\cdots$$
$$\frac{robj' = mk\text{-}ObjInfo(cl, \sigma', mk\text{-}Active(rl, k))}{(\cdots, O) \xrightarrow{st} O \dagger \{r \mapsto robj'\}}$$

The simplest statement is *Assign*: its abstract syntax and semantics only deviate from the equivalent statements in previous chapters insofar as an assignment can only affect the state of the object in which it is executed.

$$Stmt = Assign \mid If \mid \cdots$$

$$Assign :: lhs : Id$$
$$\qquad\qquad rhs : Expr$$

For such simple statements, a *Reference* is found for which the *rem*aining text of the corresponding *ObjInfo* indicates that the appropriate statement type is to be executed. For example, r_3 in Figure 9.3(b) can transition to:

$$mk\text{-}ObjInfo(Sort, \sigma, mk\text{-}Active([mk\text{-}Assign(v, x)] \frown rl, k))$$

---

[7] Section 9.5.2 deals with synchronising objects and requires more than one object to have a suitable status.

with:

$$\sigma = \{v \mapsto 6, l \mapsto r_4, x \mapsto 5\}$$

Executing the assignment should change the variable map of $O_i(r)$ to give:

$$\sigma' = \{v \mapsto 5, l \mapsto r_4, x \mapsto 5\}$$

Furthermore, the completed statement should be removed, leaving only rl in the *rem* field — the *class* and *client* fields of $O_i(r_3)$ are unchanged. Thus the resulting *ObjMap* would be:

$$O_{i+1}(r_3) = mk\text{-}ObjInfo(Sort, \sigma', mk\text{-}Active(rl, k))$$

The SOS rule for *Assign* is:

$$
\frac{
\begin{array}{l}
robj = O(r) \\
mk\text{-}ObjInfo(cl, \sigma, mk\text{-}Active([mk\text{-}Assign(lhs, rhs)] \curvearrowright rl, k)) = robj \\
robj' = mk\text{-}ObjInfo(cl, \sigma \dagger \{lhs \mapsto eval(rhs, \sigma)\}, mk\text{-}Active(rl, k))
\end{array}
}{
(\cdots, O) \xrightarrow{st} O \dagger \{r \mapsto robj'\}
}
$$

The context conditions for *Assign* should be obvious from earlier language descriptions and are spelled out in Appendix D.

It is worth repeating that methods cannot be invoked from expressions in COOL — *Call* (and *Delegate*) are statements and their semantics is covered in Sections 9.5.2 and 9.5.3 respectively.

Conditional statements should also offer few surprises given the languages covered in Chapters 3 and 4. The abstract syntax is:

$$
\begin{array}{llll}
If & :: & test & : Expr \\
& & then & : Stmt^* \\
& & else & : Stmt^*
\end{array}
$$

The context condition for *If* is given in Appendix D and should anyway be obvious: *c-type* of *test* must yield BOOLTP and both *th* and *el* must be well formed.

Turning to the semantics of conditionals in COOL, the *ObjMap* in Figure 9.3(d) contains two *ObjInfo*s indexed by r_1, r_2 that are ready to execute an *If* (i.e. *iif*). Because the concurrency in COOL requires a small-step semantics, *iif* is unrolled and, if r_1 is selected for progress, this would give rise to:

$$O_{i+1}(r_1) = mk\text{-}ObjInfo(Sort, \{v \mapsto 2, l \mapsto r_2, x \mapsto 9\}, mk\text{-}Active(p\text{-}i, r_0))$$

where:

$$p\text{-}i : \mathsf{activate}(l.insert(x))$$

The SOS rule for the then case of *If* is:

$$
\frac{
\begin{array}{l}
robj = O(r) \\
mk\text{-}ObjInfo(cl, \sigma, mk\text{-}Active([mk\text{-}If(test, th, el)] \curvearrowright rl, k)) = robj \\
eval(test, \sigma) = \mathsf{true} \\
robj' = mk\text{-}ObjInfo(cl, \sigma, mk\text{-}Active(th \curvearrowright rl, k))
\end{array}
}{
(\cdots, O) \xrightarrow{st} O \dagger \{r \mapsto robj'\}
}
$$

The else case is obvious.

The importance of unfolding the branches of the *If* is for granularity reasons: the semantics should allow other threads to execute between statements in the *th* or *el* lists.

9.4 Creating objects

The creation of new instances of classes is more interesting than the foregoing simple statements. Objects are created as instances of classes using:

$Stmt = \cdots \mid New \mid \cdots$

$New :: target : Id$

No type information is required in the statement itself because the class can be determined from the type of the variable to which the new reference is to be assigned.

The *ObjInfo* in Figure 9.3(d) that is indexed by r_4 will evolve to:

$$mk\text{-}ObjInfo(Sort,$$
$$\{v \mapsto 8, l \mapsto \text{nil}, x \mapsto 7\},$$
$$mk\text{-}Active([mk\text{-}New(l), mk\text{-}Assign(v,x)], r_3))$$

The effect of executing the *New* should change this to:

$$mk\text{-}ObjInfo(Sort,$$
$$\{v \mapsto 8, l \mapsto r_n, x \mapsto 7\},$$
$$mk\text{-}Active([mk\text{-}Assign(v,x)], r_3))$$

and create a new quiescent thread r_n with default initial values:

$$mk\text{-}ObjInfo(Sort, \{v \mapsto 0, l \mapsto \text{nil}\}, \text{READY})$$

In order for the semantics of *New* (and *Call* below) to locate information about classes, the type of the semantic relation $\xrightarrow{st}$ needs to be:

$$\xrightarrow{st} : \mathscr{P}((ClMap \times ObjMap) \times ObjMap)$$

with:

$$ClMap = Id \xrightarrow{m} Class$$

$$Class :: vars \quad : Id \xrightarrow{m} Type$$
$$methods : Id \xrightarrow{m} Meth$$

The full SOS rule is given in Appendix D — here the routine description of state initialisation is omitted in order to focus on the more interesting aspects of the semantics of *New*:

$$robj = O(r)$$
$$mk\text{-}ObjInfo(cl_r, \sigma_r, mk\text{-}Active([mk\text{-}New(targ)] \frown rl, k)) = robj$$
$$n \in (Reference - \mathrm{dom}\, O)$$
$$robj' = mk\text{-}ObjInfo(cl_r, \sigma_r \dagger \{targ \mapsto n\}, mk\text{-}Active(rl, k))$$
$$cl_n = (C(cl_r).vars)(targ)$$
$$\sigma_n = \text{initial values}$$
$$nobj = mk\text{-}ObjInfo(cl_n, \sigma_n, \text{READY})$$
$$\rule{7cm}{0.4pt}$$
$$(C, O) \xrightarrow{st} O \dagger \{r \mapsto robj', n \mapsto nobj\}$$

As can be seen, the new thread (indexed by n) is created in an inactive state. An alternative would be to have an initial method that executes on object creation — this idea is outlined in Section 9.7.

A programmer might wish to delete the value of a reference. One way of doing this would be to add nil as an option in the abstract syntax of *Expr* but this would cause a problem with defining *c-type* in this case because nil could be a value of any optional reference type. Rather than take this route, Appendix D.5.2 defines a *Discard* statement that sets the appropriate reference variable to nil.

> **Language issue 44: Anonymous values**
> Any use of values (symbols) that can belong to more than one type can be difficult in a programming language that tries to offer strong typing. One option is to have a form of type hierarchy.

Notice that *Discard* does not destroy the referenced *ObjInfo* because there could be other reference variables in the current object or in other objects that contain the same reference and might need to invoke methods in the referenced object. The subject of "garbage collection" of objects is also sketched in Section 9.7.

9.5 Method activation and synchronisation

Objects (as instances of classes) can be in a quiescent state, which is marked by the *mode* field in their *ObjInfo* containing READY. As explained in Section 9.4 objects are created in this READY state — a server also returns to this state on completion of activity on behalf of a client.

Activity in a quiescent object can be started by a request from another (client) object:

- One possibility is that –after activation– there is no need for further communication between the client and the server. This scenario is described in Section 9.5.1.
- Another possibility is that a result is required by the client and the server must return such a value before the client can progress. There are actually sub-options here depending on whether the client has useful work that it can perform in parallel with the server before the result is available. Section 9.5.2 gives the descriptions of the relevant parts of COOL.

- Another way of enhancing concurrency is for the object that acted as initial server to delegate computing a result to another object and thus free itself for work on behalf of some new client. This delegation concept is described in Section 9.5.3.

9.5.1 Method activation

Methods are activated using the statement whose abstract syntax is:

$Activate$ :: $object$: Id
            $method$: Id
            $args$: $Expr^*$

Notice that the *object* field contains the name of a variable whose value is the reference of the server object in which the *method* is to be activated (i.e. a programmer cannot write a *Reference* in a statement because they are machine generated). The context conditions are routine and are contained in Appendix D.4.1.

Executing the first call:

activate($l.insert(7)$)

in the state depicted in Figure 9.3(a) should make thread r_1 become active in order to execute its *insert* method; the previous state of the *ObjInfo* should be updated with argument values passed (in this case the identifier x gets the value 7).

The picture in Figure 9.4 serves to introduce the formal semantics — it indicates the fact that both the activated server object (r_s) and the client (r_c) continue to execute.[8]

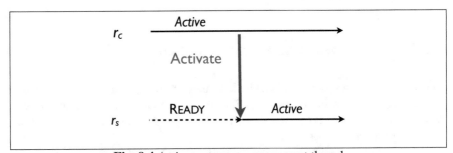

Fig. 9.4 *Activate* spawns a concurrent thread

To return to the example of activate($l.insert(7)$), the resulting state of r_1 would be:

$mk\text{-}ObjInfo(Sort,$
               $\{v \mapsto 2, l \mapsto r_2, x \mapsto 7\},$
               $mk\text{-}Active(insert, r_0))$

---

[8] The Go language also spawns — but can then communicate over channels.

The SOS rule to achieve this step has to update two *ObjInfo*s:

$$cobj = O(c)$$
$$mk\text{-}ObjInfo(cl_c, \sigma_c,$$
$$\qquad mk\text{-}Active([mk\text{-}Activate(obj, meth, args)] \frown rl_c, k)) = cobj$$
$$cobj' = mk\text{-}ObjInfo(cl_c, \sigma_c, mk\text{-}Active(rl_c, k))$$
$$sobj = O(\sigma_c(obj))$$
$$mk\text{-}ObjInfo(cl_s, \sigma_s, \text{READY}) = sobj$$
$$mk\text{-}Class(vars, meths) = C(cl_s)$$
$$mk\text{-}Meth(rtp, params, paramtps, body) = meths(meth)$$
$$\sigma_s' = \sigma_s \dagger \{params(i) \mapsto eval(args(i), \sigma_c) \mid i \in \text{inds } args\}$$
$$sobj' = mk\text{-}ObjInfo(cl_s, \sigma_s', mk\text{-}Active(body, c))$$

$$\overline{(C, O) \xrightarrow{st} O \dagger \{c \mapsto cobj', \sigma_c(obj) \mapsto sobj'\}}$$

The SOS rule above makes clear that both the object whose reference is $cobj'$ can continue actively executing rl_c and $sobj'$ begins executing *body*.

Notice that this rule can only be used if the server object (*sobj* indexed by $\sigma_c(obj)$) is in the READY mode. (Remember that all hypotheses of an SOS rule have to be satisfied for a rule to confirm the relation in its conclusion.) Any attempt to activate a method in an active object will have to wait. This of course brings danger of "deadlock", where the server never makes progress (see Section 9.7).

In the terminology of Section 5.4, the parameter passing mode in COOL is "by value": evaluated arguments are installed in local objects of the server. It is however true that passing a *Reference* confers considerable power to the receiving method: possession of a *reference* makes it possible to invoke any of its methods.

9.5.2 Method synchronisation

An obvious way to write a method for the class *Sort* that tests whether a value is present anywhere in the ladder is with a *Call* statement, whose execution has to wait until its server object returns a value:

```
test(x: ℕ) method : 𝔹
    if is-nil(l) ∨ x < v then return (false)
    elif x = v then return (true)
    else call(b, l.test(x)); return (b)
    fi
```

Such a *Call* statement has an abstract syntax that is similar to that for *Activate* but has, in addition, an *lhs* field to which the server's return value will be assigned:

```
Call :: lhs        : Id
        object     : Id
        method     : Id
        arguments  : Expr*
```

Here again, the context conditions are straightforward and are spelled out in Appendix D.4.2.

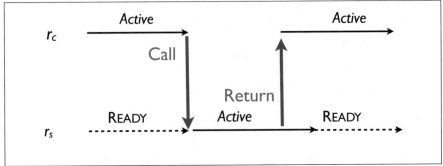

Fig. 9.5 Sequential method call

Figure 9.5 indicates the flow of control with the gap in the upper line indicating that r_c has to suspend activity until the server r_s returns a result. (The fact that r_s can continue activity after the *return* is explained below.)

The *test* method above could evolve into an *ObjMap* with:

$$
\left\{
\begin{array}{l}
r_1 \mapsto \textit{mk-ObjInfo}(\textit{Sort}, \\
\qquad\qquad \{v \mapsto 2, l \mapsto r_2, x \mapsto 7\}, \\
\qquad\qquad \textit{mk-Active}([\textit{mk-Call}(b, l, test, x), \textit{mk-Return}(b)], r_0)), \\
r_2 \mapsto \textit{mk-ObjInfo}(\textit{Sort}, \{v \mapsto 4, l \mapsto r_3\}, \text{READY}), \\
\vdots
\end{array}
\right\}
$$

The vertical ellipses are to remind the reader that there could be other threads that are also candidates for execution.

This form of call statement is in fact a special case of a more interesting "future call" present in ABC/L [Yon90]. This more general synchorisation starts with a future call whose syntax does not need the *lhs* field; the semantics allows the client object to continue execution until it needs the result from the server; at this point, the client executes an *Await* statement that indicates where (in the client) the returned value is to be stored.

Await :: *lhs* : *Id*

The flow of control is pictured in Figure 9.6 but, instead of using future call, *Activate* serves the same purpose. It can be seen that the client remains active until the *Await* statement is executed. Furthermore, the server can return a value and continue executing until the method code is exhausted.

It is simple to describe *Call* (which requires an answer before the client can make progress) in terms of the more general case and use *Await* in the description of *Call*.[9] Thus the SOS rule is:

---

[9] An alternative –but equivalent– model could add a new *mode* to the *ObjInfo* semantic object.

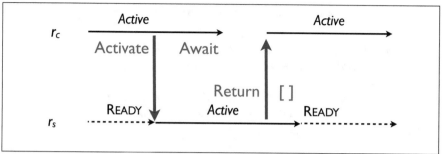

Fig. 9.6 Future call

$cobj = O(c)$
$mk\text{-}ObjInfo(cl_c, \sigma_c,$
$\qquad mk\text{-}Active([mk\text{-}Call(lhs, obj, meth, args)] \frown rl_c, k)) = cobj$
$cobj' = mk\text{-}ObjInfo(cl_c, \sigma_c, mk\text{-}Active([mk\text{-}Await(lhs)] \frown rl_c, k))$
$sobj = O(\sigma_c(obj))$
$mk\text{-}ObjInfo(cl_s, \sigma_s, \text{READY}) = sobj$
$mk\text{-}Class(vars, meths) = C(cl_s)$
$mk\text{-}Meth(rtp, params, paramtps, body) = meths(meth)$
$\sigma'_s = \sigma_s \dagger \{params(i) \mapsto eval(args(i), \sigma_c) \mid i \in \text{inds } args\}$
$sobj' = mk\text{-}ObjInfo(cl_s, \sigma'_s, mk\text{-}Active(body, c))$
_____
$(C, O) \xrightarrow{st} O \dagger \{c \mapsto cobj', \sigma_c(obj) \mapsto sobj'\}$

Thus the next state of *ObjMap* would be:

$$\left\{ \begin{array}{l} r_1 \mapsto mk\text{-}ObjInfo(Sort, \\ \qquad\qquad\qquad \{v \mapsto 2, l \mapsto r_2, x \mapsto 7\}, \\ \qquad\qquad\qquad mk\text{-}Active([mk\text{-}Await(b), mk\text{-}Return(b)], r_0)), \\ r_2 \mapsto mk\text{-}ObjInfo(Sort, \\ \qquad\qquad\qquad \{v \mapsto 4, l \mapsto r_3, x \mapsto 7\}, \\ \qquad\qquad\qquad mk\text{-}Active(\cdots, r_1)), \\ \vdots \end{array} \right\}$$

After computation further down the ladder the *ObjMap* will arrive at:

$$\left\{ \begin{array}{l} r_1 \mapsto mk\text{-}ObjInfo(Sort, \\ \qquad\qquad\qquad \{v \mapsto 2, l \mapsto r_2, x \mapsto 7\}, \\ \qquad\qquad\qquad mk\text{-}Active([mk\text{-}Await(b), mk\text{-}Return(b)], r_0)), \\ r_2 \mapsto mk\text{-}ObjInfo(Sort, \\ \qquad\qquad\qquad \{v \mapsto 4, l \mapsto r_3, x \mapsto 7\}, \\ \qquad\qquad\qquad mk\text{-}Active([mk\text{-}Return(\mathsf{false})], r_1)), \\ \vdots \end{array} \right\}$$

This brings the discussion to the return statement:

Return :: *value* : *Expr*

the semantics of which completes the *rendezvous* with the r_1 client:

$$sobj = O(s)$$
$$mk\text{-}ObjInfo(cl_s, \sigma_s, mk\text{-}Active([mk\text{-}Return(e)] \frown rl_s, c)) = sobj$$
$$sobj' = mk\text{-}ObjInfo(cl_s, \sigma_s, mk\text{-}Active(rl_s, \text{nil}))$$
$$cobj = O(c)$$
$$mk\text{-}ObjInfo(cl_c, \sigma_c, mk\text{-}Active([mk\text{-}Await(lhs)] \frown rl_c, k)) = cobj$$
$$\frac{cobj' = mk\text{-}ObjInfo(cl_c, \sigma_c \dagger \{lhs \mapsto eval(e, \sigma_s)\}, mk\text{-}Active(rl_c, k))}{(C, O) \xrightarrow{st} O \dagger \{s \mapsto sobj', c \mapsto cobj'\}}$$

In the example:

$$\left\{ \begin{array}{l}
r_1 \mapsto mk\text{-}ObjInfo(Sort, \\
\qquad\qquad \{v \mapsto 2, l \mapsto r_2, x \mapsto 7, b \mapsto \text{false}\}, \\
\qquad\qquad mk\text{-}Active([mk\text{-}Return(b)], k_m)), \\
r_2 \mapsto mk\text{-}ObjInfo(Sort, \\
\qquad\qquad \{v \mapsto 4, l \mapsto r_3, x \mapsto 7\}, \\
\qquad\qquad mk\text{-}Active([], \text{nil})), \\
\vdots
\end{array} \right\}$$

When a method has no more statements to execute (a *Return* can occur anywhere in the body of a method) it reverts to the quiescent status:

$$\frac{O(s) = mk\text{-}ObjInfo(cl, \sigma, mk\text{-}Active([], k))}{(C, O) \xrightarrow{st} O \dagger \{s \mapsto mk\text{-}ObjInfo(cl, \sigma, \text{READY})\}}$$

Thus the *ObjInfo* for r_2 changes to:

$$\left\{ \begin{array}{l}
r_2 \mapsto mk\text{-}ObjInfo(Sort, \\
\qquad\qquad \{v \mapsto 4, l \mapsto r_3\}, \\
\qquad\qquad \text{READY}), \\
\vdots
\end{array} \right\}$$

Notice however that there is a problem type checking the *lhs* in an *Await* statement and this would in general have to be a dynamic check. Furthermore, executing multiple future calls before an *Await* could give rise to dangerous program errors.

9.5.3 Delegation

The *test* method given above is unnecessarily sequential, as is shown in Figure 9.7(a). Nor can either *Activate* or future call resolve the problem because the initial client needs a value to be returned and must wait for that value. But it is possible to avoid tying up the intermediate objects, as is shown in Figure 9.7(b).

The *Delegate* statement achieves this effect by allowing the flow of control pictured in Figure 9.8. Its abstract syntax is:

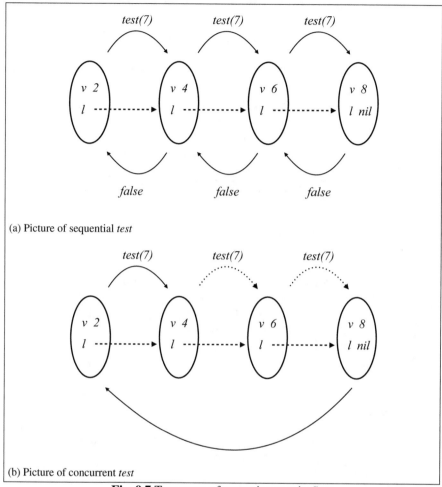

(a) Picture of sequential *test*

(b) Picture of concurrent *test*

Fig. 9.7 Two ways of executing *test* in *Sort*

$$
\begin{array}{llll}
Delegate & :: \ object & : \ Id \\
 & method & : \ Id \\
 & arguments & : \ Id^*
\end{array}
$$

Delegate statements are much like *Call* statements — the distinction is that a *Delegate* passes down its client to be the client of the newly called object whereas the object making a normal *Call* becomes the client of the called object.

A use of *Delegate* is indicated in the *test* method in Figure 9.9. Suppose that some client r_0 has called the *test* method passing 3 to r_1: r_1 cannot determine the result required by r_0 so the code of *test* reaches *Delegate*; providing the status of r_2 is READY, the situation would be:

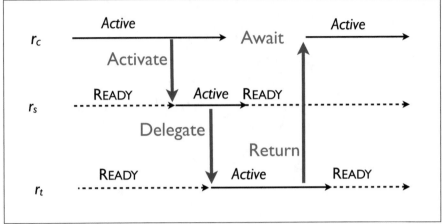

Fig. 9.8 COOL delegation

$$\left\{ \begin{array}{l} r_0 \mapsto \textit{mk-ObjInfo}(c_0, \sigma_0, \textit{mk-Active}([\textit{mk-Await}(\cdots)], k_0)), \\ r_1 \mapsto \textit{mk-ObjInfo}(\textit{Sort}, \\ \qquad\qquad\qquad \{v \mapsto 2, l \mapsto r_2, x \mapsto 3\}, \\ \qquad\qquad\qquad \textit{mk-Active}([\textit{mk-Delegate}(l, \textit{test}, x)], r_0)), \\ r_2 \mapsto \textit{mk-ObjInfo}(\textit{Sort}, \{v \mapsto 4, l \mapsto r_3\}, \text{READY}) \\ \vdots \end{array} \right\}$$

with the semantics:

$$sobj = O(s)$$
$$\textit{mk-ObjInfo}(cl_s, \sigma_s,$$
$$\qquad \textit{mk-Active}([\textit{mk-Delegate}(obj, meth, args)] \frown rl_s, k)) = sobj$$
$$sobj' = \textit{mk-ObjInfo}(cl_s, \sigma_s, \textit{mk-Active}(rl_s, \text{nil}))$$
$$tobj = O(\sigma_s(obj))$$
$$\textit{mk-ObjInfo}(cl_t, \sigma_t, \text{READY}) = tobj$$
$$\textit{mk-Class}(vars, meths) = C(cl_t)$$
$$\textit{mk-Meth}(rtp, params, paramtps, body) = meths(meth)$$
$$\sigma_t' = \sigma_t \dagger \{params(i) \mapsto eval(args(i), \sigma_s) \mid i \in \text{inds}\, args\}$$
$$\underline{tobj' = \textit{mk-ObjInfo}(cl_t, \sigma_t', \textit{mk-Active}(body, k))}$$
$$(C, O) \xrightarrow{st} O \dagger \{s \mapsto sobj', \sigma_s(obj) \mapsto tobj'\}$$

This would step to:

$$\left\{ \begin{array}{l} r_0 \mapsto \cdots \\ r_1 \mapsto \textit{mk-ObjInfo}(\textit{Sort}, \{v \mapsto 2, l \mapsto r_2, x \mapsto 3\}, \text{READY}), \\ r_2 \mapsto \textit{mk-ObjInfo}(\textit{Sort}, \{v \mapsto 4, l \mapsto r_3, x \mapsto 3\}, \textit{mk-Active}([\cdots], r_0)), \\ \vdots \end{array} \right\}$$

Notice that r_1 is now available to act as a server for another client and that the return from r_2 goes directly to r_0.

9.6 Reviewing COOL

The example class

Figure 9.9 depicts the *Sort* class with three methods (*insert*, *min* and *test*) in what is hopefully a readable concrete syntax. As in the illustrative examples in Sections 9.5.1–9.5.3:

- The *insert* method does not return a result and is invoked via an activate statement which causes the method to run concurrently with the object that caused the activation. In the case that this is the first *insert* to this object, the parameter value is stored and a new object is created; in all other cases, work is passed on to objects further down the sorting ladder.
- The *min* method is only given to illustrate that the minimum value in the ladder is always available in the first object.
- The *test* method is shown as using delegate to achieve concurrency by passing on the need to return a value to the client that called *test*.

```
Sort class
vars v: ℕ; l: ref(Sort)
insert(x: ℕ) method
    begin
        if is-nil(l)
        then {new (l); v := x; }
        else if v ≤ x
                then {activate(l.insert(x))}
                else {activate(l.insert(v)); v := x}
                fi
        fi
    end
min() method : ℕ
    return(v)
test(x: ℕ) method : 𝔹
    begin
        if is-nil(l) ∨ x < v
        then return (false)
        else if x = v
                then return (true)
                else delegate (l.test(x))
                fi
        fi
    end
```

Fig. 9.9 Concurrent *Sort*

As is shown in Appendix D.6, a *CoolProgram* contains a collection of named classes. In order to generate an initial *ObjMap*, an initial method call must also be identified. Thus the semantics of a *CoolProgram* creates an *ObjInfo* for *start-class* and then activate *start-method* (with no arguments). Adding some form of input/output statements to the language would clearly be one way to make COOL programs more useful. A more interesting alternative would be to have a way of linking a *CoolProgram* with an existing object store. Doing this is straightforward but is outside the realm of the language itself.

COOL summary

A full formal description of COOL is given in Appendix D. This section offers some observations on COOL as a language.

COOL is strongly typed with variables that contain object references only being allowed to store references to objects of the declared class (because of this, there is no need to have a class type argument to the new statement).

The context conditions for COOL are given for each language feature in Appendix D. The type information (of methods) required is:

$$ClTypes = Id \xrightarrow{m} ClInfo$$

$$ClInfo = Id \xrightarrow{m} MethInfo$$

$$MethInfo :: \begin{array}{ll} restype & : [Type] \\ paramtypes & : Type^* \end{array}$$

$$Type = Id \mid ScType$$

$$ScType = \text{INTTP} \mid \text{BOOLTP}$$

$$VarEnv = Id \xrightarrow{m} Type$$

Here again (see Section 4.2), no attempt is made to subdivide the class of *Id*. Since their written forms are taken to be the same, relating variable, method and class names is left to the context conditions.

The least conventional aspect of the semantics of COOL is the insistence that at most one method can be active in any particular object at any point in time.[10] This decison certainly increases the possibilities of deadlocks in COOL programs. On the other hand, it has the advantage that there is no possibility of data races on instance variables within an object. If a programmer wants to share data, this can be achieved by placing the data in an object whose references can be shared. This puts explicit sharing firmly in the hands of programmers and it should be exploited with great care.

Although related to POOL [AdB91], COOL is not intended to be a full language — its features have been chosen to illustrate points about semantic description.

---

[10] A similar approach is taken by Bertrand Meyer in his SCOOP proposal.

There are many ways (e.g. inheritance) in which COOL could be extended and a number of these are outlined as projects in Section 9.7.

9.7 Further material

There are many projects that can be developed from the description in Appendix D including:

1. The semantics for *Call* in Section 9.5.2 is indirect in that it employs another statement (*Await*) to put the client into a waiting state. An alternative would be to define another *mode* for *ObjInfo*.
2. Rather than have newly created objects start life in the quiescent (READY) status, an initialisation method could be added to each class that is activated on creation. This, of course, provides another source of concurrent execution. Options include whether or not *New* passes arguments to this method.
3. There is no attempt in Appendix D to make the access to objects "fair" in the sense that two attempts to call an active object will not necessarily be served in order when the called object becomes free. It is not difficult to add some form of queue to control the order of invocation.
4. A solution that is perhaps more satisfactory than the preceding point might be to add a form of conditional *Call* where the client has a list of alternative statements that are executed in the event that the sought-after server object is not Ready.
5. It would be possible to add a limited form of "self call" that either works like a local *Delegate* or is only allowed to call methods that are limited in some way as to the variables they can access or change.
6. There are several approaches to "garbage collection" of unwanted objects. An explicit *Destroy* statement should have some pre conditions; automatic collection of objects to which no reference remains is not difficult to write formally but could be expensive to implement; collecting "circular garbage" is more challenging.
7. Java allows access from object r_i to internal variables of any object for which r_i holds a reference; such an extension is not difficult to add to COOL but it is important to note that it reintroduces the danger of data races.
8. The Go language has an *activate* statement but activated "Go-routines" are closed when the *main* routine finishes. Go also offers a form of channel similar to those in the π-calculus [MPW92] in that channel names can be passed.
9. Various forms of inheritance could be added to COOL.
10. Careful addition of arrays (notably of references) can introduce extra ways of generating concurrent activity.

There is a rich literature relating to formal models of object-oriented languages. Starting with items close to COOL and working outwards:

- The debt to POOL2 has been acknowledged. An overview is given in [Ame89]; a layered semantics is given in [AR92, AdBKR89]; proof theory is considered in [AdB91, dB91].

- Bertrand Meyer's Eiffel language [Mey88] is a fully fledged and interesting language; his SCOOP proposal for simple concurrency shares many features with COOL.
- Transformations that preserve observational equivalence and can be used to introduce more concurrent threads were studied for a language referred to as $\pi o \beta \lambda$ whose semantics were given in [Jon93] by mapping to Robin Milner's π-calculus [MPW92, SW01]. (David Walker had already published [Wal91].) It proved non-trivial to justify the equivalences via bi-simulation but Davide Sangiorgi settled the issue in [San99].[11] The validity of the equivalences links to Hogg's notion [Hog91] of "islands".
- Simula [DMN68] and Smalltalk [GR83] were early object-oriented languages. The task of providing semantics was addressed in [Wol88].
- A careful look at the basic ideas behind object orientation is [AC12].

---

[11] This links to the issue raised in Section 7.1 about the tractability of denotations when a semantics is given by mapping to another language.

Chapter 10
Exceptional ordering [*]

This short optional chapter addresses the topic of modelling statements that cause execution to occur in orders different from their textual juxtaposition. The controversial goto statement provides the classic example of this modelling challenge but it is not the only manifestation of the difficulty. The discussion can be undertaken without worrying about concurrency and is limited below to consideration of sequential languages.

This chapter also moves more freely than earlier parts of the book between operational and denotational description techniques.[1] There are two aspects of the challenge of describing the semantics of the goto statement: on the one hand, it is necessary to show the change of order of execution; on the other hand, there is the question of the denotation of the label for a statement.

Normal sequential execution of $S1; S2$ dictates that execution of $S1$ is followed by execution of $S2$. This is clear in a "big-step" SOS rule for statement sequencing:

$$\frac{(s, \sigma) \xrightarrow{st} \sigma' \qquad (rl, \sigma') \xrightarrow{stl} \sigma''}{([s] \overset{\frown}{} rl, \sigma) \xrightarrow{stl} \sigma''}$$

The same sequencing is shown in denotational semantics by composition of functions (from $\Sigma \to \Sigma$). This simple model does not work if $S1$ can be a goto statement that explicitly chooses the next statement to be executed by using its label.

Language issue 45: Goto
The goto statement proved to be controversial (compare Dijkstra's original letter [Dij68b] with Knuth's [Knu74b]) but it was present in nearly all early languages. This was presumably as a direct analogue of the branch instruction in the hardware. Modern programming languages have tended to follow Dijkstra's plea to provide more structured control constructs but the challenge to be able to model exceptional ordering remains.

---

[1] Gordon Plotkin observes in [Plo04a] that ideas from operational semantics have influenced denotational semantics.

© Springer Nature Switzerland AG 2020
C. B. Jones, *Understanding Programming Languages*,
https://doi.org/10.1007/978-3-030-59257-8_10

The reason that this optional chapter considers exceptional ordering is that, even without goto statements, there remain features in most languages that present a similar challenge to providing formal models. A key interaction of language features is that abnormal execution order can cut across the structure of the syntax of a language. This requires that the semantics essentially has to perform clean up actions even though previously anticipated executions are abandoned. (Chapter 5 shows that pre-planned entry and exit from procedures and functions can be modelled without difficulty.) This chapter tackles the modelling of programming language constructs that cause execution to deviate from neat composition of statements.

Language issue 46: Exceptions
A further example of a language issue that complicates semantic description is exception handling. Unlike function calls, exception handlers can abandon previous anticipated execution.

The last of the language challenges is:

Challenge VIII: Modelling exits
How can a neat model be given for the semantics of a language in which features permit abnormal exits from structured text?

To return to the point about feature interaction, there are several language features that do cut across the phrase structure of a language but whose modelling is unproblematic.

- Premature termination of a looping construct is easy to model because nothing has to be reinstated at the end of a loop.
- A return statement from a method in COOL can be embedded within other phrase structures but OOLs leave the values of instance variables alone at method termination so all that the semantics of *Return* has to ensure is that the rest of the *rem* code is discarded.

These cases contrast with a goto that abnormally terminates a *Block* or *Procedure*. As is shown in Chapter 5, there are changes to the state (Σ) that must be made at normal termination of the text of a block or procedure; such resetting steps that clean up the state by removing locations also have to be executed when a goto statement causes abnormal termination.

Two distinct approaches to coping with Challenge VIII are described in the following sub-sections; it would however be possible to mix some aspects of the approaches described in Sections 10.1 and 10.2. A key distinguishing aspect of the approaches is whether they work forwards or backwards from labels.

10.1 Abnormal exit model

In the old VDL style of operational semantics, one component of the (grand) state of the description contained the text of the program that was being executed. Statements such as *Goto* could then be given a meaning by changing the text component. Any required cleanup operations could be programmed in terms of this tree navigation.

Operationally, this does not fit with the objective of being structural and it certainly fails to fit the homomorphic objective of denotational approaches.

A much more structural account of the way in which goto statements explicitly appoint their successor statement can be given in terms of relations that are extended (beyond $\Sigma \times \Sigma$) to mark any abnormal sequencing that results from executing a portion of program text. The range of the relation can contain an optional "abnormal" component which need only be a label in the case of a language allowing a simple goto statement:

$$\xrightarrow{st}: \mathscr{P}((Stmt \times \Sigma) \times (\Sigma \times [Id]))$$

Executing a normal statement returns a nil abnormal component:

$$\frac{(rhs, \sigma) \xrightarrow{ex} v}{(mk\text{-}Assign(lhs, rhs), \sigma) \xrightarrow{st} (\sigma \dagger \{lhs \mapsto v\}, \text{nil})}$$

In contrast the effect of something like a goto statement contains an indication of what is to be done next: in the simplest case this is just to continue execution from the appointed label:

$$\frac{(rhs, \sigma) \xrightarrow{ex} v}{(mk\text{-}Goto(id), \sigma) \xrightarrow{st} (\sigma, id)}$$

Explicitly showing the propagation of this exit field would require writing:[2]

$$\frac{(s, \sigma) \xrightarrow{st} (\sigma', abn)}{abn \neq \text{nil}}{([s] \frown rl, \sigma) \xrightarrow{stl} (\sigma', abn)}$$

and:

$$\frac{(s, \sigma) \xrightarrow{st} (\sigma', \text{nil})}{(rl, \sigma') \xrightarrow{stl} (\sigma'', abn)}{([s] \frown rl, \sigma) \xrightarrow{stl} (\sigma'', abn)}$$

It is, however, simple to adopt a convention that the default for $\xrightarrow{st}$ is to return nil unless otherwise marked, which restores the description to:

$$\frac{(rhs, \sigma) \xrightarrow{ex} v}{(mk\text{-}Assign(lhs, rhs), \sigma) \xrightarrow{st} \sigma \dagger \{lhs \mapsto v\}}$$

Such conventions are related to the use of the abnormal exit model in denotational descriptions, which is discussed further in Section 10.3. Further combinators that trap abnormal exits are also described there.

---

[2] This becomes cumbersome but was actually carried through in the ALGOL 60 description in [ACJ72].

As is explained in the next section, the use of the exit approach is the largest difference between VDM denotational descriptions[3] and those associated with Oxford (where the "continuation" approach was developed and employed). The connections between these approaches are reviewed in Section 10.3.

10.2 Continuations

The approach taken to modelling goto statements in denotational descriptions by the Oxford group looks very different from the exit mechanism described in Section 10.1; language descriptions such as SAL in [MS76] and ALGOL 60 in [Mos74] employ "continuations".

At first meeting, continuations appear to do everything backwards: the meaning of a statement is given in the context of the rest of the computation. Among other things, this immediately lifts the whole definition to:

$$Tr \rightarrow Tr$$
$$Tr = \Sigma \rightarrow \Sigma$$

The meaning of an assignment could be written:

$$M[\![mk\text{-}Assign(lhs, rhs)]\!]\{\theta\} \triangleq assign(\cdots) \circ \theta$$

to define that the overall denotation is the composition of the obvious $\Sigma \rightarrow \Sigma$ for assignment with the continuation θ.

Denotations of labels are stored in the environment and denote the entire computation from the label through to the end of the program. It is then possible to have the denotation of a goto statement simply deploy the denotation of the label. It is, however, possible to question whether the idea that the denotation of a label within a block involves its execution to the end of the surrounding context really respects the homomorphic constraint espoused by denotational semantics researchers.

10.3 Relating the approaches

Continuations can describe language constructs for which no obvious exit model has been found. But power is not necessarily an advantage: as observed in other contexts, making clear that something cannot be done can simplify reasoning about a language description. This section relates the exit and continuation approaches to

---

[3] Peter Mosses points out in [Mos11] that the "semicolon combinator" used in [BBH+74] can be related to Moggi's "monads", which were published as [Mog89]. The use of a semicolon combinator to mean either simple functional composition or a function-level version of the composition sketched above goes some way towards the reuse of formal language descriptions. Mosses goes much further in his work on component-based specifications "funcons" [BSM16],

denotational language descriptions in the context of languages –such as one containing goto statements– where what needs to be modelled is abnormal termination of part of a program.

Once a reader has overcome the feeling that a continuation description gives the meaning backwards, there are two further technical differences between continuation and exit forms of denotational semantics:

- The denotation of a label in a continuation semantics reflects the effect of starting execution at the statement with that label and continuing to the end of the entire program. In an exit formulation, the effect of a statement label extends only to the end of its enclosing block. In the former case, any clean up steps have to be composed into the denotation; in the latter, the default clean up intervenes at block end.
- The denotations of labels in a continuation description are normally stored in an environment[4] whereas an exit description tends to wrap a trapping combinator around each block. There is in fact no reason why an environment could not be used with an exit formulation — this is simply a matter of taste.

Denotational semantic descriptions exist for languages as large and complicated as PL/I [BBH+74] and Ada [Don80, HM87]. Useful comparisons between the continuation- and exit-style versions of denotational semantics can be made by looking at two descriptions of ALGOL 60: [Mos74] uses classical Oxford-style continuations and [HJ82] uses the exit combinators. Choices such as lengths of function names (and the extent of use of the Greek alphabet) make the definitions appear more different than they really are; [JA16, JA17] get below these surface issues and tease apart the more important decisions.

The existence of two ALGOL descriptions shows that both approaches to modelling language features are expressive enough to handle constructs such as goto statements. This makes it possible to look at the formal equivalence of the two approaches on non-trivial language features. An argument of equivalence is given in [Jon82b] (which is not mechanically checked). It is interesting that the observations above can be used to structure a chain of equivalences of which continuations and the most common use of exit combinators are just the extreme points.

10.4 Further material

Projects

ALGOL 60 introduced switch variables whose values are labels. (This would appear to result again from another spurious argument of orthogonality: making labels into first-class objects.) Modelling switch variables would let the reader explore the snags that this idea brings with it.

---

[4] As a consequence, the environment has to be defined using a fixed point.

Historical notes

The continuation concept is normally listed as having been separately invented by Lockwood Morris [Mor70] and Chris Wadsworth [Wad72, SW74]. In [Rey93], John Reynolds traces even more "inventions" of the idea[5] and sees the first hint of the idea in van Wijngaarden's [vW66b].

---

[5] Reynolds revisited this discussion in a talk given at the BCS Computer Conservation Society in 2004 (a video recording of this talk exists).

Chapter 11
Conclusions

This short concluding chapter begins with a review of the eight challenges discussed in the body of this book; this is followed by comments on some significant formal language descriptions or specifications.

11.1 Review of challenges

Despite the many "language issues" that are discussed and modelled in the body of this book, only eight significant "challenges" are teased out: they are summarised here.

(I) Delimiting a language (concrete representation)
How can the set of valid strings of an object language be delimited?
BNF –or a variant such as EBNF– is the most common notation used for describing concrete syntax but less common notations such as Wirth's "railroad" diagrams have equivalent expressive power.

(II) Delimiting the abstract content of a language
How can the abstract syntax of a language be defined?
In Chapter 2 and on all subsequent examples, simple parts of VDM notation for describing objects are used for describing the abstract syntax of programming languages.

(III) Recording semantics (deterministic languages)
How can the semantics of a deterministic language be recorded?
An operational semantics can be defined by a recursive function (over the abstract syntax) and is used in Section 3.1.

(IV) Operational semantics (non-determinism)
How can an operational semantics describe a non-deterministic language in a way that clearly relates the structure of the semantics to its abstract syntax?
The key step in Section 3.2 is to recognise that the semantics is a relation be-

© Springer Nature Switzerland AG 2020
C. B. Jones, *Understanding Programming Languages*,
https://doi.org/10.1007/978-3-030-59257-8_11

tween initial states and permissible final states. "Structural Operational Semantics" (SOS) defines the requisite relation by using inference rules.

(V) **Context dependancy**

How can abstract syntax objects that exhibit type errors be ruled out before semantics are tackled?

Section 4.2 shows how recursive predicates over the abstract syntax can define the set of type correct programs. These predicates are conventionally named wf-X for objects of type X.

(VI) **Modelling sharing**

How can a language description model sharing?

Section 5.2 shows how the introduction of a surrogate such as Loc as an abstraction of machine addresses makes it possible to have an environment (Env) that maps different identifiers to the same location. It is important to indicate that the environment is separate from –and changes less often than– Σ. Similarly, Section 9.1.2 uses object references to record the sharing of objects in an object-oriented language.

(VII) **Modelling concurrency**

How can shared-variable concurrency be described using SOS?

The fact that the inference rules of SOS provide a natural way of defining semantics as a relation means that non-determinacy is handled easily. The key change from big-step to small-step semantics is described in Section 8.2.

(VIII) **Modelling exits**

How can a neat model be given for the semantics of a language in which features permit abnormal exits from structured text?

Chapter 10 outlines both the use of abnormal signals and the continuation model.

11.2 Capabilities of formal description methods

Although the author has complained that insufficient use has been made of formal language description ideas, it is important to record some of the examples that indicate that formal methods can cope with realistic programming languages.

Clearly, the optimal use is in the actual specification of a programming language (rather than a *post hoc* description). The Modula-II standard uses VDM notation (see [AGLP88]). The situation with PL/I is more complicated: the repeated updatings of VDL operational semantic descriptions of PL/I were followed by the VDM denotational description [BBH+74]; the standard [ANS76] builds on this work — it has a formal description of the state of a semantics but then attempts to describe the mapping to denotations in words. The standardisation effort also came many years after IBM had gone through its normal language control processes.

A far more promising example of the use of formal methods by language designers is SML. Two versions are [MTHM97] and [HMT88]; there is also a useful web site:

http://scholarpedia.org/article/Standard_ML_language

Amongst *post hoc* descriptions of programming languages, ALGOL 60 has a special place: it has been used as a testbed for several specification methods:

- Peter Lauer's VDL description
- a "functional semantics" is given in [ACJ72]
- Peter Mosses wrote an Oxford-style denotational description [Mos74]
- A VDM-style denotational description is [HJ82].

These descriptions are analysed in detail in [JA16] (a more accessible but slightly less detailed account is given in [JA18]). ALGOL 60 is a clean and well-thought-out language that presents fewer challenges to *post hoc* description than less disciplined languages.

At the other extreme, PL/I was a nightmare for those who had to write its formal descriptions. For this author, it represents the most convincing example of where complications could have been reduced had the designers themselves employed formal modelling. PL/I is a huge language but it also presents many avoidable feature interactions. The three major versions of the VDL operational semantic descriptions of PL/I are discussed by those involved in [LW69] and with the benefit of hindsight in [JA18]. Thankfully, the ECMA/ANSI subset removed some of the complications and the VDM denotational description [BBH$^+$74] is a fraction of the length of those in VDL.

Another monster language is CHILL, whose description is in [Stu80]. The story of the Ada language could have been so much more rewarding:

- the DoD's "Ironman" requirements for the language that was to become Ada stated that there should be a formal semantics either as Hoare axioms or in VDL;
- in the event, Ichbiah's winning proposal was designed with, again, formalists attempting to model indisciplined design decisions;
- the French efforts are described in [DGKL80, Don80];
- the team around Dines Bjørner in Denmark's DDC produced a well-respected Ada compiler from their VDM description [BO80b]; the concurrency features used SMoLCS [HM87].

Although the efforts to describe the Pascal language were also conducted *post facto*, it represents a much better thought-out language: [AH82] does have to cope with some unnecessary feature interactions but fits comfortably in a chapter of a book rather than being a book itself.

An important line of operational research that looks rather different is that conducted by J Strother Moore at Austin Texas. Using Lisp, this group has, over many years, provided executable semantic descriptions. Some of these descriptions are of hardware instruction sets and have been used to verify hardware designs. Moreover, the group has tackled the key task of verifying a "stack" of languages that are implemented on the next layer down. A wide-ranging survey of this work is given in [Moo19].

Descriptions of logic programming languages include [AB87] and [And92].

Moving further afield, descriptions of database systems include [Han76, Owl79] and their interestingly different (from programming languages) concurrency issues are covered in [BHG87, L$^+$94, WV01].

The use of techniques for reasoning formally about programs in a language is much more widespread. Some historical material is contained in [Jon03]. Moreover, extremely encouraging examples of use by major corporations are reported in [CDD$^+$15, DFLO19] and [Coo18].

11.3 Envoi

A huge number of programming languages exist and there is no reason to believe that people will cease to design new ones. Perhaps one reason for there being so many languages is that there is dissatisfaction with the state of play. The challenge of designing a language that makes programs clear and easy to reason about is significant; the effort of building a translator or interpreter for a language is significant (and these days a complete development environment must be added). The argument in this book is that it is less effort to think out the ideas of languages using formal models and the resulting language should possess clearer structure.

If this book can play a small part in helping the language design process yield better thought-out languages that –in turn– make it possible to construct better programs, the effort in writing the book will be amply repaid.

Appendix A
Simple language

This appendix separates syntax, context conditions and semantics and is thus in the order in which the topics are introduced in Chapters 2–4 of the current book.

Abbreviations used in the description:

Σ	the set of all "states"
$\sigma \in \Sigma$	a single "state"
Arith	Arithmetic
Expr	Expression
Id	Identifier
lhs	left-hand side
Rel	Relational
rhs	right-hand side
Stmt	Statement

© Springer Nature Switzerland AG 2020
C. B. Jones, *Understanding Programming Languages*,
https://doi.org/10.1007/978-3-030-59257-8

A.1 Concrete syntax

A.1.1 Dijkstra style

⟨*Program*⟩ ::= **program vars**⟨*Ids*⟩: ⟨*Stmts*⟩ **end**
⟨*Ids*⟩ ::= ⟨*Id*⟩ [, ⟨*Ids*⟩]
⟨*Stmts*⟩ ::= [⟨*Stmt*⟩ [; ⟨*Stmts*⟩]]
⟨*Stmt*⟩ ::= ⟨*Assign*⟩ | ⟨*If*⟩ | ⟨*While*⟩
⟨*Assign*⟩ ::= ⟨*Id*⟩ := ⟨*ArithExpr*⟩
⟨*If*⟩ ::= **if** ⟨*RelExpr*⟩ **then** ⟨*Stmts*⟩ [**else** ⟨*Stmts*⟩] **fi**
⟨*While*⟩ ::= **while** ⟨*RelExpr*⟩ **do** ⟨*Stmts*⟩ **od**
⟨*ArithExpr*⟩ ::= ⟨*BinArithExpr*⟩ | ⟨*NaturalNumber*⟩ | ⟨*Id*⟩ | (⟨*ArithExpr*⟩)
⟨*BinArithExpr*⟩ ::= ⟨*ArithExpr*⟩⟨*BinArithOperator*⟩⟨*ArithExpr*⟩
⟨*BinArithOperator*⟩ ::= + | *
⟨*RelExpr*⟩ ::= ⟨*ArithExpr*⟩⟨*CompareOperator*⟩⟨*ArithExpr*⟩
⟨*CompareOperator*⟩ ::= =|≤
⟨*NaturalNumber*⟩ ::= ⟨*Digit*⟩ | ⟨*Digit*⟩⟨*NaturalNumber*⟩
⟨*Digit*⟩ ::= 0 | 1 | 2 | 3 | 4 | 5 | 6 | 7 | 8 | 9

A.1.2 Java-style statement syntax

⟨*Stmts*⟩ ::= [⟨*Stmt*⟩ [; ⟨*Stmts*⟩]]
⟨*Stmt*⟩ ::= ⟨*Assign*⟩ | ⟨*If*⟩ | ⟨*While*⟩
⟨*Assign*⟩ ::= ⟨*Id*⟩ = ⟨*ArithExpr*⟩
⟨*If*⟩ ::= **if** (⟨*RelExpr*⟩) ⟨*BodyStmts*⟩ [**else** ⟨*BodyStmts*⟩]
⟨*While*⟩ ::= **while** (⟨*RelExpr*⟩) ⟨*BodyStmts*⟩
⟨*BodyStmts*⟩ ::= ⟨*Stmt*⟩ | {⟨*Stmts*⟩}

A.2 Abstract syntax

SimpleProgram :: *vars* : *Id*-set
                       body : *Stmt**

Stmt = *Assign* | *If* | *While*

Assign :: *lhs* : *Id*
             rhs : *ArithExpr*

If :: *test* : *RelExpr*
       then : *Stmt**
       else : *Stmt**

While :: *test* : *RelExpr*
           body : *Stmt**

ArithExpr = *BinArithExpr* | *Id* | $\mathbb{N}$

BinArithExpr :: *operand*1 : *ArithExpr*
                   operator : PLUS | TIMES
                   *operand*2 : *ArithExpr*

RelExpr :: *operand*1 : *ArithExpr*
             operator : EQUALS | LESSTHANEQ
             *operand*2 : *ArithExpr*

A.3 Semantics

Statements

$$\Sigma = Id \xrightarrow{m} \mathbb{N}$$

The semantic transition relation for statement lists is

$$\xrightarrow{st}: \mathscr{P}((Stmt \times \Sigma) \times \Sigma)$$

$$\frac{(s,\sigma) \xrightarrow{st} \sigma'}{(rl,\sigma') \xrightarrow{stl} \sigma''}{([s] \frown rl, \sigma) \xrightarrow{stl} \sigma''}$$

$$\frac{}{([]s,\sigma) \xrightarrow{stl} \sigma}$$

The semantic transition relation for single statements is given by cases below.

$$\xrightarrow{stl}: \mathscr{P}((Stmt^* \times \Sigma) \times \Sigma)$$

$$\frac{(rhs,\sigma) \xrightarrow{ex} v}{(mk\text{-}Assign(lhs,rhs),\sigma) \xrightarrow{st} \sigma \dagger \{lhs \mapsto v\}}$$

$$\frac{(test,\sigma) \xrightarrow{ex} \text{true}}{(th,\sigma) \xrightarrow{stl} \sigma'}{(mk\text{-}If(test,th,el),\sigma) \xrightarrow{st} \sigma'}$$

$$\frac{(test,\sigma) \xrightarrow{ex} \text{false}}{(el,\sigma) \xrightarrow{stl} \sigma'}{(mk\text{-}If(test,th,el),\sigma) \xrightarrow{st} \sigma'}$$

$$\frac{(test,\sigma) \xrightarrow{ex} \text{true}}{(body,\sigma) \xrightarrow{stl} \sigma'}{(mk\text{-}While(test,body),\sigma') \xrightarrow{st} \sigma''}{(mk\text{-}While(test,body),\sigma) \xrightarrow{st} \sigma''}$$

$$\frac{(test,\sigma) \xrightarrow{ex} \text{false}}{(mk\text{-}While(test,body),\sigma) \xrightarrow{st} \sigma}$$

Expressions

Although the evaluation of expressions is deterministic, the semantics is given as a relation for consistency with semantics of statements:

Expr = ArithExpr | RelExpr

$\xrightarrow{ex}: \mathscr{P}((Expr \times \Sigma) \times (\mathbb{B} \mid \mathbb{N}))$

Given by cases below.

$$\frac{(op1, \sigma) \xrightarrow{ex} v1 \quad (op2, \sigma) \xrightarrow{ex} v2}{(mk\text{-}BinArithExpr(op1, \text{PLUS}, op2), \sigma) \xrightarrow{ex} v1 + v2}$$

$$\frac{(op1, \sigma) \xrightarrow{ex} v1 \quad (op2, \sigma) \xrightarrow{ex} v2}{(mk\text{-}BinArithExpr(op1, \text{TIMES}, op2), \sigma) \xrightarrow{ex} v1 * v2}$$

$$\frac{(op1, \sigma) \xrightarrow{ex} v1 \quad (op2, \sigma) \xrightarrow{ex} v2}{(mk\text{-}RelExpr(op1, \text{EQUALS}, op2), \sigma) \xrightarrow{ex} v1 = v2}$$

$$\frac{(op1, \sigma) \xrightarrow{ex} v1 \quad (op2, \sigma) \xrightarrow{ex} v2}{(mk\text{-}RelExpr(op1, \text{LESSTHANEQ}, op2), \sigma) \xrightarrow{ex} v1 \leq v2}$$

$$\frac{e \in Id}{(e, \sigma) \xrightarrow{ex} \sigma(e)}$$

$$\frac{e \in \mathbb{N}}{(e, \sigma) \xrightarrow{ex} e}$$

Appendix B
Typed language

The formulae in this appendix separate abstract syntax, context conditions and semantics. This is not the order used in subsequent appendices but it serves at this stage to emphasise the distinctions.

Abbreviations used in the description:

Σ	the set of all "states"
$\sigma \in \Sigma$	a single "state"
Arith	Arithmetic
Expr	Expression
Id	Identifier
lhs	left-hand side
Rel	Relational
rhs	right-hand side
Stmt	Statement
wf-	well-formed

© Springer Nature Switzerland AG 2020
C. B. Jones, *Understanding Programming Languages*,
https://doi.org/10.1007/978-3-030-59257-8

B.1 Abstract syntax

$BaseProgram$ :: $types$: $Id \xrightarrow{m} ScalarType$
$\qquad\qquad\quad body$: $Stmt^*$

$ScalarType = \text{INTTP} \mid \text{BOOLTP}$

$Stmt = Assign \mid If \mid While$

$Assign$ :: lhs : Id
$\qquad\qquad rhs$: $Expr$

If :: $test$: $Expr$
$\qquad then$: $Stmt^*$
$\qquad else$: $Stmt^*$

$While$ :: $test$: $Expr$
$\qquad\quad body$: $Stmt^*$

$Expr = ArithExpr \mid RelExpr \mid Id \mid ScalarValue$

$ArithExpr$ :: $operand1$: $Expr$
$\qquad\qquad operator$: $\text{PLUS} \mid \text{MINUS} \mid \cdots$
$\qquad\qquad operand2$: $Expr$

$RelExpr$ :: $operand1$: $Expr$
$\qquad\qquad operator$: $\text{EQUALS} \mid \text{LESSTHANEQ} \mid \cdots$
$\qquad\qquad operand2$: $Expr$

$ScalarValue = \mathbb{Z} \mid \mathbb{B}$

B.2 Context conditions

In order to define the Context Conditions below, an auxiliary object is required in which the types of declared identifiers can be stored.

$TypeMap = Id \xrightarrow{m} ScalarType$

$wf\text{-}BaseProgram : BaseProgram \rightarrow \mathbb{B}$

$wf\text{-}BaseProgram(mk\text{-}BaseProgram(types, body)) \quad \triangleq$
$\quad wf\text{-}StmtList(body, types)$

$wf\text{-}StmtList : Stmt^* \times TypeMap \rightarrow \mathbb{B}$

$wf\text{-}StmtList(sl, tpm) \quad \triangleq \quad \forall i \in \text{inds } sl \cdot wf\text{-}Stmt(sl(i), tpm)$

$wf\text{-}Stmt : Stmt \times TypeMap \rightarrow \mathbb{B}$

$wf\text{-}Stmt(s, tpm) \quad \triangleq \quad$ given by cases below

$wf\text{-}Stmt(mk\text{-}Assign(lhs, rhs), tpm) \quad \triangleq$
$\quad lhs \in \text{dom } tpm \wedge$
$\quad c\text{-}type(rhs, tpm) = tpm(lhs)$

$wf\text{-}Stmt(mk\text{-}If(test, th, el), tpm) \quad \triangleq$
$\quad c\text{-}type(test, tpm) = \text{BOOLTP} \wedge$
$\quad wf\text{-}StmtList(th, tpm) \wedge wf\text{-}StmtList(el, tpm)$

$wf\text{-}Stmt(mk\text{-}While(test, body), tpm) \quad \triangleq$
$\quad c\text{-}type(test, tpm) = \text{BOOLTP} \wedge$
$\quad wf\text{-}StmtList(body, tpm)$

An auxiliary function *c-type* is defined

$c\text{-}type : Expr \times TypeMap \rightarrow (\text{INTTP} \mid \text{BOOLTP} \mid \text{ERROR})$

$c\text{-}type(e, tpm) \quad \triangleq \quad$ given by cases below

$c\text{-}type(mk\text{-}ArithExpr(e1, opt, e2), tpm) \quad \triangleq$
    if $c\text{-}type(e1, tpm) = \text{INTTP} \wedge c\text{-}type(e2, tpm) = \text{INTTP}$
    then INTTP
    else ERROR
    fi

$c\text{-}type(mk\text{-}RelExpr(e1, opt, e2), tpm) \quad \triangleq$
    if $c\text{-}type(e1, tpm) = \text{INTTP} \wedge c\text{-}type(e2, tpm) = \text{INTTP}$
    then BOOLTP
    else ERROR
    fi

For the base cases:

$e \in Id \;\Rightarrow\; c\text{-}type(e, tpm) = tpm(e)$

$e \in \mathbb{Z} \;\Rightarrow\; c\text{-}type(e, tpm) = \text{INTTP}$

$e \in \mathbb{B} \;\Rightarrow\; c\text{-}type(e, tpm) = \text{BOOLTP}$

B.3 Semantics

An auxiliary object is needed to describe the Semantics — this "Semantic Object" (Σ) stores the association of identifiers and their values.

$$\Sigma = Id \xrightarrow{m} ScalarValue$$

$$\sigma_0 = \{id \mapsto 0 \mid id \in \text{dom } types \wedge types(id) = \text{INTTP}\} \cup$$
$$\{id \mapsto \text{true} \mid id \in \text{dom } types \wedge types(id) = \text{BOOLTP}\}$$

$$\frac{(body, \sigma_0) \xrightarrow{stl} \sigma'}{(mk\text{-}BaseProgram(types, body)) \xrightarrow{pr} \text{DONE}}$$

The semantic transition relation for statement lists is

$$\xrightarrow{stl} : \mathscr{P}((Stmt^* \times \Sigma) \times \Sigma)$$

$$\frac{}{([\,], \sigma) \xrightarrow{stl} \sigma}$$

$$\frac{(s, \sigma) \xrightarrow{st} \sigma'}{(rest, \sigma') \xrightarrow{stl} \sigma''}{([s] \frown rest, \sigma) \xrightarrow{stl} \sigma''}$$

The semantic transition relation for single statements is

$$\xrightarrow{st} : \mathscr{P}((Stmt \times \Sigma) \times \Sigma)$$

$$\frac{(rhs, \sigma) \xrightarrow{ex} v}{(mk\text{-}Assign(lhs, rhs), \sigma) \xrightarrow{st} \sigma \dagger \{lhs \mapsto v\}}$$

$$\frac{(test, \sigma) \xrightarrow{ex} \text{true}}{(th, \sigma) \xrightarrow{stl} \sigma'}{(mk\text{-}If(test, th, el), \sigma) \xrightarrow{st} \sigma'}$$

$$\frac{(test, \sigma) \xrightarrow{ex} \text{false}}{(el, \sigma) \xrightarrow{stl} \sigma'}{(mk\text{-}If(test, th, el), \sigma) \xrightarrow{st} \sigma'}$$

$$\frac{(test, \sigma) \xrightarrow{ex} \text{true}}{(body, \sigma) \xrightarrow{stl} \sigma'}{(mk\text{-}While(test, body), \sigma') \xrightarrow{st} \sigma''}{(mk\text{-}While(test, body), \sigma) \xrightarrow{st} \sigma''}$$

$$\frac{(test, \sigma) \xrightarrow{ex} \text{false}}{(mk\text{-}While(test, body), \sigma) \xrightarrow{st} \sigma}$$

The semantic transition relation for expressions is

$$\xrightarrow{ex}: \mathscr{P}((\mathit{Expr} \times \Sigma) \times \mathit{ScalarValue})$$

$$\frac{(e1,\sigma) \xrightarrow{ex} v1 \qquad (e2,\sigma) \xrightarrow{ex} v2}{(\mathit{mk\text{-}ArithExpr}(e1,\text{PLUS},e2),\sigma) \xrightarrow{ex} v1 + v2}$$

$$\frac{(e1,\sigma) \xrightarrow{ex} v1 \qquad (e2,\sigma) \xrightarrow{ex} v2}{(\mathit{mk\text{-}ArithExpr}(e1,\text{MINUS},e2),\sigma) \xrightarrow{ex} v1 - v2}$$

$$\frac{(e1,\sigma) \xrightarrow{ex} v1 \qquad (e2,\sigma) \xrightarrow{ex} v2 \qquad v1 = v2}{(\mathit{mk\text{-}RelExpr}(e1,\text{EQUALS},e2),\sigma) \xrightarrow{ex} \text{true}}$$

$$\frac{(e1,\sigma) \xrightarrow{ex} v1 \qquad (e2,\sigma) \xrightarrow{ex} v2 \qquad v1 \neq v2}{(\mathit{mk\text{-}RelExpr}(e1,\text{EQUALS},e2),\sigma) \xrightarrow{ex} \text{false}}$$

$$\frac{(e1,\sigma) \xrightarrow{ex} v1 \qquad (e2,\sigma) \xrightarrow{ex} v2 \qquad v1 \leq v2}{(\mathit{mk\text{-}RelExpr}(e1,\text{LESSTHANEQ},e2),\sigma) \xrightarrow{ex} \text{true}}$$

$$\frac{(e1,\sigma) \xrightarrow{ex} v1 \qquad (e2,\sigma) \xrightarrow{ex} v2 \qquad v1 > v2}{(\mathit{mk\text{-}RelExpr}(e1,\text{LESSTHANEQ},e2),\sigma) \xrightarrow{ex} \text{false}}$$

$$\frac{e \in \mathit{Id}}{(e,\sigma) \xrightarrow{ex} \sigma(e)}$$

$$\frac{e \in \mathit{ScalarValue}}{(e,\sigma) \xrightarrow{ex} e}$$

Appendix C
Blocks language

Unlike the preceding appendices (where the whole of the abstract syntax is given before all of the context conditions to be followed by the semantics for every construct), this appendix is in the "preferred order": that is, it is ordered by language concept. For reference purposes, this order is normally most convenient. There remains the decision whether to present the parts of a language in a top-down (from *BlocksProgram* to *Expr*) order or bottom-up: this decision is fairly arbitrary. What is really needed is an interactive support system!

Abbreviations

$\sigma \in \Sigma$	a single "state"
Σ	the set of all "states"
Arith	Arithmetic
Def	Definition
Den	Denotation
env	a single "environment"
Env	the set of all "environments"
Expr	Expression
param	parameter
Proc	Procedure
Rel	Relational
Stmt	Statement

© Springer Nature Switzerland AG 2020
C. B. Jones, *Understanding Programming Languages*,
https://doi.org/10.1007/978-3-030-59257-8

C.1 Auxiliary objects

The objects required for both context conditions and semantic rules are given first.

Objects needed for context conditions

The following objects are needed in the description of the Context Conditions.

$$TypeMap = Id \xrightarrow{m} (ScalarType \mid ProcType)$$

$$ScalarType = \text{INTTYPE} \mid \text{BOOLTYPE}$$

$$ProcType :: paramtypes : ScalarType^*$$

Semantic objects

The following objects are needed in the description of the Semantics.

$$Env = Id \xrightarrow{m} Den$$

$$Den = ScalarLoc \mid ProcDen$$

where *ScalarLoc* is an infinite set chosen from *Token*.

$$\begin{aligned} ProcDen :: \;& params \;:\; Id^* \\ & body \quad:\; Stmt \\ & context \;:\; Env \end{aligned}$$

The state only contains a "store":[1]

$$\Sigma = ScalarLoc \xrightarrow{m} ScalarValue$$

A useful predicate is:

$$uniquel : (X^*) \to \mathbb{B}$$

$$uniquel(l) \quad \triangle \quad \text{len } l = \text{card elems } l$$

---

[1] I/O as in Section 4.3.1 could, of course, be added.

C.2 Programs

Abstract syntax

$BlocksProgram$ :: $body$: $Stmt$

Context conditions

$wf\text{-}BlocksProgram : BlocksProgram \to \mathbb{B}$

$wf\text{-}BlocksProgram(mk\text{-}BlocksProgram(b)) \quad \triangleq \quad wf\text{-}Stmt(b, \{\mapsto\})$

Semantics

$\xrightarrow{pr} : \mathscr{P}(BlocksProgram \times \text{DONE})$

$$env_0 = \{\mapsto\}$$
$$\sigma_0 = \{\mapsto\}$$
$$\frac{(b, env_0, \sigma_0) \xrightarrow{st} \sigma'}{mk\text{-}BlocksProgram(b) \xrightarrow{pr} \text{DONE}}$$

C.3 Statements

Abstract syntax

$Stmt = Assign \mid If \mid While \mid Compound \mid Block \mid Call$

Context conditions

$wf\text{-}Stmt : Stmt \times TypeMap \to \mathbb{B}$

$wf\text{-}Stmt(s, tpm) \quad \triangleq \quad$ given by cases below

Semantics

The semantic relation (which is also given by cases below) for statements is:

$$\xrightarrow{st}: \mathscr{P}((Stmt \times Env \times \Sigma) \times \Sigma)$$

C.4 Simple statements

Assignment

Abstract syntax

$$Assign :: lhs : Id$$
$$\qquad\qquad rhs : Expr$$

Context conditions

$$wf\text{-}Stmt(mk\text{-}Assign(lhs, rhs), tpm) \quad \triangle$$
$$\qquad lhs \in \mathsf{dom}\, tpm \land c\text{-}type(rhs, tpm) = tpm(lhs)$$

Semantics

$$\frac{(rhs, env, \sigma) \xrightarrow{ex} v}{(mk\text{-}Assign(lhs, rhs), env, \sigma) \xrightarrow{st} \sigma \dagger \{env(lhs) \mapsto v\}}$$

If

Abstract syntax

$$If :: test : Expr$$
$$\qquad then : Stmt$$
$$\qquad else : Stmt$$

Context conditions

$$wf\text{-}Stmt(mk\text{-}If(test,th,el),tpm) \quad \triangleq$$
$$c\text{-}type(test,tpm) = \text{BOOLTP} \wedge$$
$$wf\text{-}Stmt(th,tpm) \wedge wf\text{-}Stmt(el,tpm)$$

Semantics

$$\frac{(test,env,\sigma) \xrightarrow{ex} \text{true}}{(th,env,\sigma) \xrightarrow{st} \sigma'}$$
$$\overline{(mk\text{-}If(test,th,el),env,\sigma) \xrightarrow{st} \sigma'}$$

$$\frac{(test,env,\sigma) \xrightarrow{ex} \text{false}}{(el,env,\sigma) \xrightarrow{st} \sigma'}$$
$$\overline{(mk\text{-}If(test,th,el),env,\sigma) \xrightarrow{st} \sigma'}$$

C.5 Compound statements

Abstract syntax

$$Compound :: body : Stmt^*$$

Context conditions

$$wf\text{-}Stmt : Compound \times TypeMap \rightarrow \mathbb{B}$$
$$wf\text{-}Stmt(mk\text{-}Compound(sl),tpm) \quad \triangleq \quad \forall i \in \text{inds } sl \cdot wf\text{-}Stmt(sl(i),tpm)$$

Semantics

$$\frac{(stl,env,\sigma) \xrightarrow{stl} \sigma'}{(mk\text{-}Compound(stl),env,\sigma) \xrightarrow{st} \sigma'}$$

Statement lists

$$\overline{([\,],env,\sigma) \xrightarrow{stl} \sigma}$$

$$\frac{(s,env,\sigma) \xrightarrow{st} \sigma'}{(rl,env,\sigma') \xrightarrow{stl} \sigma''}$$
$$\overline{([s] \frown rl,env,\sigma) \xrightarrow{stl} \sigma''}$$

C.6 Blocks

Abstract syntax

$$
\begin{aligned}
Block \;::\; & var\text{-}types \;:\; Id \xrightarrow{m} ScalarType \\
& proc\text{-}defs \;:\; Id \xrightarrow{m} ProcDef \\
& body \qquad\; :\; Stmt^*
\end{aligned}
$$

Context conditions

$$
\begin{aligned}
& wf\text{-}Stmt(mk\text{-}Block(vm,pm,body),tpm) \quad \triangle \\
& \quad \text{dom}\, vm \cap \text{dom}\, pm = \{\,\} \wedge \\
& \quad \left(\begin{array}{l}
\text{let } tpm' = tpm \dagger vm \text{ in} \\
\text{let } proc\text{-}tpm = \\
\quad \{p \mapsto mk\text{-}ProcType(pm(p).paramtypes) \mid p \in \text{dom}\, pm\} \text{ in} \\
\forall p \in \text{dom}\, pm \cdot wf\text{-}ProcDef(pm(p),tpm') \wedge \\
wf\text{-}Stmt(body,tpm' \dagger proc\text{-}tpm)
\end{array}\right)
\end{aligned}
$$

Semantics

$$newlocs \in (Id \overset{m}{\longleftrightarrow} ScalarLoc)$$
$$\text{dom}\, newlocs = \text{dom}\, vm$$
$$\text{rng}\, newlocs \cap \text{dom}\, \sigma = \{\,\}$$
$$penv = \{p \mapsto mk\text{-}ProcDen(pm(p).params, pm(p).body, env) \mid p \in \text{dom}\, pm\}$$
$$env' = env \dagger newlocs \dagger penv$$
$$\sigma_i = \sigma \dagger (\{env(id) \mapsto 0 \mid id \in \text{dom}\, vm \wedge vm(id) = \textsc{IntTp}\} \cup$$
$$\{env(id) \mapsto \text{true} \mid id \in \text{dom}\, vm \wedge vm(id) = \textsc{BoolTp}\})$$
$$\frac{(body, env', \sigma_i) \overset{stl}{\longrightarrow} \sigma_i'}{(mk\text{-}Block(vm, pm, body), env, \sigma) \overset{st}{\longrightarrow} \text{dom}\, \sigma \lhd \sigma_i'}$$

Procedure definition

Abstract syntax

$$
\begin{array}{llll}
ProcDef & :: & params & : & Id^* \\
        &   & paramtypes & : & ScalarType^* \\
        &   & body & : & Stmt
\end{array}
$$

Context conditions

$$wf\text{-}ProcDef : ProcDef \times TypeMap \to \mathbb{B}$$

$$wf\text{-}ProcDef(mk\text{-}ProcDef(ps, ptps, body), tpm) \quad \triangle$$
$$\quad uniquel(ps) \wedge$$
$$\quad \text{len}\, ps = \text{len}\, ptps \wedge$$
$$\quad wf\text{-}Stmt(body, tpm \dagger \{ps(i) \mapsto ptps(i) \mid i \in \text{inds}\, ps\})$$

C.7 Call statements

Abstract syntax

$$
\begin{array}{llll}
Call & :: & proc & : & Id \\
     &   & args & : & Id^*
\end{array}
$$

Context conditions

$$wf\text{-}Stmt(mk\text{-}Call(proc,args),tpm) \quad \triangleq$$
$$proc \in \operatorname{dom} tpm \wedge$$
$$tpm(proc) \in ProcType \wedge$$
$$\begin{pmatrix} \operatorname{let} mk\text{-}ProcType(ptl) = tpm(proc) \text{ in} \\ \operatorname{len} args = \operatorname{len} ptl \wedge \\ \forall i \in \operatorname{inds} args \cdot tpm(args(i)) = ptl(i) \end{pmatrix}$$

Semantics (parameter passing by reference)

$$\frac{\begin{array}{l} mk\text{-}ProcDen(parms,body,cenv) = env(p) \\ lenv = cenv \dagger \{parms(i) \mapsto env(args(i)) \mid i \in \operatorname{inds} parms\} \\ (body,lenv,\sigma) \xrightarrow{st} \sigma' \end{array}}{(mk\text{-}Call(p,args),env,\sigma) \xrightarrow{st} \sigma'}$$

Semantics (parameter passing by value)

$$\frac{\begin{array}{l} mk\text{-}ProcDen(parms,body,cenv) = env(p) \\ newlocs \in (Id \xleftrightarrow{m} ScalarLoc) \\ \operatorname{dom} newlocs = \operatorname{elems} parms \\ \operatorname{rng} newlocs \cap \operatorname{dom} \sigma = \{\,\} \\ lenv = cenv \dagger newlocs \\ \sigma_i = \sigma \cup \{newlocs(parms(i)) \mapsto \sigma(env(args(i))) \mid i \in \operatorname{inds} parms\} \\ (body,lenv,\sigma_i) \xrightarrow{st} \sigma_i' \end{array}}{(mk\text{-}Call(p,args),env,\sigma) \xrightarrow{st} \operatorname{dom} \sigma \lhd \sigma_i'}$$

C.8 Expressions

The only interesting deviation from earlier languages is the case of identifiers.

Abstract syntax

$$Expr = \cdots \mid Id$$

Semantics

$$\xrightarrow{ex}: \mathscr{P}((Expr \times Env \times \Sigma) \times ScalarValue)$$

$$\frac{e \in Id}{(e, env, \sigma) \xrightarrow{ex} \sigma(env(e))}$$

Appendix D
COOL

This appendix is –like Appendix C– in the "preferred order": i.e. the abstract syntax, context conditions and semantics are grouped under each language concept.

Abbreviations

Arith	Arithmetic
Cl	Class
Expr	Expression
Obj	Object
opd	operand
Meth	Method
Rel	Relational
rem	remaining
Sc	Scalar
Stmt	Statement
Val	(semantic) Value
Var	Variable

© Springer Nature Switzerland AG 2020
C. B. Jones, *Understanding Programming Languages*,
https://doi.org/10.1007/978-3-030-59257-8

D.1 Auxiliary objects

Types for context conditions

The following types are needed in the description of the Context Conditions.

$ClTypes = Id \xrightarrow{m} ClInfo$

$ClInfo = Id \xrightarrow{m} MethInfo$

$MethInfo :: restype \quad : \; [Type]$
$\qquad\qquad\quad\; paramtypes \; : \; Type^*$

$Type = ScType \mid Id$

$ScType = \text{INTTP} \mid \text{BOOLTP}$

$VarEnv = Id \xrightarrow{m} Type$

The types of the context condition predicates are:

$c\text{-}type : Expr \times ClTypes \times VarEnv \rightarrow Type$
$wf\text{-}Stmt : Stmt \times ClTypes \times VarEnv \times Type \rightarrow \mathbb{B}$
$wf\text{-}CoolProgram : CoolProgram \rightarrow \mathbb{B}$

Types for semantics

In addition to the abstract syntax of *ClMap* (see abstract syntax in Section D.6), the following types are needed in the description of the semantics.

$ObjMap = Reference \xrightarrow{m} ObjInfo$

$ObjInfo :: class \; : \; Id$
$\qquad\qquad\; \sigma \qquad : \; VarStore$
$\qquad\qquad\; mode \; : \; \text{READY} \mid Active$

$VarStore = Id \xrightarrow{m} Val$

$Val = \mathbb{Z} \mid \mathbb{B} \mid [Reference]$

The set *Reference* is infinite and $\text{nil} \notin Reference$.

$Active :: rem \quad : \; Stmt^*$
$\qquad\qquad client \; : \; [Reference]$

The types of the semantic relation/function are

$\xrightarrow{st} : \mathscr{P}((ClMap \times ObjMap) \times ObjMap)$

$eval : Expr \times VarStore \rightarrow Val$

D.2 Expressions

Abstract syntax

$Expr = ArithExpr \mid RelExpr \mid Id \mid Value \mid TestNil$

$$
\begin{array}{lll}
ArithExpr :: & operand1 & : Expr \\
& operator & : \text{PLUS} \\
& operand2 & : Expr
\end{array}
$$

$$
\begin{array}{lll}
RelExpr :: & operand1 & : Expr \\
& operator & : \text{EQUALS} \\
& operand2 & : Expr
\end{array}
$$

$TestNil :: object : Id$

$Value = \mathbb{Z} \mid \mathbb{B}$

Context conditions

The context conditions here are similar to those for the typed language (Appendix B) except that an additional parameter (*ctps*) carries the types of classes so that a check can be made that the argument to *TestNil* refers to an (instance) variable of type *Reference*; the result of applying *c-type* to a *TestNil* will of course be Boolean.

$c\text{-}type(mk\text{-}TestNil(id), ctps, v\text{-}env) \quad \triangle$
   if $v\text{-}env(id) \in \text{dom}\, ctps$ then BOOLTP else ERROR fi

Semantics

The semantics of *Expr* also broadly follows those for simpler languages because expression evaluation depends only on the local instance variables (cf. semantics of *Assign*) and method calls are disallowed within expressions.

$eval : Expr \times VarStore \rightarrow (\mathbb{Z} \mid \mathbb{B})$

The semantics of *TestNil* are:

$eval(mk\text{-}TestNil(id), \sigma) \quad \triangle \quad \sigma(id) = \text{nil}$

D.3 Statements

$Stmt = Assign \mid If \mid New \mid Discard \mid Activate \mid Call \mid Return \mid Await \mid Delegate$

D.3.1 Assignments

Remember that method calls cannot occur in an *Assign* — method invocation is covered in D.4.

Abstract syntax

$$Assign :: lhs : Id$$
$$rhs : Expr$$

Context conditions

$$wf\text{-}Stmt(mk\text{-}Assign(lhs,rhs),ctps,v\text{-}env,mtp) \quad \triangleq$$
$$lhs \in \text{dom } v\text{-}env \wedge$$
$$c\text{-}type(rhs,ctps,v\text{-}env) = v\text{-}env(lhs)$$

Semantics

$$robj = O(r)$$
$$mk\text{-}ObjInfo(cl,\sigma,mk\text{-}Active([mk\text{-}Assign(lhs,rhs)] \frown rl,k)) = robj$$
$$\underline{robj' = mk\text{-}ObjInfo(cl,\sigma \dagger \{lhs \mapsto eval(rhs,\sigma)\},mk\text{-}Active(rl,k))}$$
$$(C,O) \xrightarrow{st} O \dagger \{r \mapsto robj'\}$$

D.3.2 If statements

Abstract syntax

$$If \;::\; \begin{array}{ll} test & : \; Expr \\ then & : \; Stmt^* \\ else & : \; Stmt^* \end{array}$$

Context conditions

$$wf\text{-}Stmt(mk\text{-}If(test,th,el),ctps,v\text{-}env,mtp) \quad \triangle$$
$$c\text{-}type(test,ctps,v\text{-}env) = \text{BOOLT\textsc{p}} \land$$
$$\forall i \in \text{inds}\, th \cdot wf\text{-}Stmt(th(i),ctps,v\text{-}env,mtp) \land$$
$$\forall i \in \text{inds}\, el \cdot wf\text{-}Stmt(el(i),ctps,v\text{-}env,mtp)$$

Semantics

$$\begin{array}{c} robj = O(r) \\ mk\text{-}ObjInfo(cl,\sigma,mk\text{-}Active([mk\text{-}If(test,th,el)] \frown rl,k)) = robj \\ eval(test,\sigma) = \text{true} \\ robj' = mk\text{-}ObjInfo(cl,\sigma,mk\text{-}Active(th \frown rl,k)) \\ \hline (C,O) \xrightarrow{st} O \dagger \{r \mapsto robj'\} \end{array}$$

$$\begin{array}{c} robj = O(r) \\ mk\text{-}ObjInfo(cl,\sigma,mk\text{-}Active([mk\text{-}If(test,th,el)] \frown rl,k)) = robj \\ eval(test,\sigma) = \text{false} \\ robj' = mk\text{-}ObjInfo(cl,\sigma,mk\text{-}Active(el \frown rl,k)) \\ \hline (C,O) \xrightarrow{st} O \dagger \{r \mapsto robj'\} \end{array}$$

D.4 Methods

Abstract syntax

$$Meth :: \begin{array}{ll} result\text{-}type & : \ [Type] \\ params & : \ Id^* \\ paramtypes & : \ Id \xrightarrow{m} Type \\ body & : \ Stmt^* \end{array}$$

Context conditions

$$wf\text{-}Meth : Meth \times ClTypes \times VarEnv \to \mathbb{B}$$

$$wf\text{-}Meth(mk\text{-}Meth(rtp, ps, ptpm, body), ctps, v\text{-}env) \quad \triangleq$$
$$(rtp = \mathsf{nil} \vee rtp \in ScType \vee rtp \in \mathsf{dom}\, ctps) \wedge$$
$$(\forall id \in \mathsf{dom}\, ptpm \cdot ptpm(id) \in ScType \vee ptpm(id) \in \mathsf{dom}\, ctps) \wedge$$
$$uniquel(ps) \wedge$$
$$\mathsf{elems}\, ps \subseteq \mathsf{dom}\, ptpm \wedge$$
$$\forall i \in \mathsf{inds}\, body \cdot wf\text{-}Stmt(body(i), ctps, v\text{-}env \dagger ptpm, rtp)$$

The definition of *uniquel* is given in Chapter 2.

There are no semantics for methods as such — see the semantics of *Call* etc. below.

D.4.1 *Activate method*

Abstract syntax

$$Activate :: \begin{array}{llll} object & : & Id \\ method & : & Id \\ arguments & : & Expr^* \end{array}$$

Context conditions

$$wf\text{-}Stmt(mk\text{-}Activate(obj, meth, args), ctps, v\text{-}env, mtp) \quad \triangle$$
$$obj \in \mathsf{dom}\ v\text{-}env \land$$
$$v\text{-}env(obj) \in Id \land v\text{-}env(obj) \in \mathsf{dom}\ ctps \land$$
$$meth \in \mathsf{dom}\ (ctps(v\text{-}env(obj))) \land$$
$$\left(\begin{array}{l} \mathsf{let}\ mk\text{-}MethInfo(rtp, pts) = (ctps(v\text{-}env(obj)))(meth)\ \mathsf{in} \\ \mathsf{len}\ args = \mathsf{len}\ pts \land \\ \forall i \in \mathsf{inds}\ args \cdot c\text{-}type(args(i), ctps, v\text{-}env) = pts(i) \end{array} \right)$$

Semantics

$$cobj = O(c)$$
$$mk\text{-}ObjInfo(cl_c, \sigma_c,$$
$$\qquad mk\text{-}Active([mk\text{-}Activate(obj, meth, args)] \frown rl_c, k)) = cobj$$
$$cobj' = mk\text{-}ObjInfo(cl_c, \sigma_c, mk\text{-}Active(rl_c, k))$$
$$sobj = O(\sigma_c(obj))$$
$$mk\text{-}ObjInfo(cl_s, \sigma_s, \text{READY}) = sobj$$
$$mk\text{-}Class(vars, meths) = C(cl_s)$$
$$mk\text{-}Meth(rtp, params, paramtps, body) = meths(meth)$$
$$\sigma_s' = \sigma_s \dagger \{params(i) \mapsto eval(args(i), \sigma_c) \mid i \in \mathsf{inds}\ args\}$$
$$sobj' = mk\text{-}ObjInfo(cl_s, \sigma_s', mk\text{-}Active(body, c))$$
$$\overline{(C, O) \xrightarrow{st} O \dagger \{c \mapsto cobj', \sigma_c(obj) \mapsto sobj'\}}$$

D.4.2 Call method

Abstract syntax

$$Call :: \ lhs \qquad : Id$$
$$object \quad : Id$$
$$method \quad : Id$$
$$arguments : Expr^*$$

Context conditions

$$wf\text{-}Stmt(mk\text{-}Call(lhs,obj,meth,args),ctps,v\text{-}env,mtp) \quad \triangleq$$
$$lhs \in \text{dom } v\text{-}env \wedge$$
$$obj \in \text{dom } v\text{-}env \wedge$$
$$v\text{-}env(obj) \in Id \wedge v\text{-}env(obj) \in \text{dom } ctps \wedge$$
$$meth \in \text{dom } (ctps(v\text{-}env(obj))) \wedge$$
$$\left(\begin{array}{l} \text{let } mk\text{-}MethInfo(rtp,pts) = (ctps(v\text{-}env(obj)))(meth) \text{ in} \\ rtp \neq \text{nil} \wedge \\ \text{len } args = \text{len } pts \wedge \\ \forall i \in \text{inds } args \cdot c\text{-}type(args(i),ctps,v\text{-}env) = pts(i) \end{array} \right)$$

Semantics

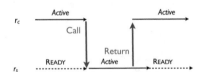

$$cobj = O(c)$$
$$mk\text{-}ObjInfo(cl_c, \sigma_c,$$
$$\qquad mk\text{-}Active([mk\text{-}Call(lhs,obj,meth,args)] \frown rl_c, k)) = cobj$$
$$cobj' = mk\text{-}ObjInfo(cl_c, \sigma_c, mk\text{-}Active([mk\text{-}Await(lhs)] \frown rl_c, k))$$
$$sobj = O(\sigma_c(obj))$$
$$mk\text{-}ObjInfo(cl_s, \sigma_s, \text{READY}) = sobj$$
$$mk\text{-}Class(vars, meths) = C(cl_s)$$
$$mk\text{-}Meth(rtp, params, paramtps, body) = meths(meth)$$
$$\sigma_s' = \sigma_s \dagger \{params(i) \mapsto eval(args(i), \sigma_c) \mid i \in \text{inds } args\}$$
$$\underline{sobj' = mk\text{-}ObjInfo(cl_s, \sigma_s', mk\text{-}Active(body, c))}$$
$$(C,O) \xrightarrow{st} O \dagger \{c \mapsto cobj', \sigma_c(obj) \mapsto sobj'\}$$

D.4.3 **Rendezvous**

An *Await* in a client thread should be matched with a *Return* in a server. (But, if no result is to be passed back, the server thread just completes the code of the method.)

Abstract syntax

Return :: *value* : *Expr*

Await :: *lhs* : *Id*

Context conditions

$$wf\text{-}Stmt(mk\text{-}Return(val), ctps, v\text{-}env, mtp) \quad \triangle \quad c\text{-}type(val) = mtp$$

Semantics

$$sobj = O(s)$$
$$mk\text{-}ObjInfo(cl_s, \sigma_s, mk\text{-}Active([mk\text{-}Return(e)] \curvearrowright rl_s, c)) = sobj$$
$$sobj' = mk\text{-}ObjInfo(cl_s, \sigma_s, mk\text{-}Active(rl_s, \text{nil}))$$
$$cobj = O(c)$$
$$mk\text{-}ObjInfo(cl_c, \sigma_c, mk\text{-}Active([mk\text{-}Await(lhs)] \curvearrowright rl_c, k)) = cobj$$
$$\frac{cobj' = mk\text{-}ObjInfo(cl_c, \sigma_c \dagger \{lhs \mapsto eval(e, \sigma_s)\}, mk\text{-}Active(rl_c, k))}{(C, O) \xrightarrow{st} O \dagger \{s \mapsto sobj', c \mapsto cobj'\}}$$

D.4.4 Method termination

When a method has no more statements to execute, it returns to quiescent status.

$$\frac{O(s) = mk\text{-}ObjInfo(cl, \sigma, mk\text{-}Active([\,], k))}{(C, O) \xrightarrow{st} O \dagger \{s \mapsto mk\text{-}ObjInfo(cl, \sigma, \text{READY})\}}$$

D.4.5 Delegation

Delegation invokes a method in another object and passes on the responsibility to return a value to its client.

Abstract syntax

$$Delegate \ :: \ object \quad : \ Id$$
$$method \quad : \ Id$$
$$arguments \ : \ Id^*$$

Context conditions

$$wf\text{-}Stmt(mk\text{-}Delegate(obj, meth, args), ctps, v\text{-}env, mtp) \quad \triangle$$
$$obj \in \mathsf{dom}\, v\text{-}env \land$$
$$v\text{-}env(obj) \in Id \land v\text{-}env(obj) \in \mathsf{dom}\, ctps \land$$
$$meth \in \mathsf{dom}\,(ctps(v\text{-}env(obj))) \land$$
$$\left(\begin{array}{l} \mathsf{let}\ mk\text{-}MethInfo(rtp, pts) = (ctps(v\text{-}env(obj)))(meth)\ \mathsf{in} \\ rtp \neq \mathsf{nil} \land \\ \mathsf{len}\, args = \mathsf{len}\, pts \land \\ \forall i \in \mathsf{inds}\, args \cdot c\text{-}type(args(i), ctps, v\text{-}env) = pts(i) \end{array} \right)$$

Semantics

$sobj = O(s)$
$mk\text{-}ObjInfo(cl_s, \sigma_s,$
$\qquad\qquad mk\text{-}Active([mk\text{-}Delegate(obj, meth, args)] \curvearrowright rl_s, k)) = sobj$
$sobj' = mk\text{-}ObjInfo(cl_s, \sigma_s, mk\text{-}Active(rl_s, \mathsf{nil}))$
$tobj = O(\sigma_s(obj))$
$mk\text{-}ObjInfo(cl_t, \sigma_t, \text{READY}) = tobj$
$mk\text{-}Class(vars, meths) = C(cl_t)$
$mk\text{-}Meth(rtp, params, paramtps, body) = meths(meth)$
$\sigma'_t = \sigma_t \dagger \{params(i) \mapsto eval(args(i), \sigma_s) \mid i \in \mathsf{inds}\,args\}$
$tobj' = mk\text{-}ObjInfo(cl_t, \sigma'_t, mk\text{-}Active(body, k))$

$$(C, O) \xrightarrow{st} O \dagger \{s \mapsto sobj', \sigma_s(obj) \mapsto tobj'\}$$

D.5 Classes

Abstract syntax

$$Class :: \begin{array}{ll} vars & : Id \xrightarrow{m} Type \\ methods & : Id \xrightarrow{m} Meth \end{array}$$

Context conditions

$$wf\text{-}Class : Class \times ClTypes \to \mathbb{B}$$

$wf\text{-}Class(mk\text{-}Class(vars, meths), ctps) \;\triangleq$
$\qquad \forall tp \in \mathsf{rng}\,vars \cdot (tp \in ScType \lor tp \in \mathsf{dom}\,ctps) \land$
$\qquad \forall m \in \mathsf{rng}\,meths \cdot wf\text{-}Meth(m, ctps, vars)$

There are no semantics for classes as such — the semantics of *New* follows.

D.5.1 *Creating objects*

Abstract syntax

New :: $target$: Id

Context conditions

$wf\text{-}Stmt(mk\text{-}New(targ), ctps, v\text{-}env, mtp)$ $\triangle$
  $targ \in \mathsf{dom}\, v\text{-}env\, \wedge$
  $v\text{-}env(targ) \in Id$

Semantics

$robj = O(r)$
$mk\text{-}ObjInfo(cl_r, \sigma_r, mk\text{-}Active([mk\text{-}New(targ)] \frown rl, k)) = robj$
$n \in (Reference - \mathsf{dom}\, O)$
$robj' = mk\text{-}ObjInfo(cl_r, \sigma_r \dagger \{targ \mapsto n\}, mk\text{-}Active(rl, k))$
$cl_n = (C(cl_r).vars)(targ)$
$mk\text{-}Class(vars, meths) = C(cl_n)$
$\sigma_n =$
  $\{v \mapsto 0 \mid v \in \mathsf{dom}\, vars \wedge vars(v) = \textsc{IntTp}\} \cup$
  $\{v \mapsto \mathsf{false} \mid v \in \mathsf{dom}\, vars \wedge vars(v) = \textsc{BoolTp}\} \cup$
  $\{v \mapsto \mathsf{nil} \mid v \in \mathsf{dom}\, vars \wedge vars(v) \notin ScType\}$
$nobj = mk\text{-}ObjInfo(cl_n, \sigma_n, \textsc{Ready})$

$$(C, O) \xrightarrow{st} O \dagger \{r \mapsto robj', n \mapsto nobj\}$$

D.5.2 Discarding references

Abstract syntax

$Discard :: target : Id$

Context conditions

$wf\text{-}Stmt(mk\text{-}Discard(targ), ctps, v\text{-}env, mtp) \quad \triangle$
$\qquad targ \in \text{dom } v\text{-}env \wedge$
$\qquad v\text{-}env(targ) \in Id$

Semantics

$robj = O(r)$
$mk\text{-}ObjInfo(cl_r, \sigma_r, mk\text{-}Active([mk\text{-}Discard(targ)] \frown rl, k)) = robj$
$robj' = mk\text{-}ObjInfo(cl_r, \sigma_r \dagger \{targ \mapsto \text{nil}\}, mk\text{-}Active(rl, k))$
$$\overline{(C, O) \xrightarrow{st} O \dagger \{r \mapsto robj'\}}$$

D.6 Programs

Abstract syntax

$$CoolProgram \; :: \; \begin{array}{lll} class\text{-}map & : & ClMap \\ start\text{-}class & : & Id \\ start\text{-}method & : & Id \end{array}$$

$$ClMap = Id \xrightarrow{\;m\;} Class$$

Context conditions

$$wf\text{-}CoolProgram : CoolProgram \rightarrow \mathbb{B}$$

$wf\text{-}CoolProgram(mk\text{-}CoolProgram(cm, start\text{-}cl, start\text{-}m)) \quad \triangleq$
  $start\text{-}cl \in \mathrm{dom}\, cm \wedge$
  $start\text{-}m \in \mathrm{dom}\, (cm(start\text{-}cl).methods) \wedge$
  $\left(\begin{array}{l} \mathrm{let}\, ctps = \{c \mapsto c\text{-}clinfo(cm(c)) \mid c \in \mathrm{dom}\, cm\} \\ \mathrm{in}\; \forall c \in \mathrm{dom}\, ctps \cdot wf\text{-}Class(cm(c), ctps) \end{array} \right)$

The following two functions extract *ClInfo* and *MethInfo* respectively.

$$c\text{-}clinfo : Class \rightarrow ClInfo$$

$c\text{-}clinfo(mk\text{-}Class(tpm, mm)) \quad \triangleq \quad \{m \mapsto c\text{-}minfo(mm(m)) \mid m \in \mathrm{dom}\, mm\}$

$$c\text{-}minfo : Meth \rightarrow MethInfo$$

$c\text{-}minfo(mk\text{-}Meth(ret, pnl, ptm, body)) \quad \triangleq$
  $mk\text{-}MethInfo(ret, apply(pnl, ptm))$

$$apply : X^* \times (X \xrightarrow{\;m\;} Y) \rightarrow Y^*$$

$apply(l, m) \quad \triangleq$
  $\mathrm{if}\; l = []$
  $\mathrm{then}\; []$
  $\mathrm{else}\; [m(\mathrm{hd}\, l)] \frown apply(\mathrm{tl}\, l, m)$
  fi

Semantics

For $mk\text{-}CoolProgram(cm, cl_0, meth_0)$, the semantics creates an *ObjMap* containing an *ObjInfo* for cl_0 and activates $meth_0$ with an empty argument list.

Appendix E
VDM notation

E.1 Logical operators

The logical operators and quantifiers are written as follows:

$$\mathbb{B} \qquad \{\text{true}, \text{false}\}$$
$$\neg E \qquad \text{negation (not)}$$
$$E_1 \wedge E_2 \qquad \text{conjunction (and)}$$
$$\qquad \qquad E_1, E_2 \text{ are conjuncts}$$
$$E_1 \vee E_2 \qquad \text{disjunction (or)}$$
$$\qquad \qquad E_1, E_2 \text{ are disjuncts}$$
$$E_1 \Rightarrow E_2 \quad \text{implication}$$
$$\qquad \qquad E_1 \text{ antecedent}, E_2 \text{ consequent}$$
$$E_1 \Leftrightarrow E_2 \quad \text{equivalence}$$
$$\forall x \in S \cdot E \quad \text{universal quantification}$$
$$\exists x \in S \cdot E \quad \text{existential quantification}$$

The Logic of Partial Functions (LPF) copes with values that fail to denote:

a	b	$\neg a$	$a \wedge b$	$a \vee b$	$a \Rightarrow b$	$a \Leftrightarrow b$
true	true	false	true	true	true	true
*	true	*	*	true	true	*
false	true	true	false	true	true	false
true	*		*	true	*	*
*	*		*	*	*	*
false	*		false	*	true	*
true	false		false	true	false	false
*	false		false	*	*	*
false	false		false	false	true	true

© Springer Nature Switzerland AG 2020
C. B. Jones, *Understanding Programming Languages*,
https://doi.org/10.1007/978-3-030-59257-8

E.2 Set notation

The symbols used in VDM for the operators of set theory are:

T-set	all finite subsets of T
$\{t_1, t_2, \ldots, t_n\}$	set enumeration
$\{\}$	empty set
$\mathbb{B}$	$\{\mathsf{true}, \mathsf{false}\}$
$\mathbb{N}$	$\{0, \cdots\}$
$\mathbb{Z}$	$\{\cdots, -1, 0, 1, \cdots\}$
$\{x \in S \mid p(x)\}$	set comprehension
$\{i, \cdots, j\}$	subset of integers (from i to j inclusive)
$t \in S$	set membership
$t \notin S$	$\neg(t \in S)$
$S_1 \subseteq S_2$	set containment (subset of)
$S_1 \subset S_2$	strict set containment
$S_1 \cap S_2$	set intersection
$S_1 \cup S_2$	set union
$S_1 - S_2$	set difference
card S	cardinality (size) of a set
$\mathscr{P}(X)$	power set

The following pictorial representation of the set operators can be a useful reminder of their signatures. The ovals contain the names of types; operators are marked with incoming arcs indicating the types of their operands and an outgoing arc indicating the type of the result.

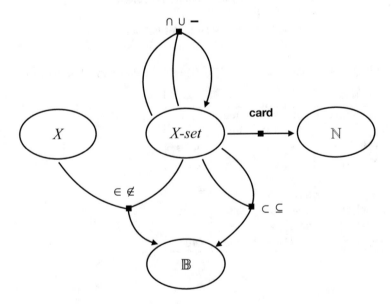

E.3 List (sequence) notation

The symbols used in VDM for the operators of sequence theory are:

T^* type defining finite sequences (elements are of type T)
len s length of a sequence
$[t_1, t_2, \ldots, t_n]$ sequence given by enumeration
$[]$ the empty sequence
$s_1 \frown s_2$ sequence concatenation
hd s the element at the head of a sequence
tl s the sequence comprising the tail of a sequence
inds s the set of indexes to a sequence
elems s the set of elements in a sequence

The pictorial representation of the sequence operators is:

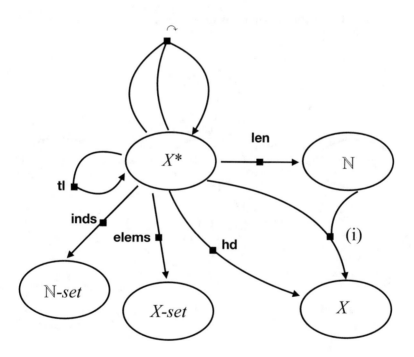

E.4 Map notation

The symbols used in VDM for the operators of map theory are:

$D \xrightarrow{m} R$	finite maps from D to R
dom m	domain of a map
rng m	range of a map
$m(d)$	map application
$\{d_1 \mapsto r_1, d_2 \mapsto r_2, \ldots, d_n \mapsto r_n\}$	map enumeration
$\{\mapsto\}$	empty map
$\{d \mapsto f(d) \in D \times R \mid p(d)\}$	map defined by comprehension
$m_1 \dagger m_2$	map overwrite
$m_1 \cup m_2$	map union
$s \triangleleft m$	domain restriction of a map
$s \triangleleft\!\!\!- m$	domain deletion of a map

The pictorial representation of the map operators is:

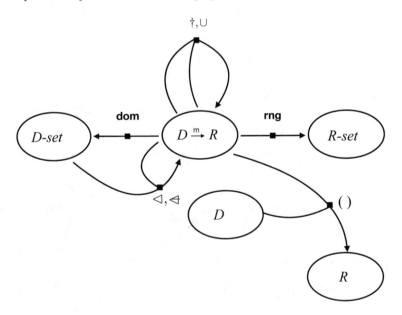

E.5 Record notation

::	record
mk-N(…)	generator
$o.s_1$	selector
$[Type]$	optional
nil	omitted object
$\mu(o, s_1 \mapsto t)$	modify a component

Each record definition gives distinct selector and constructor functions. For:

$$Program :: \quad vars \ : \ Id \xrightarrow{m} Type$$
$$body \ : \ Stmt^*$$

the pictorial representation of its types would be:

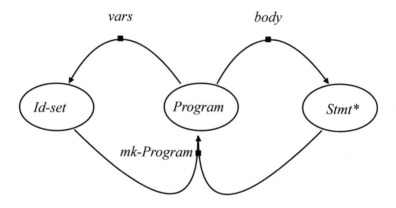

E.6 Function notation

$f: D_1 \times D_2 \to R$	signature
$f(d)$	application
if $\cdots$ then $\cdots$ else $\cdots$	conditional
let $x = \cdots$ in $\cdots$	local definition

$f \ (d:D) \ r:R$

pre $\cdots d \cdots$

post $\cdots d \cdots r \cdots$

Appendix F
Notes on influential people

This appendix contains brief notes about the main people who have played a part in the development of formal semantics and are mentioned in the body of the book. The notes are not intended to be biographies and are limited to facts related to the subject of this book. A more historical account of many of the interactions between these players can be found in [Ast19].

Hans Bekič   (1936–1982) Unlike the majority of his colleagues at the IBM Laboratory in Vienna, who were engineers, Bekič was a mathematician. He worked with Lucas on an early ALGOL 60 compiler and then on the 1960s VDL (operational) semantics of PL/I. He spent a year in London working with Peter Landin and this put him in a position where he encouraged the move towards denotational description methods for VDM. As well as his role in developing and co-authoring the VDM semantics of PL/I [BBH$^+$74], Bekič was making seminal contributions to concurrency before his untimely death. A collection of his papers was published posthumously as [BJ84].

Robert W. Floyd   (1936–2001) Bob Floyd made many contributions to the theoretical side of computing (see [Knu03] for a fitting tribute). One of his significant contributions to research on semantics was [Flo67], which provides a clear account of one way of verifying programs. Floyd's approach was predicated on flowcharts but the cited paper had a major influence on Hoare's [Hoa69], which, in turn, is the foundation stone of 50 years of productive research on the formal development of programs.

Charles Antony Richard Hoare   (b. 1934) Tony Hoare has made many key contributions to the theory of computing and has also been involved in seeing that theoretical ideas are transferred to practical applications. The major semantic avenue discussed in Section 7.3 derives from his paper [Hoa69] on "Axiomatic semantics". Hoare has tackled the search for unification of the various approaches to semantics (see [HH98]). His contributions have been recognised by the ACM Turing Award in 1983, the Kyoto Prize in 2000, two "Queen's Awards to Industry" and numerous honorary degrees. There are recorded video interviews on the ACM web site for many Turing Laureates — that for Hoare is available at:

© Springer Nature Switzerland AG 2020   207
C. B. Jones, *Understanding Programming Languages*,
https://doi.org/10.1007/978-3-030-59257-8

https://amturing.acm.org/interviews/hoare_4622167.cfm

Two *Festschriften* are [Ros94, JRW10] and a selection of his papers up to 1989 is contained in [HJ89].

Peter John Landin   (1930–2009) Peter Landin noted the link between programming languages and Church's Lambda Calculus in [Lan65a, Lan65b]; he also spoke on the subject at the 1964 "Formal Language Description Languages" conference at Baden bei Wien (Landin's paper is printed as [Lan66b] and a masterful overview of the approaches presented is [Ste66, p. 290]). His [Lan66a] is a classic paper. Together with Rod Burstall, Landin went on to consider algebraic approaches to reasoning about language descriptions.

Peter Lauer   (b. 1934) Peter Lauer was a member of the IBM Laboratory in Vienna. His interests were more philosophical than most members of the group. Two key points of contact with the material in the current book are his VDL description of ALGOL 60 [Lau68] (undertaken to show that it was the PL/I language that gave rise to the huge size of its description — not the VDL method) and his Ph.D. research supervised by Tony Hoare that showed that the axioms of a language were consistent with an underlying operational semantics [Lau71a, HL74].

Peter Lucas   (1935–2015) was one of the original members of the IBM Laboratory in Vienna. He wrote an early ALGOL 60 compiler together with Bekič and then became a key member of the team that wrote three versions of the VDL (operational) description of PL/I in the 1960s. See [LW69, Luc71]. Importantly, he then started to consider how such a description could be used as the basis from which to design compiling algorithms. He championed the idea of identifying "language concepts" that he hoped could be considered separately. A key output from this was his "twin machine" argument which was used to justify implementations of the "block concept" (locating the correct instance of an identifier with nested blocks, procedure calls etc.). References to this research include [Luc68, JL70] — Lucas managed one of the IBM Vienna groups working on the 1970s PL/I compiler and is a co-author of the VDM (denotational) semantics of PL/I [BBH$^+$74]. He left the Vienna Lab to move to IBM Research in the USA.

John McCarthy   (1927–2011) is best known as a father of Artificial Intelligence (AI) research. He did, however, also make significant contributions to formal description of programming languages: his [McC66] paper was presented at the 1964 *Formal Language Description Languages* working conference at Baden bei Wien. This paper presented a clear case for operational semantic descriptions using "Micro-ALGOL" as an example. His work on AI and formal approaches to computing coalesced in his research on support for theorem proving.

Arthur John Robin Gorell Milner   (1934–2010) Robin Milner made many important contributions to computer science including LCF [GMW79] (which influenced nearly all subsequent theorem proving assistants), Type inference and the ML programming language [HMT87]. His study of process algebras created CCS and the π-calculus. Plotkin gives credit to Milner for the way that semantics can be presented using inference rules. Milner's Turing award acceptance speech is printed as [Mil93]. A *Festschrift* in his honour is [PST00].

Peter David Mosses   (b. 1948) Peter Mosses undertook his doctoral studies with Strachey in Oxford. His thesis [Mos75] on "SIS" showed that a denotational semantics could be used to generate a prototype compiler for a language. In parallel with this research he produced one of the descriptions of ALGOL 60 [Mos74] that is discussed in [JA16]. He continued these interests with research into semantics with "Action Semantics" [Mos92], "Modular Operational Semantics" [Mos04] and attempts to build tools for compiler generation [BSM16].

John von Neumann   (1903–1957) is, of course, a legendary figure in computing and mathematics — "von Neumann architecture" is a standard phrase. The specific interest in him in this book is his use of annotations of flowcharts in [GvN47].

Gordon David Plotkin   (b. 1946) Gordon Plotkin has made many contributions to theoretical topics including "power domains" [Plo76]. The huge debt that this book owes to Plotkin's work is however "Structural Operational Semantics" which he used in his Aarhus lectures in 1981 — thankfully the lecture notes were republished as [Plo04b].

Dana Stewart Scott   (b. 1932) Dana Scott received (together with Michael Rabin) the ACM Turing Award in 1976 — see [Sco77]. The obvious link from the current book to Dana Scott is his fundamental contribution to –what became known as– "Denotational Semantics". Scott met Strachey at the April 1969 IFIP WG 2.2 meeting in Vienna and was so impressed by the latter's insights into programming languages that he immediately arranged to extend his stay in Europe and spend the last part of 1969 in Oxford with Strachey. (Scott had previously worked with Jaco de Bakker in Amsterdam — see [dBS69], which was presented during a visit to the IBM Lab in Vienna in August 1969.) Scott initially warned that the untyped Lambda calculus lacked foundations but then found models that gave birth to a whole research direction. Most of the original material was reported as monographs of the Oxford "Programming Research Group" — an accessible account is [Sco80] and Stoy's [Sto77] provides insight into this exciting period of research.

Christopher S. Strachey   (1916–75) Strachey formed and led the *Programming Research Group* at Oxford University. He wrote many wise words about programming languages (e.g. [Str67, Str73]), was a co-designer of the CPL language [BBHS63] and led the way to what became the denotational approach to language description (e.g. [Str66]). Towards the end of his life, Strachey wrote (together with Robert Milne) a submission to the Cambridge University *Adams Essay Prize*; after Strachey's untimely death, Milne completed this as [MS76]. Martin Campbell-Kelly wrote a wonderful survey of Strachey's life and achievements [CK85]. Interesting videos of the speakers and panel discussion from a conference to mark the hundredth anniversary of Strachey's birth are online at: http://podcasts.ox.ac.uk/series/strachey-100-oxford-computing-pioneer

Joe E. Stoy   (b. 1943) Joe Stoy was a key figure in the Oxford "Programming Research Group" who went on to co-found "Bluespec Inc.". In his time at Oxford he was a contributor to the development of what became known as "Denotational Semantics" and authored the classic reference on the subject [Sto77]. After Strachey's untimely death, Stoy held the group together and provided the foundation for the arrival of Tony Hoare.

Alan Mathison Turing   (1912–1954) Alan Turing's important contributions are well documented — a perfect biography was provided by Andrew Hodges and little that has been written since comes close to the insight in [Hod83]. Despite the fundamental nature of [Tur36], the link to the current material is Turing's three-page [Tur49]. ACM's most prestigious award is, of course, named after Alan Turing.

Adriaan van Wijngaarden   (1916–1987) Aad van Wijngaarden was a Dutch mathematician who both transitioned to computing and became the father of Dutch computer science. To his credit are his contributions to ALGOL 60; more controversial was his spearheading of the ALGOL 68 effort. His paper [vW66a] tackled the messy issue of reasoning about computer arithmetic (where finite representations of even integers do not match Peano's natural numbers) — this paper was cited and used in [Hoa69].

Niklaus Emil Wirth   (b. 1934) Niklaus Wirth is undoubtedly one of the most influential and successful designers of programming languages (and, in fact, systems including hardware). Landmark languages include ALGOL W, Pascal, the Modula series of languages and Oberon. A video of his Turing Award lecture is available at:[1]

https://amturing.acm.org/interviews/wirth_1025774.cfm

A lovely book noting his contributions and superb taste is [BGP00]. Two of his own influential books are [Wir73, Wir76] and he is also a co-author of [DDH72].

Heinz Zemanek   (1920–2014) Heinz Zemanek founded the IBM Laboratory in Vienna and led it through the early research on VDL — the operational descriptions of PL/I. Trained as an electrical engineer, he became a leader who furthered the careers of his many colleagues. One notable contribution that relates to the subject matter of the current book was his hosting of the Baden bei Wien IFIP Working Conference on "Formal Language Description Languages". His own interests moved more into philosophy and his energy into international affairs including the IFIP organisation. A tribute to Zemanek is contained in [FCSR15].

---

[1] Towards the end of this useful interview, Wirth says: "My idea was that programming languages allow programming on a higher level of abstraction compared to machine coding. You can abstract specific properties and facilities of a specific machine. You can abstract to a higher level and create programs that will then be available and runnable on all computers. That's called abstraction. And the term "higher-level languages" comes exactly from that. ...Look at today's situation. People program in C++, the worst disease ever created. Or C# or Java, which are a bit better. But they all suffer from their mightiness. I'm always expecting they're going to collapse under their own weight."

References

[A+97]   Samson Abramsky et al. Semantics of interaction: an introduction to game semantics. *Semantics and Logics of Computation*, 14(1):1–32, 1997.

[AB87]   Bijan Arbab and Daniel M Berry. Operational and denotational semantics of Prolog. *The Journal of Logic Programming*, 4(4):309–329, 1987.

[Abr96]   J.-R. Abrial. *The B-Book: Assigning Programs to Meanings*. Cambridge University Press, 1996.

[Abr10]   J.-R. Abrial. *The Event-B Book*. Cambridge University Press, Cambridge, UK, 2010.

[Abr13]   Samson Abramsky. Semantics of interaction. *arXiv preprint arXiv:1312.0121*, 2013.

[AC12]   Martin Abadi and Luca Cardelli. *A Theory of Objects*. Springer-Verlag, 2012.

[ACJ72]   C. D. Allen, D. N. Chapman, and C. B. Jones. A formal definition of ALGOL 60. Technical Report 12.105, IBM Laboratory Hursley, 8 1972.

[Acz82]   P. H. G. Aczel. A note on program verification. (private communication) Manuscript, Manchester, 1 1982.

[AdB91]   Pierre America and Frank S. de Boer. *A proof theory for a sequential version of POOL*. CWI, Nationaal Instituut voor Onderzoek op het gebied van Wiskunde en Informatica, 1991.

[AdBKR89]   Pierre America, Jaco de Bakker, Joost N Kok, and Jan Rutten. Denotational semantics of a parallel object-oriented language. *Information and Computation*, 83(2):152–205, 1989.

[AGLP88]   D.J. Andrews, A. Garg, S.P.A. Lau, and J.R. Pitchers. The formal definition of Modula-2 and its associated interpreter. In Robin E. Bloomfield, Lynn S. Marshall, and Roger B. Jones, editors, *VDM '88 VDM — The Way Ahead*, volume 328 of *Lecture Notes in Computer Science*, pages 167–177. Springer-Verlag, 1988.

[AH82]   Derek Andrews and Wolfgang Henhapl. Pascal. In Bjørner and Jones [BJ82], chapter 6, pages 175–252.

[AJ18]   Troy K. Astarte and Cliff B. Jones. Formal semantics of ALGOL 60: Four descriptions in their historical context. In Liesbeth De Mol and Giuseppe Primiero, editors, *Reflections on Programming Systems - Historical and Philosophical Aspects*, pages 71–141. Springer Philosophical Studies Series, 2018.

[Ame89]   P. America. Issues in the design of a parallel object-oriented language. *Formal Aspects of Computing*, 1(4):366–411, 1989.

[And92]   James H. Andrews. *Logic Programming: Operational Semantics and Proof Theory*. Distinguished Dissertations in Computer Science. Cambridge, 1992.

[ANS76]   ANSI. Programming language PL/I. Technical Report X3.53-1976, American National Standard, 1976.

[AO19]   Krzysztof R. Apt and Ernst-Rüdiger Olderog. Fifty years of Hoare's logic. *Formal Aspects of Computing*, 31(6):751–807, 2019.

© Springer Nature Switzerland AG 2020

C. B. Jones, *Understanding Programming Languages*,

https://doi.org/10.1007/978-3-030-59257-8

[Apt81]   Krzysztof R. Apt. Ten years of Hoare's logic: a survey—part I. *ACM Transactions on Programming Languages and Systems*, 3(4):431–483, 10 1981.

[AR92]   Pierre America and Jan Rutten. A layered semantics for a parallel object-oriented language. *Formal Aspects of Computing*, 4(4):376–408, 1992.

[ASS85]   Harold Abelson, Gerald Jay Sussman, and Julie Sussman. *Structure and Interpretation of Computer Programs*. MIT Press, 1985.

[Ast19]   Troy K. Astarte. *Formalising Meaning: a History of Programming Language Semantics*. PhD thesis, Newcastle University, 6 2019.

[BA90]   Mordechai Ben-Ari. *Principles of Concurrent and Distributed Programming*. Prentice Hall International Series in Computer Science. Prentice Hall, 1990.

[BA06]   Mordechai Ben-Ari. *Principles of Concurrent and Distributed Programming*. Pearson Education, 2006.

[Bac78]   John Backus. Can programming be liberated from the Von Neumann style?: A functional style and its algebra of programs. *Communications of the ACM*, 21(8):613–641, August 1978.

[Bae90]   J. C. M. Baeten, editor. *Applications of Process Algebra*. Cambridge University Press, 1990.

[Bar06]   John Barnes. *High Integrity Software: The SPARK Approach to Safety and Security*. Addison-Wesley, 2006.

[BBG$^+$60] John W. Backus, Friedrich L. Bauer, Julien Green, Charles Katz, John McCarthy, Peter Naur, Alan J. Perlis, Heinz Rutishauser, Klaus Samelson, Bernard Vauquois, et al. Report on the algorithmic language ALGOL 60. *Numerische Mathematik*, 2(1):106–136, 1960.

[BBG$^+$63] John W. Backus, Friedrich L. Bauer, Julien Green, Charles Katz, John McCarthy, Peter Naur, Alan J. Perlis, Heinz Rutishauser, Klaus Samelson, Bernard Vauquois, Joseph H. Wegstein, Adriaan van Wijngaarden, and Michael Woodger. Revised report on the algorithmic language ALGOL 60. *The Computer Journal*, 5(4):349–367, 1963.

[BBG$^+$68] Henry Bauer, Sheldon Becker, Susan L Graham, Edwin Satterthwaite, and Richard L Sites. Algol W language description. Technical Report CS89, Computer Science Dept., Stanford Univ, 1968.

[BBH$^+$74] Hans Bekič, Dines Bjørner, Wolfgang Henhapl, Cliff B. Jones, and Peter Lucas. A formal definition of a PL/I subset. Technical Report 25.139, IBM Laboratory Vienna, 12 1974.

[BBHS63]   D. W. Barron, J. N. Buxton, D. F. Hartley, and C. Strachey. The main features of CPL. *Computer Journal*, 6(2):134–143, 1963.

[BCJ84]   H. Barringer, J.H. Cheng, and C. B. Jones. A logic covering undefinedness in program proofs. *Acta Informatica*, 21(3):251–269, 1984.

[Bek64]   Hans Bekič. Defining a language in its own terms. Technical Report 25.3.016, IBM Laboratory Vienna, 12 1964.

[Bek73]   Hans Bekič. An introduction to ALGOL 68. *Annual Review in Automatic Programming*, 7:143–169, 1973. Hard copy.

[Bey09]   Kurt W. Beyer. *Grace Hopper and the Invention of the Information Age*. The MIT Press, 2009.

[BG96]   Thomas J. Bergin and Richard G. Gibson, editors. *History of Programming Languages—II*. ACM Press, New York, NY, USA, 1996.

[BGP00]   László Böszörményi, Jürg Gutknecht, and Gustav Pomberger, editors. *The School of Niklaus Wirth: the art of simplicity*. dpunkt. verlag, 2000.

[BH73]   P. Brinch Hansen. *Operating System Principles*. Prentice Hall Series in Automatic Computation. Prentice Hall, 1973.

[BHG87]   P. A. Bernstein, V. Hadzilacos, and N. Goodman. *Concurrency Control and Recovery in Database Systems*. Addison-Wesley, 1987.

[BHJ20]   Alan Burns, Ian J. Hayes, and Cliff B. Jones. Deriving specifications of control programs for cyber physical systems. *The Computer Journal*, 63(5):774–790, 2020.

[BHR84]   Stephen Brookes, Charles Anthony Richard Hoare, and Andrew William Roscoe. A theory of communicating sequential processes. *Journal of the ACM*, 31(3):560–599, 7 1984.

[BIJW75]   H. Bekič, H. Izbicki, C. B. Jones, and F. Weissenböck. Some experiments with using a formal language definition in compiler development. Laboratory Note LN 25.3.107, IBM Laboratory, Vienna, 12 1975.

[BJ78]   D. Bjørner and C. B. Jones, editors. *The Vienna Development Method: The Meta-Language*, volume 61 of *Lecture Notes in Computer Science*. Springer-Verlag, 1978.

[BJ82]   Dines Bjørner and Cliff B. Jones, editors. *Formal Specification and Software Development*. Prentice Hall International, 1982.

[BJ84]   Hans Bekič and Cliff B. Jones. *Programming Languages and Their Definition: Hans Bekič (1936-1982). Selected papers*, volume 177 of *Lecture Notes in Computer Science*. Springer-Verlag, 1984.

[Bla86]   Stephen Blamey. *Partial-Valued logic*. PhD thesis, University of Oxford, 1986.

[Bli81]   Andrzej J. Blikle. On the development of correct specified programs. *IEEE Transactions on Software Engineering*, 7(5):519–527, 1981.

[Bli88]   A. Blikle. Three-valued predicates for software specification and validation. In R. Bloomfield, L. Marshall, and R. Jones, editors, *VDM—The Way Ahead*, volume 328 of *Lecture Notes in Computer Science*, pages 243–266. Springer-Verlag, 1988.

[BM81]   R. S. Boyer and J. S. Moore. *The Correctness Problem in Computer Science*. International Lecture Series in Computer Science. Academic Press, London, 1981.

[BO80a]   D. Bjørner and O. N. Oest, editors. *The DDC Ada Compiler Development Project*, chapter 0. Volume 98 of Bjørner and Oest [BO80b], 1980.

[BO80b]   D. Bjørner and O. N. Oest, editors. *Towards a Formal Description of Ada*, volume 98 of *Lecture Notes in Computer Science*. Springer-Verlag, Berlin, 1980.

[BSM16]   L Binsbergen, Neil Sculthorpe, and Peter D Mosses. Tool support for component-based semantics. In *Companion Proceedings of the 15th International Conference on Modularity*, pages 8–11. ACM, 2016.

[BvW98]   Ralph-Johan Back and Joakim von Wright. *Refinement Calculus: A Systematic Introduction*. Springer-Verlag, 1998.

[BW71]   H. Bekič and K. Walk. Formalization of storage properties. In E. Engeler, editor, *[Eng71]*, pages 28–61. Springer-Verlag, 1971.

[CDD⁺15]   Cristiano Calcagno, Dino Distefano, Jeremy Dubreil, Dominik Gabi, Pieter Hooimeijer, Martino Luca, Peter O'Hearn, Irene Papakonstantinou, Jim Purbrick, and Dulma Rodriguez. Moving fast with software verification. In *NASA Formal Methods*, volume 9058 of *Lecture Notes in Computer Science*, pages 3–11. Springer International Publishing, 2015.

[CDG⁺89]   Luca Cardelli, James Donahue, Lucille Glassman, Mick Jordan, Bill Kalsow, and Greg Nelson. Modula-3 report (revised). Technical report, DEC SRC, 1989.

[CH72]   Maurice Clint and C. A. R. Hoare. Program proving: Jumps and functions. *Acta Informatica*, 1(3):214–224, 1972.

[CH79]   Derek Coleman and Jane W. Hughes. The clean termination of Pascal programs. *Acta Informatica*, 11(3):195–210, 1979.

[Chu41]   A. Church. *The Calculi of Lambda-Conversion*. Princeton University Press, 1941.

[CJ91]   J. H. Cheng and C. B. Jones. On the usability of logics which handle partial functions. In C. Morgan and J. C. P. Woodcock, editors, *3rd Refinement Workshop*, pages 51–69. Springer-Verlag, 1991.

[CJ00]   Pierre Collette and Cliff B. Jones. Enhancing the tractability of rely/guarantee specifications in the development of interfering operations. In Gordon Plotkin, Colin Stirling, and Mads Tofte, editors, *Proof, Language and Interaction*, chapter 10, pages 277–307. MIT Press, 2000.

[CK85]   Martin Campbell-Kelly. Christopher Strachey, 1916-1975: A biographical note. *IEEE Annals of the History of Computing*, 1(7):19–42, 1985.

[Coo18]   Byron Cook. Formal reasoning about the security of Amazon Web Services. In *International Conference on Computer Aided Verification*, pages 38–47. Springer-Verlag, 2018.

[Dat82]   C. J. Date. A formal definition of the relational model. *ACM Sigmod Record*, 13(1):18–29, 1982.

[Dav65a]   Martin Davis. *Computability and Undecidability*. Dover, 1965.

[Dav65b]   Martin Davis, editor. *The Undecidable*. Raven Press, 1965.

[dB91]   Frank de Boer. A proof system for the language POOL. In J.W. de Bakker, W.P. de Roever, and G. Rozenberg, editors, *Foundations of Object-Oriented Languages*, volume 489 of *Lecture Notes in Computer Science*, pages 124–150. Springer-Verlag, 1991.

[dBS69]   J. W. de Bakker and D. Scott. A theory of programs. Manuscript notes for IBM Seminar, Vienna, 8 1969.

[DDH72]   O.-J. Dahl, E. W. Dijkstra, and C. A. R. Hoare, editors. *Structured Programming*. Academic Press, 1972.

[DFLO19]   Dino Distefano, Manuel Fähndrich, Francesco Logozzo, and Peter W. O'Hearn. Scaling static analyses at Facebook. *Communications of the ACM*, 62(8):62–70, 2019.

[DFPV09]   Mike Dodds, Xinyu Feng, Matthew Parkinson, and Viktor Vafeiadis. Deny-guarantee reasoning. In Giuseppe Castagna, editor, *Programming Languages and Systems*, volume 5502 of *Lecture Notes in Computer Science*, pages 363–377. Springer Berlin / Heidelberg, 2009.

[DGKL80]   V. Donzeau-Gouge, G. Kahn, and B. Lang. On the formal definition of Ada. In N.D. Jones, editor, *Semantics-Directed Compiler Generation: Proceedings of a Workshop Aarhus, Denmark, January 1980*, volume 94 of *Lecture Notes in Computer Science*, pages 475–489. Springer-Verlag, 1980.

[DHMS12]   Brijesh Dongol, Ian J. Hayes, Larissa Meinicke, and Kim Solin. Towards an algebra for real-time programs. In W. Kahl and T.G. Griffin, editors, *13th International Conference on Relational and Algebraic Methods in Computer Science (RAMiCS)*, volume 7560 of *Lecture Notes in Computer Science*, pages 50–65. Springer-Verlag, 2012.

[Dij62]   E. W. Dijkstra. Over de sequetialiteit van procesbeschrivjingen. EWD35, 1962.

[Dij68a]   E. W. Dijkstra. Cooperating sequential processes. In F. Genuys, editor, *Programming Languages*, pages 43–112. Academic Press, New York, 1968.

[Dij68b]   E. W. Dijkstra. Go to statement considered harmful. *Communications of the ACM*, 11(3):147–148, 1968.

[Dij76]   E. W. Dijkstra. *A Discipline of Programming*. Prentice Hall, Englewood Cliffs, N.J., USA, 1976.

[DK15]   Alan AA Donovan and Brian W Kernighan. *The Go programming language*. Addison-Wesley Professional, 2015.

[DMN68]   O.-J. Dahl, B. Myhrhaug, and K. Nygaard. SIMULA 67 common base language. Technical Report S-2, Norwegian Computing Center, Oslo, 1968.

[Don76]   James Edward Donahue. *Complementary Definitions of Programming Language Semantics*, volume 42 of *Lecture Notes in Computer Science*. Springer-Verlag New York, Inc., 1976.

[Don80]   V. Donzeau-Gouge. *Formal Definition of the Ada Programming Language*. PhD thesis, INRIA, 1980.

[dRdBH⁺01]   Willem-Paul de Roever, Frank de Boer, Ulrich Hanneman, Jozef Hooman, Yassine Lakhnech, Mannes Poel, and Job Zwiers. *Concurrency Verification: Introduction to Compositional and Noncompositional Methods*. Cambridge Tracts in Theoretical Computer Science. Cambridge University Press, 2001.

[DYBG⁺13]   Thomas Dinsdale-Young, Lars Birkedal, Philippa Gardner, Matthew Parkinson, and Hongseok Yang. Views: compositional reasoning for concurrent programs. In *Proceedings of the 40th Annual ACM SIGPLAN-SIGACT Symposium on Principles of Programming Languages*, pages 287–300. ACM, 2013.

[Eng71]   E. Engeler. *Symposium on Semantics of Algorithmic Languages*. Number 188 in Lecture Notes in Mathematics. Springer-Verlag, 1971.

[ER64]   C. C. Elgot and A. Robinson. Random access stored-program machines: An approach to programming languages. *Journal of the ACM*, 11(4):365–399, 10 1964.

[FCSR15]   Karl Anton Fröschl, Gerhard Chroust, Johan Stockinger, and Norbert Rozsenich, editors. *In Memoriam: Heinz Zemanek*. Oesterreichische Computer Gesellschaft, 2015.

[Fen09]   Xinyu Feng. Local rely-guarantee reasoning. In *Proceedings of the 36th annual ACM SIGPLAN-SIGACT Symposium on Principles of Programming Languages*, POPL '09, pages 315–327, New York, NY, USA, 2009. ACM.

[FFS07]   Xinyu Feng, Rodrigo Ferreira, and Zhong Shao. On the relationship between concurrent separation logic and assume-guarantee reasoning. In R. De Nicola, editor, *ESOP: Programming Languages and Systems*, pages 173–188. Springer-Verlag, 2007.

[FH71]   Michael Foley and Charles Antony Richard Hoare. Proof of a recursive program: Quicksort. *The Computer Journal*, 14(4):391–395, 1971.

[Fis11]   Michael Fisher. *An Introduction to Practical Formal Methods using Temporal Logic*. John Wiley & Sons, 2011.

[Flo67]   R. W. Floyd. Assigning meanings to programs. In J.T. Schwartz, editor, *Mathematical Aspects of Computer Science*, volume 19 of *Proc. of Symposia in Applied Mathematics*, pages 19–32. American Mathematical Society, 1967.

[Fra86]   N. Francez. *Fairness*. Springer-Verlag, New York, 1986.

[Fra00]   Michael Franz. Oberon – the overlooked jewel. In Böszörményi et al. [BGP00].

[GJSB00]   James Gosling, Bill Joy, Guy Steele, and Gilad Bracha. *The Java Language Specification*. Addison-Wesley Professional, 2000.

[GMW79]   M. Gordon, R. Milner, and C. Wadsworth. *Edinburgh LCF*, volume 78 of *Lecture Notes in Computer Science*. Springer-Verlag, 1979.

[Gor86]   M. Gordon. Why higher-order logic is a good formalism for specifying and verifying hardware. In G. Milne and P.A. Subrahmanyam, editors, *Formal Aspects of VLSI Design*, pages 153–177. North-Holland, 1986.

[GR83]   A. Goldberg and D. Robson. *Smalltalk-80: The Language and its Implementation*. Addison-Wesley, 1983.

[Gro09]   Peter Grossman. *Discrete Mathematics for Computing*. Macmillan International Higher Education, 2009.

[GvN47]   Herman H. Goldstine and John von Neumann. Planning and coding of problems for an electronic computing instrument. Technical report, Institute of Advanced Studies, Princeton, 1947.

[GvRB+12]   Dick Grune, Kees van Reeuwijk, Henri E Bal, Ceriel JH Jacobs, and Koen Langendoen. *Modern Compiler Design*. Springer-Verlag, New York, NY, 2nd edition, 2012.

[Han76]   A. Hansal. A formal definition of a relational data base system. Technical Report UKSC 0080, IBM UK Scientific Centre, Peterlee, Co. Durham, 6 1976.

[Han04]   Chris Hankin. *Lambda Calculi: a guide for Computer Scientists*. Oxford University Press, 2004.

[Har09]   John Harrison. *Handbook of Practical Logic and Automated Reasoning*. Cambridge University Press, 2009.

[Hay87]   I. J. Hayes, editor. *Specification Case Studies*. Prentice Hall International, 1987.

[HC12]   Ian J. Hayes and Robert J. Colvin. Integrated operational semantics: Small-step, big-step and multi-step. In John Derrick, John Fitzgerald, Stefania Gnesi, Sarfraz Khurshid, Michael Leuschel, Steve Reeves, and Elvinia Riccobene, editors, *Abstract State Machines, Alloy, B, VDM, and Z - Third International Conference, ABZ 2012, Pisa, Italy, June 18-21, 2012. Proceedings*, volume 7316 of *Lecture Notes in Computer Science*, pages 21–35. Springer-Verlag, 2012.

[HCM⁺16]   I. J. Hayes, R. J. Colvin, L. A. Meinicke, K. Winter, and A. Velykis. An algebra of synchronous atomic steps. In J. Fitzgerald, C. Heitmeyer, S. Gnesi, and A. Philippou, editors, *FM 2016: Formal Methods: 21st International Symposium, Proceedings*, volume 9995 of *Lecture Notes in Computer Science*, pages 352–369. Springer International Publishing, 11 2016.

[Hen90]   Matthew Hennessy. *The Semantics of Programming Languages: an Elementary Introduction using Structural Operational Semantics*. John Wiley & Sons, New York, NY, 1990.

[HH98]   C. A. R. Hoare and Jifeng He. *Unifying Theories of Programming*. Prentice Hall, 1998.

[HJ70]   W. Henhapl and C. B. Jones. The block concept and some possible implementations, with proofs of equivalence. Technical Report 25.104, IBM Laboratory Vienna, 4 1970.

[HJ71]   W. Henhapl and C. B. Jones. A run-time mechanism for referencing variables. *Information Processing Letters*, 1(1):14–16, 1971.

[HJ73]   K. V. Hanford and C. B. Jones. Dynamic syntax: A concept for the definition of the syntax of programming languages. In *Annual Review in Automatic Programming*, volume 7, pages 115–140. Pergamon, 1973.

[HJ78]   Wolfgang Henhapl and Cliff B. Jones. A formal definition of ALGOL 60 as described in the 1975 modified report. In D. Bjørner and Cliff B. Jones, editors, *The Vienna Development Method: The Meta-Language*, volume 61 of *Lecture Notes in Computer Science*, pages 305–336. Springer-Verlag, 1978.

[HJ82]   Wolfgang Henhapl and Cliff B. Jones. ALGOL 60. In Dines Bjørner and Cliff B. Jones, editors, *Formal Specification and Software Development*, chapter 6, pages 141–174. Prentice Hall International, 1982.

[HJ89]   C. A. R. Hoare and Cliff B. Jones. *Essays in Computing Science*. Prentice Hall, Inc., 1989.

[HJ18]   I. J. Hayes and C. B. Jones. A guide to rely/guarantee thinking. In Jonathan Bowen, Zhiming Liu, and Zili Zhan, editors, *Engineering Trustworthy Software Systems – Third International School, SETSS 2017*, volume 11174 of *Lecture Notes in Computer Science*, pages 1–38. Springer-Verlag, 2018.

[HL74]   C. A. R. Hoare and P. E. Lauer. Consistent and complementary formal theories of the semantics of programming languages. *Acta Informatica*, 3(2):135–153, 1974.

[HM87]   A. Nico Habermann and Ugo Montanari, editors. *System Development and Ada*, volume 275 of *Lecture Notes in Computer Science*. Springer-Verlag, 1987.

[HM18]   I. J. Hayes and L. A. Meinicke. Encoding fairness in a synchronous concurrent program algebra. In Klaus Havelund, Jan Peleska, Bill Roscoe, and Erik de Vink, editors, *Formal Methods*, volume 10951 of *Lecture Notes in Computer Science*, pages 222–239. Springer International Publishing, 2018.

[HMRC87]   Richard C. Holt, Philip A. Matthews, J. Alan Rosselet, and James R. Cordy. *The Turing Programming Language: Design and Definition*. Prentice Hall, Inc., 1987.

[HMT87]   Robert Harper, Robin Milner, and Mads Tofte. The semantics of standard ML: Version 1. Technical Report ECS-LFCS-87-36, University of Edinburgh, Department of Computer Science, Laboratory for Foundations of Computer Science, 1987.

[HMT88]   Robert Harper, Robin Milner, and Mads Tofte. The definition of standard ML, version 2. Technical Report ECS-LFCS-88-62, LFCS Report Series, 1988.

[Hoa61]   C. A. R. Hoare. Algorithm 63, partition; algorithm 64, quicksort; algorithm 65, find. *Communications of the ACM*, 4(7):321–322, 7 1961.

[Hoa69]   C. A. R. Hoare. An axiomatic basis for computer programming. *Communications of the ACM*, 12(10):576–580, 1969.

[Hoa71a]   C. A. R. Hoare. Procedures and parameters: An axiomatic approach. In E. Engeler, editor, *Symposium On Semantics of Algorithmic Languages*, volume 188 of *LNM*, pages 102–116. Springer-Verlag, 1971.

[Hoa71b]   C. A. R. Hoare. Proof of a program: FIND. *Communications of the ACM*, 14(1):39–45, January 1971.

[Hoa72]   C. A. R. Hoare. Towards a theory of parallel programming. In C. A. R. Hoare and R. Perrott, editors, *Operating System Techniques*, pages 61–71. Academic Press, 1972.

[Hoa74a]   C. A. R. Hoare. Monitors: An operating system structuring concept. *Communications of the ACM*, 17(10):549–557, 1974.

[Hoa74b]   C.A.R. Hoare. Hints on programming language design. In C.J. Bunyan, editor, *State of the Art Report 20: Computer Systems Reliability*, pages 505–534. Pergamon/Infotech, 1974.

[Hoa78]   C. A. R. Hoare. Communicating sequential processes. *Communications of the ACM*, 21(8):666–677, 1978.

[Hoa81]   C.A.R. Hoare. The emperor's old clothes: The ACM Turing Award Lecture. *Communications of the ACM*, 24(2):75–83, 2 1981.

[Hoa85]   C. A. R. Hoare. *Communicating Sequential Processes*. Prentice Hall, 1985.

[Hod83]   A. Hodges. *Alan Turing: The Enigma*. Burnett Books, 1983. Vintage edition, 1992.

[Hog91]   John Hogg. Islands: Aliasing protection in object-oriented languages. *ACM SIGPLAN Notices*, 26(11):271–285, 1991.

[Hop81]   Grace Murray Hopper. Keynote address at ACM SIGPLAN History of Programming Languages conference, June c1–3 1978. In Wexelblat [Wex81].

[Hut16]   Graham Hutton. *Programming in Haskell*. Cambridge University Press, 2nd edition, 2016.

[HvS12]   Tony Hoare and Stephan van Staden. In praise of algebra. *Formal Aspects of Computing*, 24(4-6):423–431, 2012.

[HW73]   C. A. R. Hoare and N. Wirth. An axiomatic definition of the programming language Pascal. *Acta Informatica*, 2(4):335–355, 1973.

[HW90]   Maurice Herlihy and Jeannette M. Wing. Linearizability: A correctness condition for concurrent objects. *ACM Trans. Program. Lang. Syst.*, 12(3):463–492, 1990.

[IPW01]   Atsushi Igarashi, Benjamin C Pierce, and Philip Wadler. Featherweight Java: a minimal core calculus for Java and GJ. *ACM Transactions on Programming Languages and Systems (TOPLAS)*, 23(3):396–450, 2001.

[Ive62]   K. E. Iverson. *A Programming Language*. J. Wiley, 1962.

[Ive07]   Kenneth E Iverson. Notation as a tool of thought. *ACM SIGAPL APL Quote Quad*, 35(1-2):2–31, 2007.

[Izb75]   H. Izbicki. On a consistency proof of a chapter of a formal definition of a PL/I subset. Technical Report TR 25.142, IBM Laboratory Vienna, 2 1975.

[JA16]   Cliff B. Jones and Troy K. Astarte. An exegesis of four formal descriptions of ALGOL 60. Technical Report CS-TR-1498, Newcastle University School of Computer Science, 9 2016.

[JA17]   Cliff B. Jones and Troy K. Astarte. Challenges for semantic description: comparing responses from the main approaches. Technical Report CS-TR-1516, Newcastle University School of Computer Science, 11 2017.

[JA18]   Cliff B. Jones and Troy K. Astarte. Challenges for semantic description: comparing responses from the main approaches. In Jonathan P. Bowen, Zili Zhang, and Zhiming Liu, editors, *Proceedings of the Third School on Engineering Trustworthy Software Systems*, volume 11174 of *Lecture Notes in Computer Science*, pages 176–217, 2018.

[Jac00]   Michael Jackson. *Problem Frames: Analyzing and Structuring Software Development Problems*. Addison-Wesley, 2000.

[JGK+15]   Jean-Baptiste Jeannin, Khalil Ghorbal, Yanni Kouskoulas, Ryan Gardner, Aurora Schmidt, Erik Zawadzki, and André Platzer. A formally verified hybrid system for the next-generation airborne collision avoidance system. In C. Baier and C. Tinelli, editors, *International Conference on Tools and Algorithms for the Construction and Analysis of Systems*, volume 9035 of *Lecture Notes in Computer Science*, pages 21–36. Springer-Verlag, 2015.

[JH16]   Cliff B. Jones and Ian J. Hayes. Possible values: Exploring a concept for concurrency. *Journal of Logical and Algebraic Methods in Programming*, 85(5):972–984, 2016.

[JHC15]   Cliff B. Jones, Ian J. Hayes, and Robert J. Colvin. Balancing expressiveness in formal approaches to concurrency. *Formal Aspects of Computing*, 27(3):465–497, 2015.

[JHJ07]   Cliff B. Jones, Ian J. Hayes, and Michael A. Jackson. Deriving specifications for systems that are connected to the physical world. In Cliff B. Jones, Zhiming Liu, and Jim Woodcock, editors, *Formal Methods and Hybrid Real-Time Systems: Essays in Honour of Dines Bjørner and Zhou Chaochen on the Occasion of Their 70th Birthdays*, volume 4700 of *Lecture Notes in Computer Science*, pages 364–390. Springer Verlag, 2007.

[JL70]   C. B. Jones and P. Lucas. Proving correctness of implementation techniques. Technical Report TR 25.110, IBM Laboratory Vienna, 8 1970.

[JL71]   C. B. Jones and P. Lucas. Proving correctness of implementation techniques. In E. Engeler, editor, *A Symposium on Algorithmic Languages*, volume 188 of *Lecture Notes in Mathematics*, pages 178–211. Springer-Verlag, 1971.

[JL96]   Richard Jones and Rafael D Lins. *Garbage Collection: Algorithms for Automatic Dynamic Memory Management*. Wiley, 1996.

[JM94]   C.B. Jones and C.A. Middelburg. A typed logic of partial functions reconstructed classically. *Acta Informatica*, 31(5):399–430, 1994.

[Jon76]   C. B. Jones. Formal definition in compiler development. Technical Report 25.145, IBM Laboratory Vienna, 2 1976.

[Jon80]   C. B. Jones. *Software Development: A Rigorous Approach*. Prentice Hall International, Englewood Cliffs, N.J., USA, 1980.

[Jon82a]   Cliff B. Jones. Compiler design. In Bjørner and Jones [BJ82], chapter 8, pages 253–270.

[Jon82b]   Cliff B. Jones. More on exception mechanisms. In Dines Bjørner and Cliff B. Jones, editors, *Formal Specification and Software Development*, chapter 5, pages 125–140. Prentice Hall International, 1982.

[Jon86]   C. B. Jones. *Systematic Software Development Using VDM*. Prentice Hall International, 1986.

[Jon90]   C. B. Jones. *Systematic Software Development Using VDM*. Prentice Hall International, second edition, 1990.

[Jon93]   C. B. Jones. A pi-calculus semantics for an object-based design notation. In E. Best, editor, *CONCUR'93: 4th International Conference on Concurrency Theory*, volume 715 of *Lecture Notes in Computer Science*, pages 158–172. Springer-Verlag, 1993.

[Jon00]   C. B. Jones. Compositionality, interference and concurrency. In Jim Davies, Bill Roscoe, and Jim Woodcock, editors, *Millennial Perspectives in Computer Science*, pages 175–186. Macmillan Press, 2000.

[Jon01]   C. B. Jones. The transition from VDL to VDM. *Journal of Universal Computer Science*, 7(8):631–640, 2001.

[Jon03]   Cliff B. Jones. The early search for tractable ways of reasoning about programs. *IEEE Annals of the History of Computing*, 25(2):26–49, 2003.

[JP11]   Cliff B. Jones and Ken G. Pierce. Elucidating concurrent algorithms via layers of abstraction and reification. *Formal Aspects of Computing*, 23(3):289–306, 2011.

[JRW10]   Cliff B Jones, A William Roscoe, and Kenneth R Wood, editors. *Reflections on the Work of C.A.R. Hoare*. Springer Science & Business Media, 2010.

[JVY17]   Cliff B. Jones, Andrius Velykis, and Nisansala Yatapanage. General lessons from a rely/guarantee development. In Kim Guldstrand Larsen, Oleg Sokolsky, and Ji Wang, editors, *Dependable Software Engineering: Theories, Tools, and Applications*, volume 10606 of *Lecture Notes in Computer Science*, pages 3–24. Springer-Verlag, 2017.

[JY15]   Cliff B. Jones and Nisansala Yatapanage. Reasoning about separation using abstraction and reification. In Radu Calinescu and Bernhard Rumpe, editors, *Software Engineering and Formal Methods*, volume 9276 of *Lecture Notes in Computer Science*, pages 3–19. Springer-Verlag, 2015.

[Kin69]   J. C. King. *A Program Verifier*. PhD thesis, Department of Computer Science, Carnegie-Mellon University, 1969.

[Kin71]   J. C. King. A program verifier. In C. V. Freiman, editor, *Information Processing 71*, pages 234–249. North-Holland, 1971.

[Kle52]   Stephen C. Kleene. *Introduction to Metamathematics*. North-Holland, 1952.

[Knu67]   D. E. Knuth. The remaining trouble spots in ALGOL 60. *Communications of the ACM*, 10(10):611–618, 1967.

[Knu73]   D. E. Knuth. *Sorting and Searching*, volume III of *The Art of Computer Programming*. Addison-Wesley Publishing Company, 1973.

[Knu74a]   Donald E Knuth. Computer programming as an art. *Communications of the ACM*, 17(12):667–673, 1974.

[Knu74b]   Donald E Knuth. Structured programming with go to statements. *ACM Computing Surveys (CSUR)*, 6(4):261–301, 1974.

[Knu03]   Donald E. Knuth. Robert W. Floyd, in memoriam. *ACM SIGACT News*, 34(4):3–13, 12 2003.

[Kol76]   George Koletsos. Sequent calculus and partial logic. Master's thesis, University of Manchester, 1976.

[Koz97]   Dexter Kozen. Kleene algebra with tests. *ACM Trans. Program. Lang. Syst.*, 19(3):427–443, May 1997.

[KTB88]   B. Konikowska, A. Tarlecki, and A. Blikle. A three-valued logic for software specification and validation. In R. Bloomfield, L. Marshall, and R. Jones, editors, *VDM— The Way Ahead*, volume 328 of *Lecture Notes in Computer Science*, pages 218–242. Springer-Verlag, 1988.

[L+94]   Nancy Lynch et al. *Atomic Transactions*. MIT Press, 1994.

[Lan65a]   Peter J. Landin. A correspondence between ALGOL 60 and Church's lambda-notation: Part I. *Communications of the ACM*, 8(2):89–101, February 1965.

[Lan65b]   Peter J. Landin. A correspondence between ALGOL 60 and Church's lambda-notation: Part II. *Communications of the ACM*, 8(3):158–167, March 1965.

[Lan66a]   P. J. Landin. The next 700 programming languages. *Communications of the ACM*, 9(3):157–166, 1966.

[Lan66b]   Peter J. Landin. A formal description of ALGOL 60. In Steel [Ste66], pages 266–294.

[Lau68]   Peter E. Lauer. Formal definition of ALGOL 60. Technical Report 25.088, IBM Laboratory Vienna, 12 1968.

[Lau71a]   P. Lauer. Consistent formal theories of the semantics of programming languages. Technical Report TR 25.121, IBM Laboratory Vienna, 11 1971.

[Lau71b]   P. E. Lauer. *Consistent Formal Theories of the Semantics of Programming Languages*. PhD thesis, Queen's University of Belfast, 1971. Printed as TR 25.121, IBM Lab. Vienna.

[Lee72]   John AN Lee. *Computer Semantics*. Van Nostrand Reinhold, 1972.

[Lev84]   Henry M. Levy. *Capability-Based Computer Systems*. Butterworth-Heinemann, Newton, MA, USA, 1984.

[Lin93]   C. H. Lindsey. A history of ALGOL 68. In *The Second ACM SIGPLAN Conference on History of Programming Languages*, HOPL-II, pages 97–132. ACM, 1993.

[Luc68]   Peter Lucas. Two constructive realisations of the block concept and their equivalence. Technical Report TR 25.085, IBM Laboratory Vienna, 6 1968.

[Luc71]   P. Lucas. Formal definition of programming languages and systems. In C. V. Freiman, editor, *Information Processing 71. Proceedings of the IFIP Congress 1971*, volume 1, pages 291–297. North-Holland, 1971.

[Łuk20]   J. Łukasiewicz. O logice trójwartościowej (on three-valued logic). *Ruch Filozoficzny*, 5:169–171, 1920.

[LV16]   Ori Lahav and Viktor Vafeiadis. Explaining relaxed memory models with program transformations. In J. Fitzgerald, C. Heitmeyer, S. Gnesi, and A. Philippou, editors, *FM 2016: Formal Methods: 21st International Symposium, Limassol*, volume 9995 of *Lecture Notes in Computer Science*, pages 479–495. Springer-Verlag, 2016.

[LvdM80]   CH Lindsey and SG van der Meulen. *Informal Introduction to ALGOL 68*. North-Holland, revised edition, 1980.

[LW69]   Peter Lucas and Kurt Walk. On the formal description of PL/I. *Annual Review in Automatic Programming*, 6:105–182, 1969.

[McC66]   John McCarthy. A formal description of a subset of ALGOL. In *Formal Language Description Languages for Computer Programming*, pages 1–12. North-Holland, 1966.

[Mey88]   B. Meyer. *Object-oriented Software Construction*. Prentice Hall, 1988.

[Mil78a]   Robin Milner. Synthesis of communicating behaviour. *Mathematical Foundations of Computer Science 1978*, 64:71–83, 1978.

[Mil78b]   Robin Milner. A theory of type polymorphism in programming. *Journal of Computer and System Sciences*, 17(3):348–375, 12 1978.

[Mil80]   R. Milner. *A Calculus of Communicating Systems*, volume 92 of *Lecture Notes in Computer Science*. Springer-Verlag, 1980.

[Mil89]   Robin Milner. *Communication and Concurrency*. Prentice Hall, January 1989.

[Mil93]   Robin Milner. Elements of interaction. *Communications of the ACM*, 36(1):78–89, 1993.

[MJ84]   F. L. Morris and C. B. Jones. An early program proof by Alan Turing. *Annals of the History of Computing*, 6(2):139–143, 1984.

[MK99]   Jeff Magee and Jeff Kramer. *State Models and Java Programs*. Wiley, 1999.

[ML65]   John McCarthy and Michael I Levin. *LISP 1.5 Programmer's Manual*. MIT Press, 1965.

[Mog89]   Eugenio Moggi. *An Abstract View of Programming Languages*. PhD thesis, Edinburgh University Laboratory for the Foundations of Computer Science, 1989.

[Moo65]   Gordon E. Moore. Cramming more components onto integrated circuits. *Electronics*, 38(8), 4 1965.

[Moo19]   J Strother Moore. Milestones from the Pure Lisp theorem prover to ACL2. *Formal Aspects of Computing*, 31(6):699–732, 2019.

[Mor70]   F. L. Morris. The next 700 formal language descriptions. Manuscript, 1970.

[Mor88]   Carroll Morgan. The specification statement. *ACM Trans. Program. Lang. Syst.*, 10(3):403–419, July 1988.

[Mor90]   Carroll Morgan. *Programming from Specifications*. Prentice Hall, 1990.

[Mos74]   Peter David Mosses. The mathematical semantics of ALGOL 60. Technical report, Programming Research Group, 1 1974.

[Mos75]   Peter David Mosses. *Mathematical semantics and compiler generation*. PhD thesis, University of Oxford, 4 1975.

[Mos85]   Ben Moszkowski. Executing temporal logic programs. In Stephen D. Brookes, Andrew William Roscoe, and Glynn Winskel, editors, *Seminar on Concurrency*, volume 197 of *Lecture Notes in Computer Science*, pages 111–130. Springer Berlin Heidelberg, 1985.

[Mos92]   Peter D. Mosses. *Action Semantics*. Number 26 in Cambridge Tracts in Theoretical Computer Science. Cambridge Press, 1992.

[Mos04]   Peter D Mosses. Modular structural operational semantics. *The Journal of Logic and Algebraic Programming*, 60:195–228, 2004.

[Mos09]   Peter D Mosses. Component-based semantics. In *Proceedings of the 8th International Workshop on Specification and Verification of Component-Based Systems*, pages 3–10. ACM, 2009.

[Mos11]   Peter D. Mosses. VDM semantics of programming languages: combinators and monads. *Formal Aspects of Computing*, 23(2):221–238, 2011.

[MP66]   John McCarthy and James A. Painter. Correctness of a compiler for arithmetic expressions. Technical Report CS38, Computer Science Department, Stanford University, 4 1966.

[MP95]   Z. Manna and A. Pnueli. *Temporal Verification of Reactive Systems: Safety*. Springer-Verlag, 1995.

[MP99]   Dale Miller and Catuscia Palamidessi. Foundational aspects of syntax. *ACM Comput. Surv.*, 31(3es):11, 1999.

[MPW92]   R. Milner, J. Parrow, and D. Walker. A calculus of mobile processes. *Information and Computation*, 100(1):1–77, 1992.

[MS74]   Robert Milne and Christopher Strachey. A theory of programming language semantics. Privately circulated, 1974.

[MS76]   R. Milne and C. Strachey. *A Theory of Programming Language Semantics (Parts A and B)*. Chapman and Hall, 1976.

[MS13]   Faron Moller and Georg Struth. *Modelling Computing Systems: Mathematics for Computer Science*. Springer Science & Business Media, 2013.

[MTHM97]   Robin Milner, Mads Tofte, Robert Harper, and David MacQueen. *The Definition of Standard ML (Revised)*. MIT Press, 1997.

[Nau66]   Peter Naur. Proof of algorithms by general snapshots. *BIT Numerical Mathematics*, 6(4):310–316, 1966.

[New63]   Allen Newell. Documentation of IPL-V. *Communications of the ACM*, 6(3):86–89, 1963.

[Nip09]   Tobias Nipkow. *Programming and Proving in Isabelle/HOL*. Springer-Verlag, 2009.

[NPW02]   Tobias Nipkow, Lawrence C. Paulson, and Markus Wenzel. *Isabelle/HOL — A Proof Assistant for Higher-Order Logic*, volume 2283 of *Lecture Notes in Computer Science*. Springer-Verlag, 2002.

[OG76]   S. S. Owicki and D. Gries. An axiomatic proof technique for parallel programs I. *Acta Informatica*, 6:319–340, 1976.

[O'H07]   P. W. O'Hearn. Resources, concurrency and local reasoning. *Theoretical Computer Science*, 375(1-3):271–307, 5 2007.

[OS16]   Martin Odersky and Lex Spoon. *Programming in Scala*. Artima, 3rd edition, 2016.

[Owi75]   S. S. Owicki. *Axiomatic Proof Techniques for Parallel Programs*. PhD thesis, Department of Computer Science, Cornell University, 1975. Published as technical report 75-251.

[Owl79]   J. Owlett. *A Theory of Database Schemata – Studies in Conceptual and Relational Schemata*. PhD thesis, Wolfson College, Oxford University, 10 1979.

[Pai67]   J. A. Painter. Semantic correctness of a compiler for an Algol-like language. Technical Report AI Memo 44, Computer Science Department, Stanford University, 3 1967.

[Pet81]   G.L. Peterson. Myths about the mutual exclusion problem. *Information Processing Letters*, 12(3):115–116, 1981.

[Pet08]   Charles Petzold. *The Annotated Turing: a Guided Tour Through Alan Turing's Historic Paper on Computability and the Turing Machine*. Wiley Publishing, 2008.

[Pie02]   Benjamin C. Pierce. *Types and Programming Languages*. MIT Press, 2002.

[PJ03]   Simon Peyton Jones. Wearing the hair shirt: a retrospective on Haskell. *Invited talk at POPL*, 206, 2003.

[PL92]   Nico Plat and Peter Gorm Larsen. An overview of the ISO/VDM-SL standard. *ACM Sigplan Notices*, 27(8):76–82, 1992.

[Plo76]   G. D. Plotkin. A powerdomain construction. *SIAM Journal on Computing*, 5:452–487, 9 1976.

[Plo81]   G. D. Plotkin. A structural approach to operational semantics. Technical Report DAIMI FN-19, Aarhus University, 1981.

[Plo04a]   Gordon D. Plotkin. The origins of structural operational semantics. *Journal of Logic and Algebraic Programming*, 60–61:3–15, July–December 2004.

[Plo04b]   Gordon D. Plotkin. A structural approach to operational semantics. *Journal of Logic and Algebraic Programming*, 60–61:17–139, July–December 2004.

[Pra65]   Dag Prawitz. *Natural Deduction: a Proof-Theoretical Study*. Dover Publications, 1965.

[Pri18]   Mark Priestley. *Routines of Substitution: John von Neumann's Work on Software Development, 1945–1948*. SpringerBriefs in History of Computing. Springer-Verlag, 2018.

[PST00]   G. Plotkin, C. Stirling, and M. Tofte, editors. *Proof, Language, and Interaction: Essays in Honour of Robin Milner*. MIT Press, 2000.

[Rad81]   George Radin. The early history and characteristics of PL/I. In Richard L. Wexelblat, editor, *History of programming languages*, pages 551–589. Academic Press, 1981.

[Rei12]   Wolfgang Reisig. *Petri Nets: an Introduction*, volume 4 of *Monographs in Theoretical Computer Science*. Springer Science & Business Media, 2012.

[Rei13]   Wolfgang Reisig. *Understanding Petri Nets: Modeling Techniques, Analysis Methods, Case Studies*. Springer-Verlag, 2013.

[Rey93]   John C Reynolds. The discoveries of continuations. *Lisp and Symbolic Computation*, 6(3-4):233–247, 1993.

[Rey02]   John Reynolds. A logic for shared mutable data structures. In Gordon Plotkin, editor, *Proceedings of the Seventeenth Annual IEEE Symp. on Logic in Computer Science, LICS 2002*, pages 55–74. IEEE Computer Society Press, 7 2002.

[RH07]   Barbara G. Ryder and Brent Hailpern, editors. *HOPL III: Proceedings of the Third ACM SIGPLAN Conference on History of Programming Languages*, New York, NY, USA, 2007. ACM.

[RNN92]   H. Riis Nielson and F. Nielson. *Semantics with Applications: A Formal Introduction*. Wiley, 1992.

[Ros94]   Bill Roscoe, editor. *A Classical Mind: Essays in Honour of CAR Hoare*. Pearson Education, 1994.

[Sam69]   Jean E Sammet. *Programming Languages: History and Fundamentals*. Prentice Hall, Inc., 1969.

[San99]   Davide Sangiorgi. Typed π-calculus at work: a correctness proof of Jones's parallelisation transformation on concurrent objects. *Theory and Practice of Object Systems*, 5(1):25–34, 1999.

[Sat75]   Edwin H. Satterthwaite. *Source Language Debugging Tools*. PhD thesis, Stanford University, 1975.

[Sch97]   Fred B. Schneider. *On Concurrent Programming*. Texts in Computer Science. Springer-Verlag, 1997.

[Sco69]   D. Scott. A type-theoretical alternative to CUCH, ISWIM, OWHY. Typescript – Oxford, 10 1969.

[Sco77]   Dana S Scott. Logic and programming languages. *Communications of the ACM*, 20(9):634–641, 1977.

[Sco80]   Dana Scott. Lambda calculus: some models, some philosophy. *Studies in Logic and the Foundations of Mathematics*, 101:223–265, 1980.

[Sco00]   Michael L. Scott. *Programming Language Pragmatics*. Morgan Kaufmann, 2000. ISBN 1-55860-578-9.

[Seb16]   Robert W. Sebesta. *Concepts of Programming Languages*. Pearson, eleventh edition, 2016.

[Sin67]   Michel Sintzoff. Existence of a van Wijngaarden sytnax for every recursively enumerable set. *Annales Soc. Sci. Bruxelles*, 81(2):115–118, 1967.

[Sit74]   R. L. Sites. *Proving that Computer Programs Terminate Cleanly*. PhD thesis, Computer Science Department, Stanford University, 1974. Printed as STAN-CS-74-418.

[SJv19]   Elizabeth Scott, Adrian Johnstone, and J. Thomas van Binsbergen. Derivation representation using binary subtree sets. *Science of Computer Programming*, 2019.

[SN86]   Herbert A Simon and Allen Newell. Information Processing Language V on the IBM 650. *IEEE Annals of the History of Computing*, 8(1):47–49, 1986.

[SS86]   L. Sterling and E. Shapiro. *The Art of Prolog: Advanced Programming Techniques*. MIT Press, 1986.

[Ste66]   T. B. Steel, editor. *Formal Language Description Languages for Computer Programming*. North-Holland, 1966.

[STER11]   G. Schellhorn, B. Tofan, G. Ernst, and W. Reif. Interleaved programs and rely-guarantee reasoning with ITL. In *Temporal Representation and Reasoning (TIME), 2011 Eighteenth International Symposium on*, pages 99–106, 2011.

[Sto77]   Joseph E. Stoy. *Denotational Semantics: The Scott-Strachey Approach to Programming Language Theory*. MIT Press, Cambridge, MA, USA, 1977.

[Str66]   C. Strachey. Towards a formal semantics. In Steel [Ste66].

[Str67]   Christopher Strachey. Fundamental concepts in programming languages. Notes from a series of lectures given at the Summer School in Computer Programming held in Copenhagen in August 1967, 1967.

[Str73]   C. Strachey. The varieties of programming language. Technical Monograph PRG-10, Oxford University Computing Lab, 3 1973.

[Stu80]   Study Group XI. CHILL Language Definition. Technical report, C.C.I.T.T. Period 1977–1980, 5 1980.

[ŠVZN+13]   Jaroslav Ševčík, Viktor Vafeiadis, Francesco Zappa Nardelli, Suresh Jagannathan, and Peter Sewell. Compcerttso: A verified compiler for relaxed-memory concurrency. *Journal of the ACM (JACM)*, 60(3):22, 2013.

[SW74]   Christopher Strachey and Christopher Peter Wadsworth. Continuations: A mathematical semantics for handling jumps. Monograph PRG-11, Oxford University Computing Laboratory, Programming Research Group, 1 1974.

[SW01]   Davide Sangiorgi and David Walker. *The π-Calculus: A Theory of Mobile Processes*. Cambridge University Press, Cambridge, United Kingdom, 2001.

[Sym99]   Donald Robert Syme. *Declarative theorem proving for operational semantics*. PhD thesis, University of Cambridge, 1999.

[Tur36]   Alan M. Turing. On computable numbers, with an application to the Entscheidungsproblem. *Proceedings of the London Mathematical Society, Series 2*, 42:230–265, 1936. Correction published: ibid, 43:544–546, 1937.

[Tur49]   A. M. Turing. Checking a large routine. In *Report of a Conference on High Speed Automatic Calculating Machines*, pages 67–69. University Mathematical Laboratory, Cambridge, 6 1949.

[Tur85]   David A Turner. Miranda: A non-strict functional language with polymorphic types. In *Conference on Functional Programming Languages and Computer Architecture*, volume 201 of *Lecture Notes in Computer Science*, pages 1–16. Springer-Verlag, 1985.

[Vaf07]   Viktor Vafeiadis. *Modular fine-grained concurrency verification*. PhD thesis, University of Cambridge, 2007.

[vdH19]   Gauthier van den Hove. *New Insights from Old Programs: The Structure of the First ALGOL 60 System*. PhD thesis, University of Amsterdam, 2019.

[vGH15]   Rob van Glabbeek and Peter Höfner. Progress, fairness and justness in process algebra. *arXiv preprint of ACM Surveys article arXiv:1501.03268*, 2015.

[VP07]   Viktor Vafeiadis and Matthew Parkinson. A marriage of rely/guarantee and separation logic. In Luís Caires and Vasco Vasconcelos, editors, *CONCUR 2007 – Concurrency Theory*, volume 4703 of *Lecture Notes in Computer Science*, pages 256–271. Springer-Verlag, 2007.

[vW66a]   Adriaan van Wijngaarden. Numerical analysis as an independent science. *BIT Numerical Mathematics*, 6(1):66–81, 1966.

[vW66b]   Adriaan van Wijngaarden. Recursive definition of syntax and semantics. In Steel [Ste66], pages 13–24.

[vWMPK69]   A. van Wijngaarden, B. J. Mailloux, J. E. L. Peck, and C. H. A. Koster. *Report on the Algorithmic Language ALGOL 68*. Mathematisch Centrum, Amsterdam, 10 1969. Second printing , MR 101.

[vWSM+76]   A. van Wijngaarden, M. Sintzoff, B. J. Mailloux, C. H. Lindsey, J. E. L. Peck, L. G. L. T. Meertens, C. H. A. Koster, and R. G. Fisker. *Revised Report on the Algorithmic Language ALGOL 68*. Mathematical Centre Tracts 50. Mathematisch Centrum, Amsterdam, 1976.

[Wad72]   Christopher P. Wadsworth. Notes on continuations. Unpublished, 7 1972.

[Wal69]   Kurt Walk. Minutes of the 4th meeting of IFIP WG 2.2 on Formal Language Description Languages, 9 1969. Held in Colchester, Essex, England. Chaired by T. B. Steel.

[Wal91]   D. Walker. π-calculus semantics for object-oriented programming languages. In T. Ito and A. R. Meyer, editors, *TACS'91*, volume 526 of *Lecture Notes in Computer Science*, pages 532–547. Springer-Verlag, 1991.

[WC04]   Jim Woodcock and Ana Cavalcanti. A tutorial introduction to designs in unifying theories of programming. In E.A. Boiten, J. Derrick, and G. Smith, editors, *International Conference on Integrated Formal Methods*, pages 40–66. Springer-Verlag, 2004.

[Wei75]   F. Weissenböck. A formal interface specification. Technical Report TR 25.141, IBM Laboratory Vienna, 2 1975.

[Wex81]   Richard L. Wexelblat, editor. *History of Programming Languages*. Academic Press, 1981.

[WH66]   N. Wirth and C.A.R. Hoare. A contribution to the development of ALGOL. *Communications of the ACM*, 9(6):413–432, 6 1966.

[Wir67]   N. Wirth. On certain basic concepts of programming languages. Technical Report CS 65, Computer Science Department, Stanford University, 5 1967.

[Wir73]   N. Wirth. *Systematic Programming: An Introduction*. Prentice Hall, 1973.

[Wir76]   N. Wirth. *Algorithms + Data Structures = Programs*. Prentice Hall, 1976.

[Wir77]   Niklaus Wirth. What can we do about the unnecessary diversity of notation for syntactic definitions? *Commun. ACM*, 20(11):822–823, 1977.

[Wir85]   Niklaus Wirth. From programming language design to computer construction. *Commun. ACM*, 28(2):159–164, 1985.

[Wol88]   M. I. Wolczko. *Semantics of Object-Oriented Languages*. PhD thesis, Department of Computer Science, University of Manchester, 3 1988. Also published as Technical Report UMCS-88-6-1.

[WV01]   Gerhard Weikum and Gottfried Vossen. *Transactional Information Systems: Theory, Algorithms, and the Practice of Concurrency Control and Recovery*. Morgan Kaufmann Publishers Inc., 2001.

[WW66]   Niklaus Wirth and Helmut Weber. Euler: a generalization of ALGOL and its formal definition: Part I. *Communications of the ACM*, 9(1):13–25, 1966.

[Yon90]   Akinori Yonezawa, editor. *ABCL: An Object-Oriented Concurrent System*. MIT Press, 1990. ISBN 0-262-24029-7.

[Zem66]   Heinz Zemanek. Semiotics and programming languages. *Communications of the ACM*, 9(3):5, 3 1966.

Index

© Springer Nature Switzerland AG 2020
C. B. Jones, *Understanding Programming Languages*,
https://doi.org/10.1007/978-3-030-59257-8

Printed in the United States
by Baker & Taylor Publisher Services